PIER PAOLO PASOLINI
Contemporary Perspectives

Pier Paolo Pasolini is one of the most important cultural figures in postwar Italy; his influence continues to be felt in Europe and North America. A new generation of scholars has grasped Pasolini's speculative power and understood the integrity of his art, an art that usually stood in sharp opposition to the opinion of his time. *Pasolini: Contemporary Perspectives* is an anthology of new essays by several noted Pasolini scholars from North America and Europe. It is a re-examination of his life and work as poet, novelist, filmmaker, journalist, and cultural theorist.

Pasolini began his career as an award-winning poet and novelist in the 1940s and 1950s with *The Ashes of Gramsci*, *Ragazzi di vita*, and *A Violent Life*. After working as a scriptwriter for film directors like Fellini and Bolognini, he began to direct his own productions. With films such as *Accattone*, *The Gospel According to St. Matthew*, *Teorema*, *Salò*, and the *Trilogy of Life*, Pasolini's reputation spread beyond the national borders of Italy and on to the international scene. His films, articles, and fiction were an excoriating critique of an eroticized consumer culture; he was an artist always in fiery opposition.

This anthology reflects new developments in semiotics, poststructuralist theory, and historical research on Italian literature and film. Pasolini himself anticipated many of these ideas. Included are two important but previously untranslated essays by him, 'Manifesto for a New Theatre' and 'Tetis,' a late and prophetic essay on modern sexuality.

PATRICK RUMBLE teaches Italian literature and cinema in the Department of French and Italian, University of Wisconsin–Madison.

BART TESTA teaches cinema studies and semiotics at the University of Toronto. His catalogue *Back and Forth: Early Cinema and the Avant-Garde* was published by the Art Gallery of Ontario.

MAJOR ITALIAN AUTHORS
General Editors: Massimo Ciavolella and Amilcare A. Iannucci

EDITED BY
PATRICK RUMBLE AND BART TESTA

Pier Paolo
PASOLINI

CONTEMPORARY
PERSPECTIVES

UNIVERSITY OF TORONTO PRESS
Toronto Buffalo London

© University of Toronto Press Incorporated 1994
Toronto Buffalo London
Printed in Canada

ISBN 0-8020-2966-3 (cloth)
ISBN 0-8020-77374 (paper)

Printed on acid-free paper

Toronto Italian Studies: Major Italian Authors

Canadian Cataloguing in Publication Data

Main entry under title:

Pier Paolo Pasolini: contemporary perspectives

(Toronto Italian studies. Major Italian authors)
Includes bibliographical references.
ISBN 0-8020-2966-3 (bound) ISBN 0-8020-7737-4 (pbk.)

1. Pasolini, Pier Paolo, 1922–1975 – Criticism
and interpretation. I. Rumble, Patrick Allen,
1963– . II. Testa, Bart. III. Series.

PQ4835.A48Z83 1993   858'.91409   C93-095395-9

Unless otherwise indicated, illustrations are from the
Museum of Modern Art Film Stills Archive.

University of Toronto Press acknowledges the financial
assistance to its publishing program of the Canada Council
and the Ontario Arts Council.

Contents

Acknowledgments

This project originated as a conference called 'Pier Paolo Pasolini: Heretical Imperatives' held in Toronto in the spring of 1990 in conjunction with the travelling retrospective of Pasolini's films. This conference was the work of several cooperating institutions including the Fondo Pier Paolo Pasolini (Rome), the Italian Cultural Institute (Toronto), the Film Department of the Art Gallery of Ontario, the Department of Italian Studies, and the Cinema Studies Programme at the University of Toronto. The conference was held at Innis College – the home of Cinema Studies and, indeed, most film-related activities at the University of Toronto – and would not have been possible without the aid of principal John Browne and help from the Harold Innis Foundation and its then-president Roger Riendeau. Thanks are owed to Jim Shedden, who mediated between the Art Gallery and the College in critical ways; to Francesca Valente, Martin Stiglio, and Mariolina Franceschetti, of the Italian Cultural Institute in Toronto; to James Quandt, chief programmer of the Cinematheque Ontario, who looked after the retrospective; to Martha De Souza of Innis College, who handled a myriad of practical tasks; and to Kate MacKay.

The book would not have developed without the encouragement from start to finish of professors Massimo Ciavolella and Amilcare Iannucci, who initiated the publication process through the Major Italian Authors series at the University of Toronto Press, and saw the project through to completion. We would like to thank Ron Schoeffel of the University of Toronto Press for his assistance and encouragement as well. A great deal of appreciation is also due to Laura Betti, director of the Associazione Fondo Pier Paolo Pasolini in Rome, and to her assistant Giuseppe Iafrate for all his help, and for furnishing us with some of the illustrations for the book. Thanks as well to Nico Naldini for permission to publish the translation of his essay, which originally appeared in *Nuovi argomenti*. Graziella Chiarcossi granted permission to publish the translations of Pasolini's 'Manifesto for a New Theatre,' which originally appeared in *Nuovi argomenti*, and for his 'Tetis,' which originally appeared in a Vittorio Boarini's *Erotismo, eversione, merce* (Bologna: Cappelli, 1974), and we thank Esa Di Simone for her assistance in this matter. We would also like to thank Walter Siti for permission to translate his essay, which first appeared in *Quaderni piacentini*. Thanks are due as well to *Cinema Journal* for permission to publish Giuliana Bruno's essay, which, like P. Adams Sitney's, originated at the Pasolini conference held at New York University within weeks of the Toronto colloquium. Small but indispensable grants were provided through the Social Sciences and Humanities Research Council of Canada and the Harold Innis Foundation to cover editorial costs. At the University of Toronto Press, we would like to thank Anne Forte and Jim Leahy for reading the volume and providing many helpful suggestions. At Innis College, Lisa Lanns, and especially Maureen Murney, provided invaluable help in preparing the manuscript. We would like to thank Adrienne Ward for her translating skills, and Richard Kidder for providing invaluable advice concerning one of the translations. Thanks are due to Grazia Menechella, as well, for her excellent suggestions and support, and to Lisa Morch who transcribed the tapes that eventually became Paolo Fabbri's essay and provided important research assistance throughout. Finally, thanks are due to Nicola Sani and Antonella Baldino, and to their families, for their hospitality in Rome during research for the project.

Chronology

1922–1942

Pier Paolo Pasolini is born 5 March 1922 in Bologna. His father, a native of Ravenna, is an officer in the Italian military, his mother a schoolteacher from Friuli. Pasolini completes high school in Bologna where he also develops friendships with other young intellectuals that would last his entire life. Every summer the family returns to Pasolini's mother's home in Casarsa della Delizia in the province of Udine, and it is here that he, along with his mother and older brother Guido, spends most of the years of the war (Guido, a member of the Resistance, was killed in 1945). In 1942, Pasolini registers in the Faculty of Letters of the University of Bologna. Also in 1942, he publishes his first book of poems, *Poesie di Casarsa*, in the Friulian dialect.

1943–1959

Pasolini receives his Laurea in 1945 with a thesis on Pascoli, directed by Carlo Calcaterra. An earlier thesis on twentieth-century Italian painting, directed by Roberto Longhi, is lost during the war. He becomes secretary of the local section of the Italian Communist Party, and he teaches in Casarsa and in neighbouring towns. In 1949, after allegations of sexual misconduct with some local boys, Pasolini is ejected from the Communist party (never to rejoin), and moves to Rome. He finds work as a teacher in a private school in Ciampino. He commences his associations with Attilio Bertolucci, Alberto Moravia, Elsa Morante, Paolo Volponi, and various other important writers. In 1952 he publishes an anthology of dialect poetry entitled *Poesia dialettale del Novecento*. He begins to receive work as a screenwriter. He collaborates on screenplays for directors such as Federico Fellini, Mauro Bolognini, Franco Rossi, Florestano Vancini, and Bernardo Bertolucci. In 1955, he publishes his first novel, *Ragazzi di vita*, for which he will be brought to trial. Along with Roberto Roversi, Francesco Leonetti, and Franco Fortini, he collaborates on the journal *Officina*. He wins the Premio Viareggio in 1957 for a collection of poems entitled *Le ceneri di Gramsci*. In 1959, he wins the Premio Crotone for his second novel, *Una vita violenta*.

1960–1975

In 1961 Pasolini turns his attention to cinema, directing his first film, *Accattone*. In the next few years he will average roughly one feature-length film per year: *Mamma Roma* (1962), *La ricotta* (1963), *La rabbia* (1963), *Il vangelo secondo Matteo* (1964), *Uccellacci e uccellini* (1966), *Edipo re* (1967), *Teorema* (1968), *Porcile* (1969), *Medea* (1969). In 1970, he begins work on the *Trilogia della vita*: *Decameron* (1971), *I racconti di Canterbury* (1972), and *Il fiore delle mille e una notte* (1974). Other 'occasional' film projects are undertaken around this schedule, including such short films as *Comizi d'amore* (1964), *Sopralluoghi in Palestina* (1964), *La terra vista dalla luna* (1966), *Che cosa sono le nuvole?* (1967), *La sequenza del fiore di carta* (1968), *Appunti per un film sull'India* (1969), *Appunti per un'Orestiade africana* (1970), and *Le mura di San'A* (1974). During this period Pasolini undergoes a series of trials for his films. He continues to write poetry and criticism, and a collection of theoretical essays, *Empirismo eretico*, is released in 1972 (see Bibliography). From the late 1960s until his death, he collaborates on the journal *Nuovi argomenti*. He begins more intense journalistic activities in the early seventies, especially in his weekly column for the newspaper *Il corriere della sera*; these essays are collected in *Scritti corsari* and *Lettere luterane* following his death. He is violently murdered on 2 November 1975 at Ostia, near Rome, apparently by a sole assailant, though the circumstances of his death remain unclear. He is buried in Casarsa after a massive public display of grief in Rome by thousands of mourners. Pasolini's last film, *Salò o le 120 giornate di Sodoma*, appears posthumously in 1975, and instantly is met with a series of court injunctions that effectively remove the film from circulation for years. In 1992 his last, unfinished novel *Petrolio* is published, giving rise to controversy and scandal in the Italian press.

Pier Paolo Pasolini

Accattone (1961)

Mamma Roma (1962)

Il Vangelo secondo Matteo (1964)

Il Vangelo secondo Matteo (1964)

Teorema (1968)

Seventeenth-century Rajput miniature (Phyllis and Eberhard Kronhausen, *The Complete Book of Erotic Art*. New York: Bell Publishing, 1978)

Il fiore delle mille e una notte (1974)

Pier Paolo Pasolini as Giotto in *Il Decamerone* (1971)
(Fondo Pier Paolo Pasolini)

Two scenes from *Salò o le 120 giornate di Sodoma* (1975)

PIER PAOLO PASOLINI: CONTEMPORARY PERSPECTIVES

Introduction

PATRICK RUMBLE AND BART TESTA

For Pier Paolo Pasolini, the visual language of film was a 'transnational' and 'transclass' language, one that could embrace a community of spectators from all over the world, and from all levels of society. This was certainly one of the reasons Pasolini began making films in the early 1960s, after more than a decade in which his reputation as a poet and novelist had been secured. Thereafter, while much else in his thinking, in his poetry, and in his politics underwent strong transformations, Pasolini never abandoned the transnational aspirations of his filmmaking, which indeed climaxed in his *Trilogy of Life*, the project that occupied him during the penultimate phase of his production.

The present volume was conceived two years ago – keeping very much in mind Pasolini's idea of working in an ever more 'global' community – during a period in which economic and cultural forces were dissolving national boundaries, calling national identities into question, and indeed causing people to reconsider the very basic principles of democracy, federalism, and national-popular culture. This collection of essays, including articles by scholars from (though often not citizens of) Canada, Italy, France, and the United States, and with translations of some of Pasolini's own work, is a product of an international community of people, whose writing is brought together out of a dedication to Pasolini's work and to the types of issues that concerned him most. Our tasks as editors of this volume, living and working in two different countries, were facilitated by various communication technologies, such as fax machines, modems, and electronic mail, that helped to render rather minimal any potential difficulties resulting from distance and national boundaries.

The timing of the inception of this collective project is not accidental. In the 1980s, and for the first time in North America, Pasolini's literary and filmic work began to receive serious attention, long overdue, on the part of scholars, critics, and translators (important in this regard are Pia Friedrich's 1982 volume *Pier Paolo Pasolini*; Beverly Allen's volume of the same year, *Pier Paolo Pasolini: The Poetics of Heresy*; the special issue of *The Italianist*, edited by Zygmunt Barański, devoted to Pasolini in 1985; and Louise Barnett and Ben Lawton's translation, *Heretical Empiricism*, in 1988). In the late 1980s, this interest in Pasolini was further energized by the efforts of the Fondo Pier Paolo Pasolini in Rome to circulate his films outside of Italy. In 1989, due to the commitment of the Fondo Pier Paolo Pasolini, under the direction of Laura Betti, new archival-quality prints with new English subtitles (by William Weaver), and accompanied by a fine assembly of documents, *Pier Paolo Pasolini: A Future Life*, were exhibited throughout the United States and Canada as the circulating retrospective entitled 'Pier Paolo Pasolini: The Eyes of a Poet.' During the retrospective's 'tour,' which at the date of publication has included exhibitions in Toronto, New York, Los Angeles, Chicago, and other cities, universities and art institutes organized symposia and conferences devoted to Pasolini's work, and these events have both reflected and generated renewed interest in Pasolini's films. The present volume bears many of the fruits of this period of intense and fresh engagement in Pasolini's life and art. Indeed, except for the translations of Walter Siti, Nico Naldini, and Pasolini himself, all of the articles found here grew directly out of work presented at conferences held in Toronto, New York, and Chicago. Thus, this volume is the product of that period, and offers a scholarly photograph of the most recent approaches to Pasolini by established and also new writers and critics committed to his work.

What has become more and more apparent in recent years is the regrettable impatience that characterizes the ways Pasolini has traditionally been approached both in North America and Europe. Up until now, Pasolini criticism has been dominated by hagiographic and auteurist tendencies (understandable given the horrible circumstances of Pasolini's violent death in 1975) that have led critics to view his texts and films as 'illustrations' of the artist's life, or as explanations – and indeed sometimes as legitimations – of his tragic death. Exemplary in this respect are Giuseppe Zigaina's positively gnostic interpretation, *Pasolini Between Enigma and Prophecy*, and Enzo Siciliano's often overwrought biography *Pasolini* (which seems to have been displaced by the recent publication of Barth Schwartz's exhaustive English-language biography, *Pasolini Requiem*). This tendency is compounded by many of Pasolini's own, often contradictory, accounts of his own individual works, especially as found in the countless interviews that he gave throughout his life. The type of approach that we are describing, which might be termed 'biographical,' though the word is rather too pale to catch the passions invested in such charged depictions of Pasolini, has certainly produced invaluable and often foundational work. But it has also tended to set certain limits upon interpretation, including a prevalent desire to frame any analysis in extremely simplistic psychoanalytic terms. The limits of this approach, on the one hand, insufficiently recognizing the extraordinarily sophisticated self-consciousness – and self-directed irony – Pasolini brought to both his polemical and artistic writing and, on the other, lacking a proper understanding of Pasolini's experience, especially as a child and young man, are at once methodological and informational.

Nico Naldini's introductory essay to this volume gives a first-hand account of Pasolini's years spent in his mother's region of Friuli during and immediately following the fascist government of Italy. Naldini begins to fill in the gaps in our knowledge of this formative period in Pasolini's life, essential to gain an understanding of a time and place that greatly determined his later attitudes concerning sexuality, political engagement, and agrarian communities. Naldini's work here and elsewhere helps to overcome the conjecture and speculation that has dominated much of the discussion of Pasolini's family life and adolescence.

While Naldini is concerned with Pasolini's beginnings, Walter Siti's essay deals with Pasolini's literary production during the later years of his life, a period more than any other the object of much ill-informed dispute. Siti analyses how Pasolini's last book of poems forms a critical and often bitter reconsideration of the lyrical and idyllic poems Pasolini wrote in the Friulian dialect during the 1940s. Siti charts Pasolini's gradual rejection of his own early poetic enthusiasm, and how his last major literary project, a novel entitled *Petrolio* (left unfinished at his death), expresses many of the scandalous and polemical themes concerning the alienating effects of consumer society that Pasolini developed as well in his journalistic writings (collected in *Lettere luterane* and *Scritti corsari*) and in his last film, *Salò*.

The necessity to engage in such political and cultural issues of national and international significance is considered by Jennifer Stone to be one of Pasolini's 'pedagogical' responsibilities. Stone studies the ideological significance of Pasolini's poetic and film work according to a perspective offered by Andrea Zanzotto, Pasolini's friend and himself an extremely important dialect poet, and through a Freudian, yet post-Lacanian approach. Likewise, Joseph Francese examines the issue of political engagement and literary notions of realism, focusing on the later years of the 'neorealist season,' when Pasolini published his 'Roman novels,' *Ragazzi di vita* (1955) and *Una vita violenta* (1959). Francese situates the narrative and stylistic departures of those novels in relation to the conventions of the 'engaged' neorealist novel, as associated with the work of Vasco Pratolini, in particular. In the process, and through a meticulous, month-by-month tracing of the unusually sharp critical debate Pasolini sparked, Francese develops an historical account of Pasolini's vexatious relationship with the cultural apparatus of the Italian Communist Party (PCI), itself in a period of intellectual and political crisis following Khrushchev's denunciation of Stalin at the Twentieth Congress of the Soviet Communist Party in 1956, and the invasions of Poland and Hungary.

Pasolini's great ambivalence toward the PCI was to a large extent the result of two very painful experiences: first, the murder of his Partisan brother Guido at the hands of other Partisans during the period of the Resistance; and second, his own ejection from the party in 1949 in Friuli after he was arrested on allegations of sexual misconduct (a matter Naldini touches upon in his piece). In spite of his attitude toward the party, and the PCI's ongoing criticism of his work, and suspicions about the man, Pasolini's philosophy remained Marxist, a point raised by Silvestra Mariniello in her essay on Pasolini's 'Gramscian' conception of language and ideology. The tendency since the mid-1960s was to approach Pasolini's theories of language, ideology, and film semiotics through a rigid structuralist optic. This tendency has largely obscured the significance and suggestive insights of those essays (subsequently collected in *Empirismo eretico* in 1972) that constitute Pasolini's sustained meditation on the diverse media at play in his diverse artistic practice.

Mariniello shows how Pasolini considered structuralism to be only one of his interlocutors, along with various other, then less predominant approaches, including Russian formalism, as well as the theories of Bakhtin, Medvedev, McLuhan, and others. The failure to recognize the plurality of Pasolini's interrogations has led a number of commentators to misrecognize Pasolini's theories and to write them off simply as the musings of a structuralist dilettante. For Pasolini, it was a mistake to conceive of language instrumentally, as a simple system of 'nomination,' as a tool kit responsible for the simple communication of meanings and mental thoughts. As Mariniello shows, Pasolini elaborated a non-instrumental notion of language as a productive, material practice of active and potentially renovating mediation between reality and understanding: an idea based on insights, she suggests, derived in part from his analysis of the language or codes of film, as thematized later in the screenplay for the unproduced film *Il padre selvaggio*.

Likewise, Giuliana Bruno's essay resumes the rescue (begun, for English readers at least, by Naomi Greene in the fourth chapter of her recent book-length study) of Pasolini's 'heretical' linguistic and semiotic theories from accusations, such as Umberto Eco's, of his semiotic naïvety. Bruno examines Pasolini's theory of filmic language as 'the written language of reality,' and his idea of reality as being 'cinema in nature.' She explains that the relation between film and the world has typically been conceived as being one of the reflection of the latter by the former. For Pasolini, rather, reality is not an extra-discursive, or 'monolithic, unitary, ontological entity' that is 'communicated' by the realistic medium of film, but is rather already the contradictory, discursive site of social negotiation. Both film and reality (and subsequently language and body) are seen as interrelated, and not simply distinguishable modes of communication. Thus, in response to Eco's famous, and largely accepted, criticism that Pasolini makes the mistake of reducing the facts of culture to natural phenomena, Bruno shows how Pasolini actually intended to reveal all apparently 'natural' relationships between humans and reality as cultural relationships, not only open to renegotiation, but always already under renegotiation.

In this regard, Bruno shares in Mariniello's concern with clarifying how Pasolini's semiotic theories often anticipate more recent Marxist, feminist, and poststructuralist approaches to problems of signification and ideology. In his turn, Paolo Fabbri examines how Pasolini's writings concerning the 'cinema of poetry' and 'free indirect discourse' (also known as *oratio obliqua* or reported speech), as found in *Heretical Empiricism*, anticipate the recent work in film semiotics, and that of Gilles Deleuze, in particular. In the process, Fabbri also revisits the theoretical debates between Pasolini, Eco, and Christian Metz. These debates involved such issues as the possibility of drawing analogies between literary and cinematic narrative models, and the appropriateness of applying analytical paradigms derived from linguistics to the study of film. Fabbri takes as his starting point an argument over whether or not there was a 'double articulation' in film language, based upon André Martinet's semiotic analysis of the double articulation in spoken-written language. According to his analysis, language can be divided into morphemes, or units of meaning that form the first articulation; these units can then be broken down into smaller but meaningless units of sound, the phonemes, that form the 'second articulation.' Fabbri discusses Pasolini's notion of the cinematic second articulation, but also suggests its limits for the interpretation of films. More productive in this regard are Pasolini's formulations concerning 'free indirect discourse' and how they help to explain Pasolini's often unconventional approach to montage in his films. Pasolini adopts editing procedures that avoid classical conventions of narrative continuity, and subsequently provoke an ambivalent reaction in the spectator.

For Pasolini, the style associated with the 'cinema of prose' was based upon classical conventions of spatial and temporal continuity whose perfection is generally associated with classical Hollywood filmmaking. Its hegemonic narrative film practice is one in which 'naturalism' in representation and narrative ordering depended upon the 'invisibility' of formal procedures and stylistic elements. In his essay, David Ward charts Pasolini's shifting views concerning narrative organization and the problem of narrative voice, by offering an analysis of the 'Roman novels' and the shifts Pasolini took in formulating, and in revising, his film theory. In the novels of the late 1950s, Ward discerns a faith on Pasolini's part in the organizing capacities of the analytical narrator (which Pasolini termed the 'genial analytic mind') and the necessity of narrational mastery over the 'chaos' of events, as seen especially in the authoritative narrative voice in *Una vita violenta* (*A Violent Life*). Nevertheless, after this novel, Pasolini appears to have lost faith in the epistemological certainty offered by the figure of the 'genial analytic mind' when he turns to film at the start of the sixties. Indeed, Pasolini begins, almost at once, to avoid the constraints of conventional narrative in his films, and he offers an explanation of his own 'open-ended' films as examples of a 'cinema of poetry.' For Pasolini, the visual language of film was based on oneiric and irrational foundations of reality itself, and his own 'poetic' cinema reveals the repressive, disciplining, and rational nature of narrative ordering. Insofar as the language of the novel – a language redeployed in classical cinema using visual means – involves symbolic, rational mediation between people and reality, it necessarily betrays the irrational nature of reality.

Pasolini's attitude toward narrative films (and, in particular, his antagonism toward Hollywood-style practices) and his prescriptions for a stylistic renovation of cinema find certain echoes in the verse tragedies Pasolini wrote in the late 1960s, in which the problem of narrative 'mastery' is translated into the unstable and open-ended narrative structure of the plays, and thematized as conflictual relationships between fathers and sons, or between rational and irrational social forces (see, for example, *Affabulazione*, *Pilade*, or *Bestia da stile*). Pasolini's 'Manifesto for a New Theatre,' translated for the first time in English in this volume, calls for a poetic reconceptualization of bourgeois theatrical practices. According to Pasolini, theatre should disengage from the naturalism in narrative, recitation, set design, and costumes found in conventional 'theatre of chatter' but without opting to become another version of its specular opposite, the avant-garde theatre of the 'gesture' or 'scream.' Theatre should concentrate more on the dialogical and pedagogical power of the poetic word. What is original about the style of theatre Pasolini proposes in his 'Manifesto' is that it

consists in being of the Word: it stands against two typical theatres of the bourgeoisie, the theatre of Chatter and the theatre of the Scream or Gesture, whose basic unity is confirmed by their both having: a) the same public (which the former entertains, the latter shocks), and b) a common hatred for the word ... The theatre of the Word does not seek out its theatrical space in any setting other than the head.

Once again, the desired effect of Pasolini's work is a challenging of the spectator, called upon to react and contribute as a 'co-author' of the work-in-progress.

Pasolini's ethical concern with the effects of narration and representation upon spectators grew consistently with each film he made. We can discern this in the way Pasolini's films continually call attention to the camera (the defining trait of the cinema of poetry, according to Pasolini), as seen in his oft-noted 'frontal' style, in his use of the unstable hand-held camera, or in his studied lapses in continuity. In this manner, his films spotlight issues of point of view, narrative address, and the codes structuring perception. All of the essays dealing with film in this volume remark upon such preoccupations in aesthetic, ideological, narratological, or theological terms. Both P. Adams Sitney and Bart Testa account for Pasolini's stylistic choices in terms of aesthetic and theological motivations. Sitney situates Pasolini's first film, *Accattone* (1961), within the genre of spiritual biography, and explains Pasolini's frontal style, his use of pans and close-ups, and the rawness of his images, in terms of a 'sacred style,' influenced by medieval and renaissance iconographic traditions as well as by the films of Dreyer, Bresson, and Rossellini. Revising many of the critical clichés about Pasolini's first film, which have suggested he was engaged in a revival of neorealist stylistics, Sitney analyses the structure and rhyming cadences of *Accattone* and traces Pasolini's allusions to biblical sources; he develops an account of the importance of Dante's medieval allegory for a proper understanding of both *Accattone* and *Mamma Roma* (1962).

The 'sacred' qualities of Pasolini's style are also taken up in Testa's analysis of Pasolini's adaptation of the gospel of St. Matthew in 1964. Testa sidesteps the dominant auteurist approach to this film, which has tended to read far too much biographical or anecdotal information into any interpretation, and focuses instead upon a detailed analysis of Pasolini's adaptation, his stylistic solutions in filming a pre-modern text of the gospel. He asserts the historic significance of Pasolini's film through a comparison with other examples in the 'Jesus film' genre, which have avoided confronting problems of filming gospels directly by the feint of novelization. Indeed, Martin Scorsese's *The Last Temptation of Christ* is offered as an example, though not the only one, of what Pasolini avoided: an adaptation of the gospel that lends the character of Jesus modern psychological attributes and motivations. This tendency in 'Jesus films,' which he explains as the result of the 'laconism' of the original gospel text, was not followed by Pasolini, who was actually attracted by the pre-modern, even 'primitive' character of the text, and sought to film the gospel directly. This led Pasolini to abandon certain editing conventions (such as the 'interval') and to revise other devices (such as shot/counter-shot and panning) as filmic equivalents of narrative accelerations and elliptical jumps in Matthew's original. Moreover, Pasolini's 'epic' or 'sacred' style, with partial repression of establishing and point-of-view shots, leads to a de-psychologization or de-individualization of point of view. This process of de-individualization is repeated in the later film *Teorema* (1968), which Testa describes as a drama in which the characters in the film undergo a traumatic loss of self-identity after their encounter with an allegorically divine 'visitor.' In the process of his analysis, Testa finds that most previous interpretations of this film relied far too heavily on Pasolini's own pronunciations regarding the film's narrative structure and allegorical message.

Pasolini's interest in pre-modern and non-Western cultures and liter-ary/pictorial traditions is maintained throughout the 1960s – as seen es-pecially in many of his poems, and in such writings as *L'odore dell'India* (1962), *Il padre selvaggio* (1963), and the films *Appunti per un film sull'India* (1969) and *Appunti per un'Orestiade africana* (1969). This interest con-tinues into the 1970s, when he makes the films of the *Trilogy of Life: Decameron* (1971), *Canterbury Tales* (1972), and *Arabian Nights* (1974). In his essay, Patrick Rumble studies Pasolini's motivation for adapting these 'proto-novels,' arguing that their anthological plurality of sto-ries and *mise-en-abyme* forms suggested eversive strategies of narrative construction. He then goes on to examine Pasolini's experimentation with Oriental pictorial traditions in the *Arabian Nights*. By translating non-Western figural models into film, Pasolini stages a conflict between perceptual codes or visual 'dialects.' Rumble offers another explanation of Pasolini's 'mixed' style as found in the *Trilogy of Life* in terms of the 'contamination' of diverse codes or ways of seeing, seen ultimately as the practical expression of Pasolini's politics of spectatorship.

It is precisely this ethical concern with visual pleasure, voyeurism, and cinema that becomes the focus of Naomi Greene's essay on Pa-solini's last film, *Salò* (1975). Greene interprets Pasolini's Dantesque adaptation of the Marquis de Sade's novel *120 Days of Sodom* as an allegory of how 'society had turned everything, including the human body, into pure merchandise.' In making *Salò*, Pasolini's intent, she ex-plains, was to shock and scandalize his spectators, and present issues concerning the exercise of power, exploitation, alienation, and the con-sumerist manipulation of desire in an 'indigestible' form. Greene also shows how Pasolini not only thematizes such issues, in the horrifying sado-masochistic world of the Republic of Salò, but also formally impli-cates the spectator and filmmaker in this drama, and calls attention to the sadistic nature of visual pleasure, through the film's manipulation of point of view.

Salò was produced during the same period in which Pasolini was writing the proposed 2,000 pages of his novel *Petrolio*. Thus, the essays by Greene and Siti complement one another, and offer the best image of Pasolini's aesthetic and political concerns during the last months of his life. Moreover, Pasolini's essay 'Tetis' (from the ancient Greek word for sex), translated here for the first time in English, represents one of the last places in which Pasolini clearly expressed himself con-cerning the issues of sexual tolerance and alienation, visual pleasure and pornography, and the significance of censorship in his own life. As he wrote in his other condemnation of the so-called sexual revolution of the sixties and seventies, the 'Abiura della *Trilogia della vita*,' sexual tolerance, and the apparent relaxation of certain forms of repression connected to human comportment, must be seen as pernicious forms of the ideology of a new 'consumerist Power' in the process of attaining global hegemony. According to Pasolini, the survival and reproduction of this new Power depended upon its ability to manipulate or channel human desire, to impose certain models of consumption, through the transnational avenues of mass media. To the extent that his own films have participated in this process (and he singles out the *Trilogy of life* in particular), Pasolini finds it necessary to recant them.

However, to paraphrase Gramsci, Pasolini's pessimism of the intellect was ever matched by an optimism of the will. As we mentioned at the outset of this introduction, Pasolini's move to filmmaking in the early sixties is partially explained by his overriding desire to engage in a severe and sustained critique of the globalizing culture of postwar consumer society. His response to multinationalist cultural paradigms would be articulated in the transnational medium of film. That is, Pasolini foresaw the victory of a global consumer culture, but not in terms of new liberties and the end of ideologies, as is being celebrated so much today, but rather in terms of new obligations and new forms of individual and collective identification, which cannot be discerned according to previous national or nationalistic coordinates. All of Pasolini's writings and films of the last years, as seen in the novel *Petrolio*, in the articles of *Scritti corsari* or *Lettere luterane*, in the poems of *La nuova gioventù*, in the film *Salò*, or in the screenplay *Porno-Teo-Kolossal*, comment both explicitly and allegorically upon the new obligations of subjects and communities mentioned above as the results of the consumerist revolution of late capitalism – an economic mode that sees in national borders and identities either trade barriers or sources of identification to be manipulated during the various negotiations and renegotiations of hegemony, as required during a period of such rapid transition. And insofar as any text in some way reflects or mediates the tensions and forces governing the historical moment in which it was composed, this collection of essays presents itself, paradoxically, as both the expression of such tensions and forces and often, at the same time, as an internal contestation of them – a paradox inherent in any responsible endeavour, pedagogical or otherwise.

References

Allen, Beverly, ed. *Pier Paolo Pasolini: The Poetics of Heresy.* Saratoga, CA: Anma Libri, 1982

Barański, Zygmunt, ed. *The Italianist* 5 (1985). Special issue on Pasolini

Friedrich, Pia. *Pier Paolo Pasolini.* Boston: Twayne, 1982

Greene, Naomi. *Pier Paolo Pasolini: Cinema as Heresy.* Princeton: Princeton University Press, 1990

Pasolini, Pier Paolo. *Heretical Empiricism.* Translated by L. Barnett and B. Lawton. Bloomington: Indiana University Press, 1988

Schwartz, Barth David. *Pasolini Requiem.* New York: Pantheon, 1992

Siciliano, Enzo. *Pasolini.* Translated by John Shepley. New York: Random House, 1982

Viano, Maurizio. *A Certain Realism: Making Use of Pasolini's Film Theory and Practice.* Berkeley: University of California Press, 1993

Zigaina, Giuseppe. *Pasolini Between Enigma and Prophecy.* Preface by Jay Scott. Translated by Jennifer Russell. Toronto: Exile Editions, 1991

Pier Paolo, My Cousin …

NICO NALDINI

With the publication of his *Pasolini: Una vita* in 1989, Nico Naldini firmly established himself as the most insightful and authoritative of Pasolini's biographers (besides being himself a noted poet). This is due in part to the fact that Naldini is Pasolini's first cousin, and he was also one of his closest friends and collaborators throughout Pasolini's life. For a period during the war, Pasolini's family shared the Naldini home in Casarsa della Delizia, in Friuli. Subsequently, Naldini was present during the much-discussed, indeed nearly 'mythical,' period of Pasolini's adolescence in Friuli. Naldini was also on hand when in 1949 Pasolini was forced to abandon Friuli and move to Rome, after being charged with the corruption of minors and with public obscenity. The details of this difficult moment in Pasolini's life have remained quite vague ever since, though with the publication of Naldini's work, it appears that these allegations may have formed part of a strategy to drastically limit Pasolini's political engagement in the region as a member of the Italian Communist Party (PCI). In its turn, the PCI denounced Pasolini's 'decadence,' and expelled him from its membership (see Naldini, *Lettere 1940–1954*, and *Pasolini: Una vita*, 133–5). From his privileged vantage point, Naldini fills in the gaps in our knowledge of the period preceding Pasolini's transfer to Rome. Thereafter, Pasolini would only rarely find himself out of the public eye.

Perhaps the only thing that drives me to recall distant moments in Pasolini's life would be the existence of such a long family history – so many years lived under the same roof, with my cousins Pier Paolo and Guido and their mother Susanna. Although I am not entirely sure of how it might be of use, I will rummage around in my memories, which are so numerous and sharply defined, and I will simply recall such memories as they occur to me.

Eighteen years ago, in November 1974, to be exact, we were in Paris in order to buy furniture for the sets in his last film, *Salò*, and Pier Paolo told me that in no other city can one take in the sun as well as in Paris. This is one of the last recollections I have of him. My first recollection is of Pier Paolo angry, with me as the cause of his anger. We are beneath one of the huge canopies that covered a part of the courtyard of our house in Casarsa. There is an air of summer vacation and my sisters, seated around a basket full of rags, are playing at sewing clothes. I am nearby with a stomach ache. I am two or three years old. A large patch of diarrhea is the result of my *malessere* and, arriving suddenly, Pier Paolo steps in it. I am myself irritated by his exaggerated complaining.

Our two families had interwoven their maternal lineage much more closely than the paternal lineage, and the old house in Casarsa was the symbol of our affections for one another. Nevertheless, the older Pasolini cast an alien shadow over our days whenever he made his rare appearances. He was an officer in the military, a man full of arrogance and of few words; one addressed him using the formal *Lei*. But my mother and her sisters were ready to confront him whenever he tried to assert his authority over the family, and more than once I saw him retreat, defeated, from their arguments.

Carlo Alberto Pasolini was born on the poorest branch of a large family of Ravenna, the Pasolinis of Onda – the branch of Corso Giovecca, completely ignored by those of our rich relatives who held noble titles. Carlo's own father's name was Argobasto, and his brother was a poet named Pier Paolo, both registered in the *Albo d'oro* of the Italian nobility. Carlo guarded this volume, bound in red cardboard with golden flourishes, as proof of his blue blood. According to gossip overheard during my infancy, his mother died an alcoholic, and when her body was removed a mountain of Chianti bottles fell from beneath her bed.

Carlo had an authoritarian's voice, with an acid tone designed precisely to be heard and obeyed even from a distance. The voice, the scowl, the uniform, the military rigidity, as suggested in the most simple Freudian theories, masked a sentimental, even passionate nature. The object of Carlo's passion was my aunt Susanna. He was short and stocky, with bushy eyebrows, with a scruffy neck like von Stroheim. He peered at us through a monocle. Since he appeared in Casarsa only during the summer, I remember him with impeccable white uniforms and white suede shoes.

Susanna was beautiful and slight, with the profile of a Venetian miniature. From my grandmother she inherited the grace of her smile, which sometimes was transformed into a brooding and desperate little laugh because she was extremely timid. Anecdotes of her timidity followed her until old age, and she would always respond to them with sweetly comical gestures.

She had never been in love with her husband.

Her only love, which she perhaps preserved forever in her memory, had been a very handsome young Venetian man to whom she had given her only work of embroidery, a pillowcover for his bed. After the disappearance of this young Attilio, sometime before the First World War, she met Carlo Pasolini, who was an infantry sergeant climbing the ladder of a military career in order to escape his ruined family. They were married three years after the war when he was promoted as an officer, and she was already thirty years old. For many years the only object of her attention was herself and only herself, until the birth of Pier Paolo; thereafter, it was herself and Pier Paolo as if they were one, inseparable and elusive.

Susanna was extremely elegant, though without exaggeration. The long years of engagement were accompanied by her attitude of indifference along with periods of capricious silence and Carlo Pasolini's own exasperation. Could there have been a shadow, a memory of some violence, between them?

At the beginning of their engagement, between 1914 and 1915, Susanna became pregnant – a fact that had the effect of a never detonated bomb lodged within the family. The scandal (since that is what it would have been) was hushed up with much effort. With a falsified medical certificate that permitted her to take time off from the elementary school where she taught, Susanna went to a town in the province of Mantova where she secluded herself in the house of some of our relatives. She stayed for a few months, until the birth of a son. The child was immediately recognized by Pasolini, and given the name Carlo. Born extremely delicate, he lived only a few months, and there remains only a single faded photograph of him in a crib. But his secret was kept forever, and no one, least of all the two sons born later, had even the slightest suspicion of his existence.

Susanna continued to deny Carlo's passion, even after the marriage and the birth of their sons. He was always prepared to offer the greatest of courtesies. But there were also certain moments of crisis in which he, perhaps overcome by frustration, left the family house and, out of complete vendetta, squandered all of his salary at gambling, leaving the family penniless.

Many years later, Carlo began to show the first signs of disequilibrium – a form of persecution paranoia – and his tantrums in the family were no longer limited to rare occasions but became a permanent attitude of grim protest against everyone. Faced with the bewilderment and eternal intoxication of his father, Pier Paolo searched for a possible interpretation of what had rendered his father's conjugal life so difficult and desolate, and he detected in his father's past some half-forgotten guilt.

Pier Paolo mentioned it to me only once. Many years earlier, at Bologna during the trial of the young Zaniboni, who had been accused of attempted assassination of Mussolini, Pasolini's father testified not only that he recognized the youth who had fired, but that he himself, with his own arm, had deflected the bullet, aimed at the Duce. Now it is known that this attempt on the life of Mussolini was nothing but a stunt carried out by a regime in need of pretexts for repression and of occasions to divinify Mussolini, to strengthen his cult, and make him appear to be protected by the heavens. What is certain is that the testimony of Carlo Pasolini is there in the trial records. It would be worth finding them in order to understand the significance of this event in Carlo Pasolini's life, to the extent that it may offer insights into the guilt that Pier Paolo detected in his father's past.

Carlo was a nationalist-fascist, and he was fanatical enough to denounce one of my father's brothers who was a communist living in Ferrara, where all my family, on my mother's side, had sought refuge during the last years of the war (this was after the invasion of Friuli by the Austrian army). My mother had worked out a sort of compromise with the Fascist party, accepting, or perhaps scheming to obtain, the position of secretary of Casarsa's *Fascio femminile*. This position mainly involved the responsibility of organizing charity projects such as health camps for children during the summer, and providing gifts from the Befana during the winter. Besides such functions, there was also the occasional parade in Rome, in which my mother, dressed in her coarse woollen uniform, participated happily. During such times, a smile of satisfaction – extraordinary given its rarity – would pass over Carlo Pasolini's lips. The corner of his lower lip was calloused and yellow from the ever-present cigarette hanging there. He was especially happy when people addressed him as Signor Conte (Sir Count), and whoever did so assured himself of Carlo's consideration forever. Besides this, he had a gentle temper, but he had been brutalized by the military life more than by any other experience.

Pier Paolo was born in March 1922; his brother Guidalberto in 1925. From the time of his infancy, Guido had a large head and my mother was certain that its abnormal size was caused by undernutrition during the first months of his life – that is, during a period of great financial hardship following one of the frequent conjugal battles that so often beset the family. It was the general opinion of the family that Guido had inherited his father's character – arrogant and courageous. Some of the portraits of Guido by Pier Paolo show him in bed with a shadow over one eye. When Guido was around fifteen years old, he spent some time in a hospital in Bologna after a fight with some unknown men. No explanation was ever offered of this incident, but, by piecing together various allusions to it heard afterwards, the story can be reconstructed as follows: some unknown persons had slandered Pier Paolo, perhaps calling him a homosexual, and Guido confronted them all by himself. He was beaten up very badly, and suffered a cerebral concussion. When he found out about the incident, Pier Paolo rushed to the hospital to be with his brother. Guido later admitted having been overwhelmed by Pier Paolo's affection and concern. Like his father, Guido was afraid of not being loved enough, and maybe he wasn't loved to the extent his temperament required. Consequently, within the family he belonged more to an area of shadow and resentment associated with his father (taking the occasional outlet of infantile cruelty of which I was usually the victim) than to the light and harmonious area of his mother and Pier Paolo. I am quite certain that father and son alike felt the painful effects of this missing osmosis (which resulted in real nervous crises) between the two family parts. But, without any precise recollection, this may only be my perception.

The years of my childhood blend with the lights and odours of one single summer, which began the day in which I went to the train station of Casarsa to await the arrival of my cousins. From that day onwards, for about three months, we made countless trips to the Tagliamento River, played countless soccer games in the playing field behind the train station; and then there were so many evenings when Pier Paolo and Guido left on bicycle with their friends, and I was left alone with the women of the house to dream about my future.

In 1942, the Pasolinis moved to Casarsa permanently in order to escape the bombings of Bologna. They occupied half of our house, and around the chimney of the old kitchen were arranged five thousand volumes of twentieth-century literature. Carlo was away fighting in Africa. After lengthy make-up sessions, Susanna would put the house into order, prepare lunch, and work in the garden (she had rediscovered many of the habits of country life). Guido attended the *liceo scientifico* [a science-oriented high school] at Pordenone. Pier Paolo was completing his *tesi di laurea* [his university degree thesis], the one on twentieth-century Italian painting that he later lost, while his little white book of poems entitled *Poesie a Casarsa*, along with congratulatory letters and the articles of his first critics, were making the rounds of the house, and they were greatly admired.

Zanzotto (1982) has described Pasolini's pedagogical passion. From the very beginning of his family's relocation in Casarsa, Pier Paolo began to give lessons in Latin, Italian literature, and English to me and my friends. These were the most wonderful lessons I have ever participated in during my entire life. We read classical poetry, then Baudelaire and the Spanish poets. Ungaretti was everyone's favourite. Wonderful hours were spent around the black table in the living room of the Pasolini house, listening for the echoes of Petrarch in the poets that came after him, composing aesthetic analyses of Virgil's verses, reading all of Leopardi, gaining our first inkling of modern poetry. In those days, Pier Paolo intoxicated us, forever, with the elixir of stylistic criticism.

It strikes me that, today, I am writing down these memories as if I were describing lunar mountain ranges, because they concern a world that is utterly destroyed, that no longer exists, and sometimes I even wonder if these sentimental memories arise from anything that ever actually occurred. I have been distanced, even 'legally,' from the objects belonging to Pasolini, from his homes, from his books. I no longer have anything around me to help me to recognize myself. I could die from a starvation of memories, or else continue to pursue those few that have remained with me, but only if it is my own desire to remember them (and only those that give me pleasure).

For example, something that I would like to recall is that great homosexual ghost of our youth. Today it is a ghost even in the technical sense. It is a shadow of a corpse, because the erotic energy of the peasant world that then surrounded us and that condensed into innumerable physical apparitions, each with an aesthetic individuality like unique works of natural art, no longer exists. It is objectively gone; it has disappeared. To anyone who would dispute this declaration, I can only repeat it like a saint abandoned by his God.

The homosexuality of that world, which filled the heart of anyone who practised it with happy wisdom, began to intrigue us very early. It was an extra statuette among those little saints in our mothers' house, half-hidden but stubborn in sending us its messages. These messages reached us more or less at the same time, even though Pier Paolo was seven years older than I. But I was the last to arrive in the family, and I always imagined that those who had come before me, Pier Paolo among them, had relieved me of the labour of puzzling over whatever should have appeared immediately evident.

I was jealous. I had many friends with whom I would play in the courtyard of my house. After ten years of age, some of them had become very good-looking, and I was already attracted to them at a distance. Pier Paolo, instead, was surreptitiously kissing them. In particular one named Dilio. He would have Dilio sit on his lap and he would caress his blond hair. Pier Paolo also painted his portrait, which has been shown in exhibits of the many sketches and paintings Pier Paolo made throughout his life. Little Dilio was quickly using up his natural gifts, and was already a falling star, and Pier Paolo forgot him as soon as he was no longer so attractive.

But it was only during the tumultuous period of the war that our erotic dream was realized in the form of the ingenuous and strong peasant boys with whom we sought shelter when our house was half-destroyed during a bombardment. It was here that Pier Paolo had the long and painful love described in *Atti impuri*. Besides the novel, there are also some letters addressed to this brown-haired and handsome boy. But as soon as he showed signs of the changes that come with age – those deformations that afflict the most pure and vulnerable peasant physiognomy – Pier Paolo once again could not wait to disappear from his life, and he fell into the most obvious embarrassment whenever they accidentally met.

After the war, other loves attracted him – or rather an entire world inhabited only by boys whom we would meet on river banks, in taverns, at festivals, along the roads of countless villages, day or night, in any weather. We travelled by bicycle. These loves did not always occur happily. There was also an element of obsessive repetition, while the construction of Pier Paolo's own *persona* had taken a bit of the upper hand. He built up his own image with so many little proofs of his devotion, but also with such an extremely exclusive and superb idea of himself based, like a challenge, upon his natural gifts, that I felt it might suffocate me.

After a period of great happiness, immediately following the war, a series of small incidents and insistent alarms began to punctuate his life. More than once I saw Pier Paolo risk lynching, and indeed it was this risk that precipitated his move to Rome. The incident that led to his departure from Friuli resulted from Pier Paolo's behaviour, which was somewhere between naïve and deliberately provocative. He was tempting fate. There were initially only small and obscure indications of danger but these nevertheless began to raise a perennial state of anxiety, during a period in which Pier Paolo's devotion to the Friulian peasant world was fully unfolding, and this devotion was returned to him everywhere with the same intensity. These obscure little warnings continued to gather invisibly until he was caught up in a spider's web. The clerical bourgeois class, long overlooked and underappreciated, was taking its revenge, as much as their power allowed. Faced with homosexuality, they resorted to the law, and produced a scandal. It is certain that the peasants would have sheltered and concealed Pier Paolo in silence, given their natural aversion to such condemnations. Instead, the bourgeoisie grew so proud of their power to condemn that they conceded Pier Paolo some clemency when they were sure that his presence in the Friulian peasant world would be erased. At every step during these events, the Friulian bourgeoisie enjoyed the complicity of the Communist party – without having requested it, and without having any real need of it.

Translated by Patrick Rumble

References

Naldini, Nico, ed. *Lettere 1940–1954*. Turin: Einaudi, 1986

–, ed. *Lettere 1955–1975*. Turin: Einaudi, 1988

– *Pasolini: Una vita*. Turin: Einaudi, 1989

Pasolini, Pier Paolo. *Poesie a Casarsa*. Bologna: Libreria Antiquariata, 1942

– *Amado mio-Atti impuri* Milan: Garzanti, 1982 [1943–48]

Zanzotto, Andrea. 'Pedagogy,' in Beverly Allen, ed., *Pier Paolo Pasolini: The Poetics of Heresy*, 30–41. Saratoga, CA: Anma Libri, 1982

Pasolini's 'Roman Novels,' the Italian Communist Party, and the Events of 1956

JOSEPH FRANCESE

In 1956, Nikita Khrushchev delivered his denunciation of Joseph Stalin, an event with seismic repercussions in the Communist parties throughout Western Europe, including Italy. In this tactful and thorough essay, Joseph Francese focuses discussion of Pasolini's often troubled relationship with the Italian Communist Party at just that moment. In this account of the polemics occasioned by the first of his two 'Roman novels,' *Ragazzi di Vita* (*The Ragazzi* [1955]), a critical debate coinciding with the 'events of '56,' Francese draws directly on the exchanges between Carlo Salinari and the other editors of the Communist review *Contemporaneo* and Pasolini concerning his novel and two poetry anthologies Pasolini edited. The debate they played out was at once revelatory and doomed. Revelatory because, in his polemical rejoinders to critics who called his book before the bar of Communist aesthetics, Pasolini raised important questions pertaining to issues of linguistics (i.e., the dialect question), narrational techniques, characterization, and the structure of the novel as they arose in the context of a 'socialist realist' aesthetic coming into crisis. Doomed because, as Francese observes, the ill-defined poetics of the Neorealist novel, belatedly clarified around another novel of 1955, *Metello*, were soon to collapse. Be that as it may, Pasolini's second 'Roman novel,' *Una Vita Violenta* (*A Violent Life*), in 1959, proved to be a far less experimental exercise. As Francese suggests, Pasolini was actually more receptive to some of the Communist critics with whom we was 'in dialogue' than his often acerbic attacks might superficially indicate.

Subsequent to his 'discovery of Marx,' Pier Paolo Pasolini's preferred interlocutors were intellectuals aligned, to a greater or lesser degree, with the Italian Communist Party (the PCI). This is so to an extent that it is possible, particularly in the 1950s, to chart Pasolini's development as both thinker and literary artist by examining his fortune in the Communist press, and his responses to critics with whom he engaged significantly on matters of crucial importance to Italian Marxism.

Pasolini's sensitivity to his critics becomes clear when we compare his two 'Roman novels,' *Ragazzi di vita* (1955) and *Una vita violenta* (1959). In the former we note the manner in which the lack of a traditional protagonist limits the scope of the narration. Rather than develop the intricacies of character, Pasolini presents his reader with a series of sketches of urban Roman life. With *Ragazzi di vita* Pasolini introduced a new social stratum into Italian letters, the urban subproletariat. In order to reflect the lives of his characters, he attempted to recreate their language, a hybrid of 'Romanesco' and the myriad dialects of the workers who had migrated to the capital from points throughout Italy's Mezzogiorno. Consequently, his narrative and linguistic experimentation of *Ragazzi di vita* differed from the neorealism of other leftist authors and critics, and Pasolini reacted vehemently to the unfavourable reception afforded *Ragazzi di vita* by those Communists who took issue with his perspective on urban life and his linguistic pastiche. Although linguistic experimentation was likewise fundamental to *Una vita violenta*, the second 'Roman novel' was equipped with chronological narration and a more conventionally edifying protagonist and so it more faithfully adhered to many of the unofficial tenets of neorealism,[1] particularly those that had come forth during the debate sparked by the publication of Vasco Pratolini's *Metello* in 1955.

Ragazzi di vita was published in the latter part of May 1955 and quickly became a focal point for debate. In early 1956 Pasolini wrote 'La posizione,' an essay in which he rebuked the PCI's cultural politics. Published barely two months after Khrushchev's denunciation of Stalin at the Twentieth Congress of the CP of the USSR in February 1956,[2] his comments surprised the reader because the paragraph in which Pasolini criticized the Italian Communist Party does not appear to be directly related to the rest of the article in which it appears:

Quanto al posizionalismo, per cosí dire, 'tattico' dei comunisti, o nella fattispecie dell' 'Unità' o del 'Contemporaneo,' sarebbe atto da Maramaldo, in questo momento, infierire. La crudezza e la durezza ideologico-tattica di Salinari e di altri era viziata da quello che Lukács – in un'intervista concessa a un inviato appunto dell' 'Unità' durante i lavori del Congresso del PCUS – chiama 'prospettivismo'. L'ingenua e quasi illetterata (e anche burocratica) coazione teorica derivava dalla convinzione che una letteratura realistica dovesse fondarsi su quel 'prospettivismo': mentre in una società come la nostra non può venire semplicemente rimosso, in nome di una salute vista in prospettiva, anticipata, coatta, lo stato di crisi, di dolore, di divisione. ('La posizione')

If I were to insist on the issue of the 'tactical positionalism,' so to speak, of the Communists, particularly that of *Unità* or of the *Contemporaneo*, it would be tantamount, at this point in time, to attacking the defenceless. The hard-line ideological and strategic harshness of Salinari and others is vitiated by what Lukács, in an interview with *Unità*'s correspondent during the Congress of the Communist Party of the USSR, calls *'prospettivismo.'* The ingenuous and almost illiterate (and bureaucratic) theoretical coercion derived from the belief that a realistic literature should be founded on that *'prospettivismo'*: while in a society such as ours the state of crisis, pain, and division simply cannot, in the name of an anticipated, compulsory, health, be repressed.

Pasolini suggested the implicit presence of an ulterior motive in the literary criticism of the Communists, namely that writers were being encouraged to adopt a certain ideological stance. This 'position' was intended to promote in the writer's creative work the prospect of a better, socialistic future, i.e., *'prospettivismo.'*[3]

The *Contemporaneo*, a Communist party weekly directed by Carlo Salinari, responded to Pasolini's essay with an unsigned note, 'Maramaldi e Ferrucci,' in which the editorial board categorically denied any a priori ideological prejudice or 'tactical' stance in its treatment of contemporary literature, or of Pasolini's work in particular.[4] Accusing Pasolini of trying to exploit the Twentieth Congress of the Soviet party to compensate for his own creative shortcomings, the note claimed that, angered by Salinari's criticisms of *Ragazzi di vita*, Pasolini was attempting to give his pique a theoretical and artistic legitimacy.[5] The note also charged Pasolini with a hasty and superficial reading of Lukács and of the writings of members of the board of the *Contemporaneo*, particularly those that addressed 'socialist realism.' The note then made clear the journal's readiness to continue the dialogue with Pasolini, but only if he would desist from seeking out an ulterior motive in each of their affirmations.

This controversy was not lost on Pasolini's friends.[6] Italo Calvino, for example, in a letter to Pasolini dated 1 March 1956, asked why those 'simpletons' at the *Contemporaneo* had yet to dedicate a centrefold to Pasolini's other book, that is, to the *Canzoniere italiano* edited by Pasolini in

1955 for Guanda. Calvino's wish was soon granted but the article that appeared in the *Contemporaneo* was hardly what he and Pasolini had hoped for. In June 1956, the weekly published an unfavourable review. Vann'Antò[7] harshly criticized Pasolini's lack of philological rigour in the sampling of Sicilian poetry reprinted in his *Canzoniere*. In a subsequent issue the *Contemporaneo* printed a letter to the editor in which Vincenzo Talarico underlined what he considered the shortcomings of Pasolini's selection of representative Neapolitan poets and criticized his interpretation of texts published in an earlier anthology edited by Pasolini, *Poesia dialettale del Novecento*.

Pasolini responded to Vann'Antò and Talarico with a letter to the editor, 'La poesia popolare.' He accused the *Contemporaneo* of debating trifles and claimed that the criticism of his *Canzoniere* was based on 'aesthetically insignificant, minimal philological imprecisions.' Pasolini did not reply to points raised by Vann'Antò but asked the weekly's editors why they published an article by someone whose world-view differed so markedly from their own, particularly since the *Contemporaneo*, in his words, was usually so insensitive to questions that could not be exploited within the context of political contingency. He then accused the journal of organizing a campaign to discredit him. Pasolini concluded by challenging the *Contemporaneo* to discard its 'hypocritically objective periphrasis' and discuss directly with him their views on contemporary literature.

Together with this public letter to the editor, Pasolini sent personal correspondence to Antonello Trombadori who, along with his uncle Gaetano Trombadori and Salinari, comprised the *Contemporaneo*'s editorial board.[8] The nephew had invited Pasolini to the *Contemporaneo*'s offices to convey to the novelist his personal dissent from his magazine's appraisal of *Ragazzi di vita*.[9] Pasolini specified in his letter to Antonello that his quarrel was not with all Communist critics, but with Salinari and with his uncle, both of whom Pasolini described as 'rigid, incapable of sentiment, aprioristic.' He specifically excluded from his invective other Communist intellectuals of note, including Niccolò Gallo, the author of a favourable review of *Ragazzi di vita*, Carlo Muscetta, and Cesare Cases. There were Marxist critics whose different interpretation of 'socialist realism' caused them to disagree with Salinari, for example, on the merits of Pratolini's *Metello*. At the same time, Pasolini sought to placate those Communists with whom he had dealt acrimoniously in 'La posizione,' and claimed to be 'substantially in agreement' with them, adding

Quanto al resto non capisco perché ve la siate presa tanto per la mia espressione, puramente cromatica, dato che non vorrete negare la realtà di un vostro momento di crisi, di ripensamento e di disagio. Naturale, giusto, e, se voi sarete veramente onesti e sinceri con voi stessi, produttivo, pieno di futuro. Non si tratta più di fare la solita 'autocritica,' scontata aprioristicamente. La cosa è molto più grave e importante: e questo ve lo dico non da avversario, ma da amico. E un amico dice talvolta le cose molto più violentemente di un avversario, come sai. (Letter to Antonello Trombadori of 7 June 1956)

For that matter I do not understand why you were angered by that purely chromatic expression of mine, since you would not want to deny the reality behind your own moment of crisis, rethinking and discomfort. Natural, just, and, if you want to be truly honest and sincere with yourselves, productive, full of promise for the future. You cannot undergo the usual 'self-criticism,' whose results are taken for granted even before you begin. This is much more serious and important: and I am telling you this as a friend, not as an adversary. And a friend sometimes says things much more violently than an adversary, as you know.

The controversy arrived at a temporary resolution in the issue of 30 June with letters to the editor from Calvino[10] and Pasolini, and a response from Salinari.[11] For his part, Pasolini stated that although the *Contemporaneo* had depicted him as 'the "darling" of the literary Establishment' he was in truth the victim of unjust and inordinate attacks in the clerical and conservative press. He was forced to defend himself against criminal charges, brought against him by that same official culture, because of what had been called the 'pornographic content' of the novel. While promising to discuss the matter more calmly in the forthcoming issue of *Officina*, he also stated that his disagreement with what he indiscriminately labelled Communist literary criticism was twofold. He saw in the *Contemporaneo*'s inability to comprehend *Ragazzi di vita* a manifestation of that journal's habitual exhortation to values that he branded *'prospettivistici,'* that is, evoking a happier, socialistic future. His other objection more closely regarded the development of his prose:

Il fatto è che nei confronti della critica letteraria comunista ... sono rimasto troppo profondamente deluso da quella incomprensione da parte non di avversari ma da parte di amici (o almeno ritenuti tali da me, se, scrivendo *Ragazzi di vita,* pensavo di scrivere un documento d'accusa sociale e di poetica realistica, secondo proprio i vostri desiderata, anche se non secondo le vostre esplicite o implicite norme 'prospettivistiche') ('La poesia e il dialetto').

The fact is, that as far as Communist literary criticism is concerned ... I was profoundly, and excessively disappointed by the incomprehension not of adversaries, but of friends (or, at least those whom I believed to be my friends, if while writing *Ragazzi di vita,* I thought I was writing a document of social denunciation that was faithful to a realistic poetics, exactly according to your own desiderata, even if not according to your explicit or implied 'perspectivistic' norms).[12]

While contradicting himself, alternately considering the Communist literati as a monolithic entity and, then, as individuals each with his own critical method, Pasolini also made two important concessions. He admitted that the *prospettivismo* of which he had accused Salinari was more implied than explicit. More significantly, he acknowledged the importance of the opinion of those critics who were members of, or close to, the Communist party *during the creative process* (and not, as is often the case, to criticism that appears subsequent to a work's publication).

Together with the change in narrative strategy that occurs between *Ragazzi di vita* and *Una vita violenta,* we must consider those 'desiderata' referred to above in 'La poesia e il dialetto' and the manner in which they influenced what was to be the story of Tommaso Puzzilli.[13] While neorealism as a literary concept was never sharply delineated, it received its most precise characterization as a result of the discussion of Pratolini's *Metello,* a novel published several months prior to *Ragazzi di vita.* It is possible to deduce from that discussion the criteria by which Pasolini assumed *Una vita violenta* would be judged.

Metello was greeted with great interest. As Ferretti has indicated, the exchange of views concerning Pratolini's novel offered the first indications of problems that would become explosive issues among Marxist critics and intellectuals in the aftermath the events of 1956.[14] The debate began soon after the novel's publication in early 1955, was protracted over seventeen months, and did much to define literary neorealism, although, as it turned out, on the eve of its eclipse. While readers such as Carlo Bo and Leone Piccioni disapproved of Pratolini's abandonment of his previous lyrical vein, critics who were attempting to provide neorealism with a theoretical basis considered *Metello* a proving ground for concepts of both 'novel' and 'realism.'

Pratolini's most enthusiastic support came from Salinari. In his review for the *Contemporaneo* of 12 February 1955, Salinari attributed to Pratolini the merit of having avoided the pseudo-objectivity of nineteenth-century *verismo*. More important for Salinari, Pratolini had, he claimed, produced a work of literature that had overcome many of the shortcomings of previous neorealist narrative. This was especially evident in the representation of the 'organic development' of the novel's central characters. 'The real problem,' Salinari argued, 'is that of acquiring a new perspective from which to observe the world, to rebuild from inside the persona a human personality and to recognize in mankind human sentiments.'

Salinari's appraisal provoked sharp disagreement among Marxist critics. Carlo Muscetta's extremely caustic rebuttal in *Società* launched the debate into a second phase. No longer were the battle lines drawn between opponents and proponents of neorealism, rather the discussion took place almost exclusively within the Left. However, neither Muscetta nor other critics like Cases and Franco Fortini, who stressed the limitations of Pratolini's novel, disagreed with Salinari when he insisted on the fundamental importance of the protagonist.[15] They all concurred that a novel needed a central character who reflected the internal struggle of the apolitical individual who gradually achieves class consciousness to become an organic part of the workers' movement. Calvino, in a contemporary essay, suggested a way of considering the concept of the novel that did not differ significantly from what other progressive intellectuals were proposing (Calvino 1955).[16] Calvino's main preoccupation was also the protagonist, and the central character of the novel was, for him, a measure of the individual's active participation in society. For this reason, the narrator was obligated to believe in the individual and fight against the individual's dissolution. According to Calvino, the novel, therefore, was called upon to represent the manner in which the individual overcomes internal and social conflict. 'Every true poem,' he declared, 'contains a "leonine core," nourishment for a rigorous morality, and for a mastery of history' (Calvino 1955).

Pasolini's narrative style was influenced by the discussion of *Metello*. This can easily be deduced from a reading of *Una vita violenta*. To use Giuliano Manacorda's phrasing, this novel represented an 'obligatory, socially liberating journey that coincided with a biographical journey that, in its turn, takes place within a normal temporal dimension, within the chronology of the calendar.' The process of maturation of an edifying protagonist is represented in *Una vita violenta*, and as such the narrative contrasted sharply with what Pasolini had done in *Ragazzi di vita*. Pasolini's earlier book could be described as a collection of distinct works of brief narratives artificially grouped into a unitary format. Pasolini himself admitted that his earlier novel 'lacks a frame. The new novel (*Una vita*) is infinitely more structured' (Naldini 1989). More important for Pasolini's critics at that time, the youthful idealism of *Ragazzi di vita*'s protagonist, Riccetto, does not progress into class consciousness but deteriorates into a cynical individualism.

During the period between the publication of the first and second of his 'Roman novels' Pasolini showed himself to be closer to the PCI than to any other faction within the Italian left despite his adamant criticism of the party.[17] In a footnote to *Una polemica in versi*, published soon after the Soviet Union's armed intervention in Poland and Hungary, Pasolini reprinted the paragraph of 'La posizione' that had incurred the ire of the *Contemporaneo* while reiterating his accusations of Communist '*prospettivismo*.' However, he softened his charges of '*tatticismo*,' and left open the possibility of an eventual reconciliation:[18]

Quanto poi al tatticismo letterario di Salinari, sono stato evidentemente, e pessimisticamente, frainteso; la mia accusa (come risulta da questi versi) era molto meno offensiva di quanto egli abbia creduto; implicava la sua buona fede e non era affatto circoscritta alle operazioni letterarie.

Regarding Salinari's literary *tatticismo*, I was obviously, and pessimistically misunderstood; my accusation (as shown by this poem) was much less offensive than his perception of it. I took for granted his good faith, and not only in literary matters.

At the same time, in another note, Pasolini warned against the tendency of other Italian Marxists (particularly Fortini and the journal *Ragionamenti*) toward creating a new myth, that of the working masses.[19] In Pasolini's words these intellectuals nullified themselves in 'a rigid and moralistic anonimity [sic].' By drawing such battle lines Pasolini at once aligned himself with the Communists while underscoring the points of disagreement. Pasolini could not accept the necessarily bureaucratic and 'institutionalized' nature of a major political party. Nor would he accept the necessary union, within any political movement, of the moment in which the individual would – as he would say in the 1970s – 'trasumanar' (that is, come to embody an ideal)[20] on the one hand and the inevitable bureaucratic organization of those collective energies on the other.[21]

The essays on literature written by Pasolini in the aftermath of the crisis of 1956 show a tendency to sublimate political differences with the Communist party into a literary context through his renewed proposal for the use of dialect in literary discourse. As we have seen, the linguistic pastiche of Ragazzi di vita had been a major point of contention, and Pasolini returned to the issue.

'La confusione degli stili' was written in October 1956, concurrent with Una polemica in versi.[22] In this essay, Pasolini identified three distinct strata within the Italian language: the literary argot, the interregional koiné of the petty bourgeoisie, and the various local dialects. Pasolini understood the practical application of Gramsci's notion of a literature – one at once national and popular in scope – differently from most progressive writers. The difference rested on Pasolini's insistence on the use of dialect in his prose. Those who eschewed dialect, opting for the more accessible middle ground of the koiné, preferred the safety afforded by conforming to the guidelines set down by the majority of Marxist critics. The neorealists' espousal of the koiné entailed subordinating literary research to a Communist strategy directed at a nation-wide middle-class electorate. To be more precise, Pasolini believed that the use of the koiné, while acceptable in the political arena, precluded the literary representation of individual parlance. Moreover, he believed the use of the koiné was based on a misreading of Gramsci.[23] Although Gramsci considered dialect a residue of subaltern cultures, Pasolini nonetheless felt that the Contemporaneo's admonishment against dialect was a 'Stalinistic' interpretation of Gramsci.[24] Pasolini believed that any realistic description of the present necessarily captured the 'the soul of the times.' Admixtures taken from the popular dialects made representation of the country's linguistic fragmentation and economic stratification possible. If a writer was to express reality, the language of subaltern culture must be incorporated. Pasolini's evaluation of the regional dialects as a source of renewal for literary language provided theoretical justification for what he was attempting in his prose.[25]

With Una vita violenta he brought forth his attempts at incorporating dialect into literary discourse while again proposing the subproletariat as literary and political subject. At the same time, he 'reduced the social space' of this novel[26] to concentrate on a single character whose gradual attainment of class consciousness was exactly what leftist critics had found lacking in *Ragazzi di vita*. Tommaso Puzzilli, the protagonist, was not 'naturally' inclined toward socialism, but reached a certain level of class consciousness as a result of a process of maturation catalysed by external events.[27]

Immediately after the fall of Mussolini's government, Pasolini had written of the 'pedagogical duty' that awaited Italian intellectuals of his generation.[28] Then, in an essay written in 1959, 'Marxisants,' he attributed a 'priestly function' to the progressive intellectual. To a significant degree, the uneasiness of Pasolini's relationship with the PCI was an effect of his never explicitly challenging the hegemonic role ascribed to the party by Gramsci. Pasolini never attempted to redefine the intellectual's social function but, faithful to his Crocean formation, he continued to consider intellectuals as a sort of aristocracy distinct from the working class and the workers' movement. For this reason, he chose to contribute to the PCI's internal debate from the outside. 'Marxisants' and *Una vita violenta* are two important manifestations of the manner in which this conflictual encounter with the PCI took shape at the end of the 1950s.

In 'Marxisants,' Pasolini noted the development of neocapitalism in Italy and its effects on the petty bourgeoisie and the working classes. As he was to state repeatedly in the early 1960s, the workers were gradually being corrupted by consumerism and absorbed into the lower middle class. Consequently, the revolutionary fervour of the proletariat was on the wane and the PCI was being forced to rethink its strategy. In his opinion, the Communist party would benefit by becoming the 'party of the poor.' He believed this to be a fertile political strategy that was also applicable to literature. *Una vita violenta* can be cited as an example of this politically strategic adjustment and, at the same time, as he said, of the rethinking of the means by which the subproletariat could be reproposed as literary subject through channels other than 'populism' and the populist documentarism of the post–World War II period. For this reason, it is essential to look beyond the differences that separated Pasolini from the intellectuals of the Italian Communist Party, particularly during the early stages of his career. We must note his attempts to influence their reception of his work through his contributions to the various discussions of literary methodology and the positive, dialectical value he attributed to the Communists' interpretation of his artistic production.

Notes

1 *Ragazzi di vita* comprises a series of loosely connected narrative fragments that describe the life of a gang of street urchins. The principal character, Riccetto, is at the outset an idealistic youth who dives into the Tiber to save a drowning swallow. He gradually becomes a cynical young man who turns his back on a drowning boy. On the other hand, *Una vita violenta* adheres more closely to traditional novel form. The protagonist, Tommaso Puzzilli, initially averse to politics, becomes involved with reactionary and conservative groups in order to satisfy egoistical concerns. He slowly acquires an understanding of his lot in life and enrols in the PCI. When torrential rains cause the Aniene River on the outskirts of Rome to overflow, Tommaso, a resident of the affected area, voluntarily guides rescue workers through the flood waters. As a result of his efforts, he contracts a fatal illness.

2 In his 'secret report' Khrushchev gave a lengthy description of Stalin's crimes. Details of the speech began to filter out of the Soviet Union immediately after the Congress. Subsequent workers' uprisings in Hungary and Poland were suppressed by armed Soviet intervention. These events threw the Italian Left into disarray and triggered an 'exodus' of intellectuals from the Italian Communist Party. For a more complete overview and analysis, see Ajello and Vittoria (1979).

3 By calling them to task for their 'tactical positionalism,' Pasolini accused those critics in or near the PCI of setting literary and aesthetic criteria aside in favour of the party's cultural politics. In his view, negative reviews were the expression of a contingent 'position' conditioned more by political than by literary considerations. Hence, the reviews were to be read as part of a long-term 'tactic' that saw culture subordinated to politics and in which literature took on the function of helping readers to adapt their perspective (*prospettiva*) in order to foresee a more just – i.e., socialist – society.

4 It may be assumed that Salinari penned this response to Pasolini. In his letter to Italo Calvino ('La poesia e il dialetto') Salinari, speaking of this editorial, states, 'I stand by my polemical notes.'

5 In a debate held earlier in Rome, Salinari had, in fact, criticized what he called the two ambiguities of the novel's narrational style, its mixture of dialect, Italianized dialect, and literary Italian on one hand, and what he characterized as the morbid curiosity of the would-be documentarist on the other (see 'Un equivoco libro sulle borgate romane'). Pasolini was present at this debate, organized to mark the publication of the second edition of his book, and offered the closing arguments in which he 'vehemently defended' his work (*L'Unità*) while verbally attacking Salinari.

6 See Naldini 1989, 190.

7 Pseudonym of the Sicilian poet Giovanni Antonio Di Giacomo

8 See the letter of 7 June 1956 in Pasolini, *Lettere: 1956–1975*, 204–5.

9 Letter to Livio Garzanti of 17 August 1955, in *Lettere*, 113

10 See 'La poesia e il dialetto.' In his letter Calvino criticized the manner in which the *Contemporaneo* followed contemporary Italian letters. He asked why the magazine had ignored the poem *Le ceneri di Gramsci*. Calvino, however, did agree with most of what Salinari had said about *Ragazzi di vita* and also found *Le ceneri di Gramsci* to be less than perfect. Calvino considered the work in prose to be a 'minor work' and believed that Pasolini's gift was as a poet and a critic. Although he could not condone the combination of 'revolutionary rigor and panic love of life' to be found in *Le ceneri di Gramsci*, Calvino nonetheless believed the poem had overcome many of the limits of hermeticism and of neorealism. Nor was Calvino happy with certain poems included in Pasolini's anthology, but he did believe that the introductory essay was an important contribution to a field of study that was of particular interest to all progressive Italian intellectuals. In his opinion, the *Contemporaneo* erred by not promoting a debate on the introductory theoretical essay and on the criteria used in selecting the works to be anthologized. This initial error was compounded by the publication of an essay for specialists in the field that, rather than encourage the discussion of Pasolini's collection, tended to discourage the average reader from consulting it at all. Since the *Contemporaneo* had chosen to ignore Pasolini's most exemplary work, he asked why had the dozen or so superficial and banal polemical lines dedicated by Pasolini to the *Contemporaneo* (and published in an obscure literary journal, *Officina*) not be given the same treatment. In Calvino's opinion, the *Contemporaneo* was wasting its energy and that of its readership with matters of little import while neglecting the more substantial contributions. He admonished the Communist weekly to highlight and discuss those rare new ideas that could be culled from contemporary literature and criticism.

11 In concluding the debate, Salinari substantially ignored Pasolini's comments and responded exclusively to Calvino. Citing an unwillingness to discuss work directly with artists for fear of compromising his critical perspective, Salinari agreed with Calvino that the *Contemporaneo* had committed a grave oversight in not discussing *Le ceneri di Gramsci* and went on to speak of the poem in encomiastic terms. For Salinari, the clash of irrationality and rationality in *Le ceneri di Gramsci* reflected an historical tendency. For Salinari the microcosm depicted in the verse reflected the travail of his generation as he and his contemporaries moved from the coerced fascism of their youth towards a definition of Marxism: formally striking, the verse

found its inner strength in this important ideological and moral problematic. Because of this, the last person with whom Salinari wished acrimony was Pasolini. He did, however, defend the editorial 'Maramaldi e Ferrucci': 'While Pasolini reserves the right to cast rough and hurried judgements on our actions, he complains if we reply.' For this reason, rather than publish the hasty and superficial discussion of the *Anthology* proposed by Calvino, the journal had preferred to entrust the treatment of the work to a well-known specialist of Italian dialect poetry. (For further documentation on the relationship between Pasolini and Salinari as it evolved against the backdrop of Italian letters of the late 1950s and earlier 1960s, the reader may consult the pages dedicated to Pasolini in Salinari's *Preludio e fine del realismo in Italia*; Salinari's review of *In morte del realismo* ('Significato dello "Strega",' *Vie Nuove*, 16 July 1960); and the exchange of views published in *Vie Nuove* to which both Salinari and Pasolini contributed weekly columns in the early 1960s. Salinari's remarks may be found in 'Diagnosi per Pasolini' (23 September 1961) and in 'Gli schemi non fanno poesia' (18 October 1961). Pasolini's comments have been reprinted in *Le belle bandiere* (155–65). Also of interest, within this context, is Pasolini's appraisal of Salinari's *Miti e coscienza del decadentismo italiano*. See 'La reazione stilistica,' now in Pasolini, *Il Portico della Morte*. See also Francese (1991).

12 The poetic tension toward a conciliation with Communist intellectuals within the 'work in progress' continued to influence Pasolini's creative production in the 1960s. According to Naldini (285), in 1963 Pasolini wrote, but perhaps did not mail, a letter to Mario Alicata in which he affirmed, 'Having just completed Matthew [*The Gospel According to St. Matthew*] I would like to remind you of this phrase: "Say yes if the answer is yes, no if it is no: everything else comes from the Evil One." You and your coterie must have the courage to say either yes or no to me. Not because this will have any effect on my real and profound Communist ideology and faith, but so that it might help me see things more clearly and help facilitate my everyday choices.' What is reaffirmed here is the importance Pasolini attributed to the Communists' approval of his work, his willingness to adapt his work to their guidelines and the tendency on his part to perceive them as a band of conspirators when that approval was not given wholeheartedly and immediately.

13 In July 1956, Tommaso Fiore published a favourable review of *Ragazzi di vita* in the Party daily *Il Paese* in which he nonetheless called Pasolini to task for purportedly maintaining a documentarist's impartiality, a criticism first advanced by the Liberal Giancarlo Vigorelli. Adriano Seroni, in the Party weekly *Vie Nuove*, discerned a 'tourist's attitude' that prevented the novelist

from truly rendering the life of Rome's subproletariat. In Seroni's opinion, *Ragazzi di vita* was a well-written work that unfortunately was not of the same calibre as Pasolini's poetry and critical writings. Giovanni Berlinguer decried the novel in the Communist party's daily, *L'Unità*, but two weeks later that same journal published a review by Gaetano Trombadori that reiterated to a great degree the salient points of Seroni's article. Faithful to the Crocean opposition of poetry and non-poetry, Trombadori relegated Pasolini's first 'Roman novel' to the latter category because the lack of 'a significant and profoundly felt content.' But Trombadori's review was not entirely negative. In fact, he was very careful to underline Pasolini's technical elaboration of literary Italian. Niccolò Gallo praised Pasolini's important and partially successful attempt to submit a difficult reality to moral and cultural reflection.

While grateful for the positive comments forthcoming from Fiore and Gallo, Pasolini could be said to have been excessively preoccupied with the unfavourable reviews. He perceived them as indicative of a campaign organized by the Communist hierarchy against him (see the letter of 17 August 1955 to Livio Garzanti in Pasolini, *Lettere: 1955–1975*). Several years after the reviews came more scholarly treatments of Pasolini's work. Piero Pucci (1958), in an important analysis of *Ragazzi di vita*, noted the manner in which Pasolini imposed on his characters his own impressionistic dialect. Pucci compared Pasolini's pastiche to that created by Gadda for his *Pasticciaccio*. According to Pucci, while Gadda's 'plurilinguism' contributed to the creation of a multiplicity of psychological strata within the text, Pasolini failed in his attempt to create 'flesh and blood' characters. In Pucci's opinion, Pasolini's success was merely one of 'philological transcription' of his own empirical observations. Mario Costanzo spoke of Pasolini's refusal to examine the psychological make-up of his street urchins in *Ragazzi di vita* while limiting the scope of his narration to the construction of an 'outline of facile effects.'

14 For a summary of the debate and bibliographical documentation of its process, see Gian Carlo Ferretti (1956).
15 Cases considered Metello a 'good savage' and for this reason faulted the character's spontaneity that, for him, was all too reminiscent of 'the usual distinction between innately good Italians and their phoney counterparts.' He explained that 'Metello's evolution as a person should be the result of the dialectic between his individual destiny and society, class conflict. Now this element is completely lacking.'

In Fortini's view, the promotion of *Metello* was equal to a defence of the pre-1956 cultural politics of the Left. Pratolini and Salinari erred by ignoring the pressure exerted on Italy's intellectuals, at once victims and accomplices of a culture industrialized by Atlantic capitalism.

16 For Calvino's views on *Metello*, see Calvino (1956).

17 What we are proposing can be verified by contrasting the diverse perspectives of poems composed by Pasolini before and after Khrushchev's 'secret report.' The persona of *La terra del lavoro* (1956) adopts a markedly different perspective from the earlier *Recit* and *Il pianto della scavatrice*. *La terra del lavoro*, due undoubtably to the intensity of Pasolini's reaction to the tumult of 1956 and his disagreement with Salinari and other Communists, is one of the few instances in which his persona goes beyond poetic autobiography (a tendency of *Recit* and *Il pianto della scavatrice*) to gain a broader perspective on the events of the day. In *Le ceneri di Gramsci* (1954) Pasolini, a bourgeois intellectual, had called himself a traitor to his own dying class; in *Il pianto della scavatrice* the persona sees himself in the process of overcoming his youthful passions and attaining a rational world-view grounded in Marxism. However, in *La terra del lavoro*, this persona does not ignore his own internal torment, but nonetheless is able to focus on extrinsic reality. Pasolini had hoped that external circumstances would facilitate his attempt to overcome his 'passions,' those irrational rushes of idealism that had caused him and many others of his generation to seek out an alternative to fascism, even when none was at hand. However, in *La terra del lavoro*, the persona realizes that it is necessary to return to those passions in order to combat the disarray into which the Left had fallen. In this poem a return to that youthful vision, once again unbridled by Party organization, is proposed.

18 Pasolini revised this note prior to the publication of the poem as part of the collection *Le ceneri di Gramsci* in 1957. I am quoting here the version reprinted in the anthology of *Officina* edited by Ferretti. The most noticeable difference in the texts is the elimination of all direct references to Salinari.

19 For an exposition of *Ragionamenti*'s political stance, see 'Proposte per un'organizzazione della cultura marxista in Italia,' Supplement to no. 5–6, September 1956, and 'I fatti d'Ungheria,' no. 7, November 1956. Pasolini objected to what Fortini's journal claimed should be the Italian Left's domestic response to the events in Eastern Europe. *Ragionamenti* equated the unwillingness to engage in dialogue on the part of the governing Parties of Eastern bloc countries with the hegemonic role the PCI tried to hold within the Italian worker's movement. The *'operaismo'* of *Ragionamenti*, that is, the call for autonomous workers' self-direction, aided by progressive intellectuals, was in reality a positing of the intellectuals' right to directly guide the working classes without the mediation of a workers' party.

20 Pasolini borrowed this verb from *Paradiso*, III, 70. Dante, speaking there of Glauco's metamorphosis, wished to represent the elevation of the individual to a sublime state.

21 Pasolini's uneasy relationship with the PCI reached a low point after the abrupt closure of 'Dialoghi con Pasolini,' published in another Communist weekly, *Vie Nuove* (see Ferretti's introduction to Pasolini, *Le belle bandiere*). Nonetheless, after the isolation brought about by his vocal opposition to the 'anti-literariness' of the *Neoavanguardia* and then of the student movement of 1968, he was able to find a common ground with the PCI (see *Trasumanar e organizzar* in the homonymous collection).

I would like to add, in passing, that Pasolini spoke in public about his expulsion from the Italian Communist Party with extreme reluctance. In the first of his two interviews with Jean Duflot, Pasolini did mention his exit from the PCI, but altered the facts significantly. As he said, 'I must say that I frequented the Communist Party for about a year, in '47–48 ... I, like many other comrades, did not renew my membership when it expired. The ever-increasing Stalinism of Togliatti's leadership, his mixture of authoritarianism and of suffocating paternalism, did not, in my view, build on the great hopes of the post-War period.' However, in the second Duflot interview he spoke of the expulsion but refused to equate a local office with the entire Party: 'In 1948, several Communists thought I should be expelled from the Party; I had to leave what I loved, it was a death in my soul' (Pasolini, *Il sogno del centauro*, 26–27, 156).

22 See the letter to the other editors of *Officina* of 3 and 16 October and 7 November 1956, in Pasolini, *Lettere: 1955–1975*. The article first appeared in *Ulisse*, Autumn-Winter 1956–1957, prior to its inclusion in *Passione e ideologia*.

23 Salinari, in 'La poesia e il dialetto,' had called for 'a linguistic reintegration that would work against the disintegration brought about at the end of the nineteenth century by Pascoli and by the *verismo* school, or, more recently, by so-called neorealism.'

24 To use Pasolini's own words, 'Look at how many Marxist critics (unable to free themselves of their ancient, provincial backwater servilism) attempt to aristocratically coerce others, interpreting for tactical (or, dare I say it, at the risk of seeming the bully, Stalinistic) ends the anything but rigid Gramscian notion of National-popular literature' (*Passione e ideologia* 343–4).

25 In concluding the essay 'La libertà stilistica,' he implicitly responded to Salinari's admonishment against allowing oneself to drown in a sea of phenomena. To use Pasolini's words, 'our experiments will result in an avenue of love – physical and sentimental love for the world's phenomena, and

intellectual love for their spirit, History' (*Passione e ideologia*, 487). It is clear
from this statement that Pasolini's view of history was less Gramscian than
Crocean. However, discussions of such matters reach beyond the scope
of this study. However, see Zygmunt Barański and Joseph Francese, 'The
Latent Presence of Crocean Aesthetics in Pasolini's "Critical Marxism",'
forthcoming in a collective volume edited by Barański to be published
through *The Italianist*.
26 According to Dallamano, by concentrating on a more limited sociological
sampling, Pasolini was able to view society with a 'more organic and
dialectic ideology,' and this gained him general approval from those same
critics who had criticized the 'aestheticism' of *Ragazzi di vita* (see Dallamano
1959).
27 Salinari called *Una vita violenta* a particularly important book because in it
he saw 'the relaunching of the character, that is the attempt to give back
to the human being that sense of completeness that was destroyed by
Decadentism' (*Preludio e fine del realismo in Italia*, 176).
28 See letter to Luciano Serra of July-August 1942, in Pasolini, *Lettere agli amici
(1941–5)*, 33–4.

References

Ajello, N. *Intellettuali e PCI 1944–1958*. Rome-Bari: Laterza, 1979
Barański, Z.G. 'Pier Paolo Pasolini: Culture, Croce, Gramsci.' In Z.G. Barański
    and R. Lumley, eds., *Culture and Conflict in Postwar Italy. Essays on Mass and
    Popular Culture*, 139–59. London: MacMillan, 1990
Berlinguer, G. 'Il vero e il falso delle borgate di Roma.' *L'Unità* (29 July 1955)
Calvino, I. 'Il midollo del leone.' *Paragone* (June 1955)
– 'Opinioni su *Metello* e il neorealismo.' *Società* (February 1956): 207–11
Cases, C. 'Opinioni su *Metello* e il Neorealismo.' *Società* (December 1955)
Costanzo, M. 'Pasolini filologo e poeta.' *Letteratura*, nos. 31–2 (1958)
Dallamano, R. 'Popolo romano e società nell'ultimo Pasolini,' *Contemporaneo*,
    nos. 14–15 (1959). In A. Luzi and L. Martellini, eds., *Pier Paolo Pasolini*,
    243–64. Urbino: Argalìa, 1973
Ferretti, G.C. 'Il dibattito intorno al *Metello* di Pratolini.' *Belfagor* no. 1 (1956)
– 'Introduzione.' *'Officina': Cultura, letteratura e politica negli anni cinquanta*.
    Edited by G.C. Ferretti. Turin: Einaudi, 1975
Fiore, T. 'Ragazzi di vita.' *Il Paese* (22 July 1955)
Fortini, F. 'Il Metellismo.' *Ragionamenti* (January-February 1956)
Francese, J. *Il realismo impopolare di Pier Paolo Pasolini*. Foggia: Bastogi, 1991

Gallo, N. 'Pasolini al tribunale dei giudici e dei critici.' In N. Gallo, *Scritti letterari*, 138–9. Milan: Il polifilo, 1975

Manacorda, G. 'Dalla faticosa conquista della storia della sublimazione nella bellezza.' In *Pier Paolo Pasolini nel dibattito culturale contemporaneo*, 35–48. Pavia: Comune di Alessandria, Amministrazione Provinciale di Pavia, 1977

'Maramaldi e Ferrucci.' *Il Contemporaneo* (9 June 1956)

Muscetta, C. '*Metello* e la crisi del neorealismo.' *Società* (August 1955)

Naldini, N. *Pasolini, una vita*. Turin: Einaudi, 1989

Pasolini, P.P. *Ragazzi di vita*. Milan: Garzanti, 1976 [1955]

– 'La posizione.' *Officina* 6 (April 1956)

– 'La poesia popolare.' *Il Contemporaneo* (23 June 1956)

– 'Una polemica in versi.' *Officina* (November 1956)

– *Le ceneri di Gramsci*. Milan: Garzanti, 1976 [1957]

– 'Marxisants.' *Officina* 2 (May–June 1959)

– *Una vita violenta*. Milan: Garzanti, 1976 [1959]

– *Passione e ideologia*. Milan: Garzanti, 1977 [1960]

– *Trasumanar e organizzar*. Milan: Garzanti, 1976 [1971]

– *Lettere agli amici (1941–1945)*. Edited by L. Serra. Milan: Guanda, 1976

– *Le belle bandiere*. Edited by G.C. Ferretti. Rome: Editori Riuniti, 1977

– *Il sogno del centauro*. Edited by J. Duflot. Rome: Editori Riuniti, 1983

– *Il Portico della Morte*. Edited by C. Segre. Rome: Associazione 'Fondo Pier Paolo Pasolini,' 1988

– *Lettere: 1955–1975*. Edited by N. Naldini. Turin: Einaudi, 1988

Pasolini, P.P., I. Calvino, and C. Salinari. 'La poesia e il dialetto.' *Il contemporaneo* (30 June 1956)

Poesia dialettale del Novecento. Edited by P.P. Pasolini and M. Dell'Arco. Parma: Guanda, 1952

Pucci, P. 'Lingua e dialetto in Pasolini e in Gadda.' *Società* 2, (1958)

Salinari, C. 'Metello.' *Il Contemporaneo* (2 February 1955)

– *Preludio e fine del realismo in Italia*. Naples: Morano, 1968

– *Miti e coscienza del decadentismo italiano*. Milan: Feltrinelli, 1960

Seroni, A. 'Ragazzi di vita.' *Vie Nuove* (24 July 1955)

Talarico, V. 'Dialetti meridionali.' *Il Contemporaneo* (16 June 1956)

Trombadori, G. 'Ragazzi di vita.' *L'Unità* (11 August 1955)

'Un equivoco libro sulle borgate romane.' *L'Unità* (5 July 1955)

Vann'Antò. 'La Baronessa di Carini.' *Il Contemporaneo* (2 June 1956)

Vittoria, A. *Togliatti e gli intellettuali. Storia dell'Istituto Gramsci negli anni Cinquanta e Sessanta*. Roma: Editori Riuniti, 1992

Pasolini, Zanzotto, and the Question of Pedagogy

JENNIFER STONE

'And I have dreamt of making love to women of stone' – Pasolini, 'Why That of Oedipus Is a Story' (1967)

In this essay Jennifer Stone examines Pasolini's writing and cinema in the context of the centuries-old debates, that began with Dante but continue to this day, concerning the standard language and dialects of Italy (the *questione della lingua*). During his entire lifetime, Pasolini constantly experimented in linguistic pastiche, mixing standard Italian and regional dialects in his poetry, novels, and films; and he was an energetic, if often discounted, participant in arguments concerning the fortunes of the Italian national language (as noted in Francese's essay in this volume). Stone discusses the pedagogical and psychological significance of Pasolini's linguistic pluralism and his interest in stylistic 'contamination.' She focuses on the psychoanalytic dimension of Pasolini's theory of pedagogy and she relates it to fellow-poet and teacher Andrea Zanzotto's interest in the language acquisition of children. Stone analyses how throughout his work Pasolini approached such problems as the third world, the commodification of bodies, beauty, and knowledge, according to a Freudian understanding of the Oedipal trauma, and from this perspective she surveys several of Pasolini's literary, theoretical, and cinematic works.

A Poetics of Pedagogy

The question of pedagogy in Italian culture is inseparable from the question of language – *la questione della lingua* – and even more so from the questions of dialect and love. Dante's medieval *Vita Nuova* is both an exemplum of the vernacular in action (as with Dante's realistic use of slang in the *Divina Commedia*) and a handbook for women students: 'Ladies, refined and sensitive in Love' (1992, 35) ('Donne ch'avete intelletto d'amore' – literally 'Ladies who know by insight what love is').

Central to the exchange between Pier Paolo Pasolini and Andrea Zanzotto is a discussion of the interrelationship between questions of pedagogy and language. The distinctly modern element of their thinking on these matters is the inclusion of Marx (in the form of Gramsci) and, more enduring perhaps, the reliance on Freud. One recalls Pasolini's orgastic sighs in 'Plan of Future Works' ('Progetto di opere future') from *Poetry in Form of a Rose* (*Poesia in forma di rosa*) of 1964: 'Oh Marx – all is gold – oh Freud – all is love' ('Oh Marx – tutto è oro – oh Freud – tutto è amore') (1982, 197). In this article, I focus on the psychoanalytic dimension of Pasolini's theory of pedagogy and on its close ties to Zanzotto's interest in the infant's acquisition of language. To formulate their treatises on learning, love, and life, both these poets share the common vehicle of poetry and poetics – a poetics of pedagogy.

Without Dialect

Of all the linguistic studies of Pasolini, an essay of 1985 by Tullio de Mauro, 'Pasolini critico di linguaggi,' is most striking for the way it underlines the paradoxes inherent in Pasolini's enterprise. The most 'shocking' sentence, and one that De Mauro repeats, is the following: 'Pasolini is a writer biographically without dialect' ('Pasolini è uno scrittore biograficamente senza dialetto'). He bases his conclusion that Pasolini had no dialect on the fact that Pasolini's right-wing *romagnolo* father spoke official standard Italian and that his *friulana* mother, a teacher, adopted the use of Italian over Friulian in the domestic setting. Since Pasolini has become emblematic of the literary use of dialect over standard Italian, it is startling to realize that his inversion consisted of acquiring dialect in order to recuperate his lost and irretrievable linguistic origins which had been annihilated in the family setting and in the compulsory school system (exacerbated by the numerous schools in different regions he attended – these include Belluno, Conigliano, Casarsa, Sacile, Cremona, Scandiano, and of course, Bologna). De Mauro writes that 'he thus did not know a dialectally univocal and homogeneous familial and environmental background' ('Egli non conosce dunque un retroterra ['*inland*,' '*interior*'] familiare e ambientale dialettalmente univoco e omogeneo') (9). De Mauro is building on Gianfranco Contini's observation that Pasolini did not use 'official' Friulian dialect either, added to the fact that Friulian has the scientific status of a minor language (a variety of the Rheto-Romance idioms) rather than that of a dialect, 'which indicates that Pasolini's dialect has in as much the fascination of the unwritten' ('ciò indica che il dialetto di Pasolini ha già in quanto materia il fascino dell'inedito') – thus a kind of 'virgin language' ('lingua vergine'), 'a language that is not known any more' ('lingua che più non si sa') or a 'dead language to recuperate' ('lingua morta da recuperare') (1978, 151; and see Haller 1986, 258). In this context, one is reminded of Luigi Meneghello's definition of Italy as a place 'where the language spoken is not written' ('dove si parla una lingua che non si scrive'). Contini writes that even Pasolini's *romanesco* only gives his 'hooligans' (*teppisti*) an unprinted form convenient for experimentation; and I would not be my own teachers' student if I did not mention Anna Laura and Giulio Lepschy's comment that Pasolini aimed 'to reproduce, with sometimes misleading precision and objectivity, the violent language of boys who have grown up in the general deprivation and linguistic Babel of the Roman outskirts' (1988, 32–3). Nico Naldini, in conversation, claims that it is not so that Pasolini knew no dialect and narrates how he and his cousin would play football speaking in *friulano* with the local boys! The serpent bites its own tail when one realizes that Pasolini's plurilingualism in imitation of Dante's comic strip, fashionable, and escapist discourse was partly inspired by Contini's study of Francesca! (see Pasolini, 'Comments on Free Indirect Discourse,' 1988, 83, 103).

If Pasolini had no dialect, I argue here, he also had no pedagogy – his own term 'apedogogical pedagogy' goes to the empty heart of his ambivalence about the institution and his disdain for the profession. As a teacher dismissed for violating the acceptable framework, Pasolini's defence is to devote his creative energies and indeed, his life, to teaching. After Pasolini's death, Zanzotto, in the essay of 1976, 'Per una pedagogia,' wrote that Pasolini silenced, like Wittgenstein, 'is a [hi]story of pedagogies, of pedagogy' ('è una storia di pedagogie, di pedagogia') (47). It is as if the extension of the posture of listening is necessarily a mortal silence – for those familiar with the techniques of psychoanalysis, there is a parallel to be drawn between the posture of the analyst and Pasolini's deliberated refusal of an institution geared toward encouraging classist and racist attitudes and toward constructing permanent consumers instead of thinkers (or persuaders, in Gramsci's term).

The (Maternal) Body of Teaching

Schoolteachers both, Pasolini and Zanzotto refute all patriarchal values in a system of instruction. I do not dwell in great detail here on
Zanzotto's poem, 'Mysteries of Pedagogy' ('Misteri della pedagogia')
(from *Pasque*, 1968–73) (1975, 269–80), except to invoke, like Pirandello's
Madama Pace, the figure of Maestra Morchet teaching Dante *a memoria*,
while knitting, like Madame Defarge. In this poem, Zanzotto, autodi-
dact and self-taught ('autodidàascolo mi autopedagogizzo'), is a tautological teacher in a continuing education reading course at a reading
centre organized by the minister of public education. He exercises a
healthy disdain for an impossible profession that fails in its nonsensical
attempts at the transmission of codes, as he noted in 'Childhoods, Po-
etries and School (notes)' ('Infanzie, poesie, scuoletta (appunti)') (1973):
'the relation between teacher and learner – which is in itself a non-
sense' ('il rapporto fra docente e discente – che è per sè un non-senso').
Zanzotto's regressive appeal to *petèl*, to the nexus of poetry, infancy,
and school, is a desperate attempt to maintain the serenity of the pre-
Oedipal state of infancy in a school setting that will serve rather than
dampen poetic creativity. It is worth referring here to Pasolini's review
of Zanzotto's *La Beltà* in which he identifies (or rather, analyses) Zanzotto's elegiac narcissism as a resistance to separation from the mother,
which is made evident in his flight into the physiological and the vernacular ('the atrocious speech' ['l'atroce parlare'] of TV), into technical,
rhetorical, and historical terms (1971b). Pasolini's ambivalence in regard to the maternal body of teaching is more marked as he is always
in anticipation of the Oedipal trauma, which in his terms consists of
the commodification of bodies, beauty, and knowledge. Pasolini's language is strong. Consider the following quotation from 'Plan of Future
Works':

> *Shit!* To try to describe the condition
>
> of language without assuming,
> political accompaniments! linguistic
> unity without base economic
>
> motives, without the insensibility
> of a class that doesn't give a shit about slang –
> literary choice! Fucking professors,

neo or paleo patriots, assholes up to their ears
in all that knowledge, who see twelfth- to fourteenth-
century texts only as functions

of other texts . . . Stop, my blind love!
I'll employ you in translinguistic
research, and to one text I'll oppose a veto,

to three texts three saints, to a literary
circle, traditions of cooking, border
disputes . . .

Merde! Cercare di spiegare come vanno

le cose della lingua, senza inferire
concomitanze politiche! unità
linguistica senza ragioni di vile

interesse, senza l'insensibilità
di una classe che se ne frega di elezione
gergale-letteraria! Professori del ca.,

neo o paleo patrioti, teste coglione
in tanta scienza, che dal XII al XIV secolo
vedono solo testi in funzione

di altri testi . . . Basta: cieco
amore mio! Ti eserciterò in ricerche
translinguistiche, e a un testo opporrò un Veto

e a tre testi tre Santi, e a una cerchia
letteraria tradizioni di cucina,
liti di confine   (1982, 184–7)

Unlike Zanzotto's somewhat stable imaginary position, Pasolini is
continually in aggressive movement, adopting a war of position in
which he realizes that his counterstatements, in time, will be recuper-
ated under a regime of repressive tolerance (as in the model of Mar-
cuse and the Freudian Frankfurt School). As Zanzotto wrote in 'Per una
pedagogia,' 'It was a present in which any pedagogical ambition whatsoever, or any tragic desire for ethico-pedagogic reformation, could not
help but be crushed, leveled down to its opposite' ('Un presente in cui
non poteva non restare stritolata, livellata al suo contrario, qualsiasi

velleità pedagogica, o tragica volontà di rifondazione etico-pedagogica' [49]). Thus Pasolini's strategy is self-contradiction, or in more transcendental and complicated terms, abjuration. All religious history of retraction is deconstructed in his renunciation of what he himself has helped make acceptable – a kind of negative theology that outwits his detractors. I have in mind, of course, his confounding abjuration of the *Trilogy of Life* (Pasolini 1983 [1976], 49–52), which forestalled sexual liberation; and compare, of course, his prescient comments on the government of women's bodies through contraception and abortion (see Macciocchi 1987a [1978], 147; and Stone 1984, 111–12). It is in this profound sense that Pasolini is pedagogically perverse: his are not the polymorphous manoeuvres of the (an)aesthetic avant-garde, but tactics of negation. Zanzotto recognizes this in Pasolini's adventure of words outside themselves ('parole fuori di sé') and in the way Pasolini as poet was always positing his own irrelevance as a pedagogic-therapeutic act (see 'L'avventura della poesia,' 1985, 222–8). So, when obscurity was hip, Pasolini told it straight: thus the first period from 1954–63 of relatively realist narrative, screenplays, and film. When the going got plainer, Pasolini became didactic and difficult: the 'unpopular' essay period of 1966–9 – *Love Meetings* (*Comizi d'amore*) (1964), *Hawks and Sparrows* (1966), *Oedipus Rex* (1967), *Notes for an African Orestes* (1969), and *Notes for a Film on India* (1969) – all to be discussed in more detail further on. And when sex was out, Pasolini made his promiscuous *Trilogy of Life* (1971, 1972, and 1974). When mass sexual repression appeared to be liberated, Pasolini renounced sex, Marx, and Freud (see 'Why That of Oedipus Is a Story' (1971a [1967]), but Freud will come off best! As in the Kantian imperative, Pasolini's was an appeal to a higher law beyond morals – an heretical ethics.

In Pasolini's model, teacher and disciple oscillate, and the best students will teach their teachers. It is at this point that I take issue with Enzo Golino's (1985) naturalized view of Pasolini's inner vocation as a born teacher, and with his partialized understanding of the Freudian aspects of Pasolini's preoccupation with sexuality. The principal difficulty the critics have is with the perturbation they experience when questions of love arise in the pedagogic situation. The Socratic model as a pretext for Greek homophilia offers no solace. The Pauline model of a poetics of conversion, and of the role of conversion, and of the role of *agape* over *eros*, finds a stumbling block in Pasolini's own conduct (see Zanzotto 1976). Golino refers to the case of Judge Schreber to offer some kind of interpretation of a pantheistic transsexuality in which *padre sole* is God. As in the case of the Marquis de Sade, Pasolini's own sexual practices are beside the point. To read Kant with Sade (à la Deleuze and Lacan) or as Pasolini did, Sade with Salò, is to understand the ethics of transgression which invokes the law. This fundamental Freudian (if not Mosaic) dictum displaces the debate about conflicting behaviours into the realm of an ethics of not giving up on (or, for that matter, giving in to) one's desires – *an ethics of no surrender* (as I conclude in my forthcoming *Italian Freud*). The paradox of Lacan's psychoanalytic ethics (*ne pas céder son désir*) helps explain Pasolini's about-faces, his standing for both at once – the simultaneity of Pasolini's contradictory feelings about Gramsci's communism, 'the scandal of contradicting myself, of being with you and against you' ('lo scandalo del contraddirmi, dell'essere con te e contro te') in *The Ashes of Gramsci* (*Le ceneri di Gramsci*) (1954). The structure of ambivalence that underpins Pasolini's pedagogic ethics is summed up in his motto that love, in the pedagogic relation, is a means and not an end. In 'From the Diary of a Teacher' ('Dal diario di un insegnante,' 29 February 1948), Pasolini, in his eerie, if not prophetic, way (1949 being the year of his dismissal from teaching for corruption of minors and for obscene acts in public) insists that his 'pedagogic passion' ('passione pedagogica') should be a pure and impersonal vehicle of teaching: 'I understood that I erred in thinking that our relationship should be one of reciprocal love: no, I should put myself aside, ignore myself, I should be a *means*, not an *end* of love' ('Capii che erravo credendo che il nostro rapporto dovesse essere un rapporto di reciproco amore: no, io dovevo mettermi in disparte, ignorarmi, dovevo essere *mezzo*, non già *fine* d'amore') (Golino 1985, 26). The process is not to be confused with a Machiavellian manipulation of the ends as means (so reminiscent of the sixties!), and whether Pasolini is conscious of it or not, his motto duplicates Freud's theory of the transference developed in the essay of 1915.

Within the analytic relation, transference love prevails or is resisted, but it is never acted out (a means, and not an end). The transference is a pre-condition for the possibility of an analysis taking place, yet it is also understood as the means whereby the unconscious shutters itself off. Through the repetition of ancient loves, the analysand unwittingly projects onto the analyst – in an astoundingly realistic (and almost compulsive) way – unconscious desires from other relationships outside the special theatre of the analysis. The game of hide-and-seek in order to gain self-knowledge, a game that necessarily cannot preclude love, but is not for the sake of that love, but for the sake of knowledge, is what

Anna Freud calls the 'double game' of psychoanalysis: to mobilize and forestall desire in the same gesture. Pasolini understood almost intuitively the mechanisms of this process and it seems appropriate that his own theories of pedagogy should find an echo in the marginal and so-called dubious practice of psychoanalysis. Freud himself knew that the institutions of knowledge were dispensable when he wrote in 'On the Teaching of Psychoanalysis in Universities' (1918) that 'the inclusion of psycho-analysis in the University curriculum would no doubt be regarded with satisfaction by every psycho-analyst. At the same time it is clear that the psycho-analyst can dispense entirely with the University without any loss to himself.' Similarly, Pasolini as teacher could do without the school system. It is precisely because of the way in which love interrogates the educational institution that Pasolini found some compatibility with Freud.

In a letter of 1941 to Franco Farfoli, he wrote that he was busy preparing a paper on Tasso and that he so abhorred the work of rhetoric and erudition that he would pan him when he gave his paper for Professor Carlo Calcaterra (compare the 'Professori del ca.' of the poem 'Plan of Future Works' cited above): 'What do I care, I who idolize Cézanne, feel for Ungaretti, cultivate Freud, about these thousands of yellowed and aphonic lines of a minor Tasso?' ('Cosa può importare a me che idolatro Cézanne, che sento forte Ungaretti, che coltivo Freud, di quelle migliaia di versi ingialliti e afoni di un Tasso minore?') (1986, vol. 1, 28). We learn from a letter written while he was a university student in Bologna to Fabio Luca Cavazza (11 February 1947), that he wanted a subscription to *Psicanalisi* 'if it still comes out' ('se esce ancora') (287). When handing out advice to the lovelorn Massimo Ferretti, Pasolini writes from Rome on 15 June 1957: 'Read Freud: things will take on a scientific aspect, with the connected detachment and connected serenity ('Leggi Freud: le cose prenderanno un aspetto scientifico, con l'annesso distacco e l'annessa serenità') (1986, vol. 2, 329).

Golino seems to be bewildered by the scope of Zanzotto's definition of Pasolini's pedagogic attitude as one of infantile polymorphous perversity, and misconstrues perversity (after Schérer) when he offers the view that the pedagogic relation is perverse precisely because it excludes the pederastic relation (a misguided perception of both terms which space does not allow me to criticize here). Golino (1985) fails to answer his own question: 'Eroticism is thus a fundamental component of the master-student relation: but in what measure do pedagogy and pederasty confront one another or merge or remain incompatible?' ('L'erotismo dunque è una componente fondamentale del rapporto maestro-allievo: ma in che misura pedagogia e pederastia si confrontano o si fondono o si ritengono incompatibili?') (39–40). His vision of 'pedagogic vice' has nothing to do with Freudian psychoanalysis. I would suggest that by developing a Freudian theory of pedagogical transference in Pasolini, one averts the dialectical trap and binary oppositions that seem to oppress his critics – how to comprehend the role of sexuality (or more bluntly, of Pasolini's paraphilia) in teaching.

The Cinema of Transference

To those familiar with Pasolini's theories of the cinema of poetry, of free indirect style, and of contamination, the question of the transference of the spectator becomes crucial. While I spell out elsewhere in detail how I think such juxtapositions lead us to rethink psychoanalytic film theory, I do want to make the point that repetition and acting out in the transference resemble Pasolini's notion of cinema as a *reproduction* of reality (see 'The End of the Avant-garde,' *Heretical Empiricism*, 1988). For instance, contamination in the transference is exactly that action of one subject on another with whom it finds itself associated; the question of the conflicting gazes of peasant and bourgeois (analysand/analyst); and what Deleuze so deftly names 'bringing the whole to the power of the false' through bizarre visions of camera whereby objective and subjective images lose their distinction and identification in favour of a new circuit. Zanzotto, in the essay, 'L'avventura della poesia,' makes the clarificatory point that while Pasolini's cinema may be realistic, it is reality itself that is codified! 'Cinema becomes the immediate contact with reality, but reality is already in itself crowded with "conventions," is already codified – and woe is us if we conceive our relation with it as a "language of reality"' ('Il cinema diventa l'immediato contatto con la realtà, ma la realtà è già di per sé gremita di "convenzioni," e già codificata – e guai a noi se si concepisse il nostro rapporto con essa come un "linguaggio della realtà"') (225). For Freud, the analytic circumstances prevent the subjects from taking real desires and emotions for reality itself. In the essay 'Why That of Oedipus Is a Story,' Pasolini emphasized the uncanny dimension of the cinematic (rather than the filmic, which is always the dead aftermath of subjectivity) in the vivid debate concerning whether a dustman (or a porter, as in the essay on the fear of naturalism [1988, 244–8]) should be able to spout Hegel or not. His parable is pedagogic for it is Pasolini's suspicion of all ideology (including his own) that distinguishes him so from Bertolucci or Godard. This is not a facile debate about the end of neorealism – 'the age of Brecht and Rossellini is finished' (*Hawks and Sparrows*) – but an important meditation on the specificity of cinema (the uncanny of the unconscious, if you will). It is also a theory that leads us to understand how, for Pasolini, almost any man could play Orestes, for he is projecting a structure (the unconscious is structured as a cinema) and not an image.

This mention of Orestes will allow me, in the second part of this article, to zoom in on Pasolini's more difficult works in which the question of pedagogy is prominent: namely, *Love Meetings* (1964), *Hawks and Sparrows* (1966), *Notes for an African Orestes* (1969–70), *Notes for a Film about India* (1969), and of course, *Oedipus Rex* (1967). I will also dwell on his film treatment, *The Savage Father* (*Il padre selvaggio*) (1975 [1967]).

The tale of Orestes, like that of Electra, is a variation on the theme of Oedipus. Orestes is a Hamlet avenging his father, Agammemnon's betrayal by Clytemnestra (the murder in the bath, in Sophocles' version, anticipates Marat-Sade). Luchino Visconti's *Sandra* (*Vaghe stelle dell'orsa*) (1965) also comes to mind –a film which I have dubbed as *Notes for a Jewish Orestes*! My comments on Pasolini's abjuration, above, make it obvious why, even if Pasolini later disavowed the Marxian ideological dimension of his 'third world' films, then they must be read historically, at the time of their production, as well as structurally, in relation to Pasolini's pedagogic mission. One of Pasolini's chief defenders, Maria-Antonietta Macciocchi, shares in the harsh criticism of Enzensberger who, in 1983, accused Pasolini of utopian naïvety in his depriving the subproletariat of their dreams for consumer goods – those apartments, TVs, and cars so brutally satirized in Ettore Scola's *Down and Dirty* (*Brutti, sporchi e cattivi*) (1976). Enzensberger cruelly goes as far as to suggest that Pasolini's misrecognition of this fact led to his auto-destruction – killed in his own sports car (see Macciocchi 1987b, 198–9). An even more chilling version of Pasolini's disaffection from the very boys he was cruising, including his assassin, Pelosi, is provided in a new biography which curdles one's blood as it feeds one's intellect with a fluent array of oftentimes fresh facts, insights, and speculations (see Schwartz 1992).

If Pasolini's murder was a travesty – killed by assassins disguised as students (as Zanzotto writes) – its very falseness points to a truth: 'Murderers because they are put in the role of students. Murderers because they are not put well enough in the "right" role as students' ('Assassini perché collocati nel ruolo di allievi. Assassini perché non abbastanza collocati in un 'giusto' ruolo di allievi') (1973, 50). The end of successful pedagogy, as of a Freudian analysis, is the metaphorical immolation of the transference relation – the teacher/analyst/crow turned to ashes. More than a gesture of Hegelian sublation, this cure consists of self-invention through the Other.

Pasolini's disdain for academic conventions, those Dantean dentists in *Hawks and Sparrows*, where I always see an omen of Umberto Eco, is offset by the view of the poor peasant in the Maoist scenes in the same film. The third world inside Italy is a precursor of the third world of Italy (compare Enzensberger) that Pasolini so dangerously enters through the western classical myth of Orestes overlaid on Africa. In *Notes for an African Orestes*, whether the African students in Rome can recognize the process of decolonization through Pasolini's eyes is debatable (and here mention must be made of the travesty of their speech, which was not translated in the subtitles in the version before William Weaver's – and even Weaver fails to render colonial French!). Yet once again critics get caught in the details rather than in the allegorical imperative of the Law and justice that metaphorically transform the ancient Erinnyes (Furies) into Eumenides (Benevolent Ones) and moreover, Pasolini emphasizes, without the latter having to lose their furious trace. Within the terms of neocolonialism, this film has a guilty imprint, yet Pasolini is saying much more: apart from the stunning nonanthropomorphic vision of trees blowing furiously instead of women travestied as gods, the film offers a devastating critique of the educational apparatus (to evoke Althusser's term) in the neocolonial context. The University buildings are paid for by the Chinese government and designed according to the anodyne (and riot-proof) 'Anglo Saxon neo-capitalist' model to offer a mirage of learning and justice in the barren veld. The country is without the paper industry to produce the imported and useless books on sale in the University College of Dar Es Salaam's bookstore, with titles such as *American Education Today*, *Nyerere as Caesar*, *The Culture of English Phonetics*, and *Larousse-French*. The mimetic imperative is unrealizable, as the uneasy students in Rome indicate. Pasolini's irony is withering – the University as a Temple of Apollo 'bears an external aspect that is elegant and confident in its internal contradictions' for students whom he describes as looking on knowledge in a passive, obedient, and respectful way. The overcrowded classrooms and the false lures of compulsory education endorse rather than betray the narrative power of Pasolini's ancient myth.

If his *Notes for an African Orestes* are, as he says, 'style without style,' so the screenplay, *The Savage Father*, is Pasolini's 'structure of a structure.' He was impeded from realizing it as a film due to the trial and lawsuit against *La ricotta* (1962), he explains, and thus dedicates an envoi poem, 'E l'Africa?' to the minister of law and to the judge who condemned him. Once again, Pasolini's brilliant meditation on the textuality of translation in 'The Screenplay as a Structure That Wants to Be Another Structure' (1988, 187–96), that is, on how to read a screenplay as a film, relates to a theory of psychoanalytic transference (in all its metaphoricity): the least one can say is that a reading of *The Savage Father* necessarily positions us as Western readers in a voyeuristic relation. My subtitle to this screen treatment could be *Bach in the Bush*, an oxymoron with which I intend to have brutal echoes of Beethoven at Auschwitz: 'There they listen to Bach. A sublime motif which, with its sweet power, appears to erase everything all around, the reality of Africa. To swallow it up back through the centuries, there where Europe is Christian, supremely civil' ('Là ascoltano Bach. Un sublime motivo che, con la sua dolce potenza, pare cancellare tutto lì intorno, la realtà dell'Africa. Risucchiarla indietro nei secoli, là dove l'Europa è cristiana, supremamente civile') (22). Pasolini's recognizable contrapuntal score should not be mistaken for Western logocentrism. The music tracks that he projects are dissonant and anti-folkloristic (as is the Polish revolutionary song in *Notes for an African Orestes*). The main protagonist, Davidson 'Ngibuini (and remember Colgate of *Hawks and Sparrows*), finally refuses the missionary position in a rebellion against books at the end of this treatment – the rejection is not some trace of anti-intellectual Papini-like futurism in Pasolini (see Papini's pamphlet of 1914, 'Let's Close the Schools,' discussed by Zanzotto 1973). Instead, it is the quest for anti-knowledge as the only knowledge writ large.

If Pasolini's unconscious is displaced in a romance of Africa, he lost it (while still in Africa) in the more autobiographical rage (to use Sandro Petraglia's phrase) of *Oedipus Rex*. Unlike *The Gospel According to Matthew* (1964), *Oedipus Rex* (set principally in Africa) includes the classist signifier – Freud's 'his majesty the baby' – of those wonderful *alba pratalia* ('white fields') opening long sequence shots so obviously located in an Italy seen through Idrain embroidery (see Zanzotto 1973 and Schwartz 1992, 508). Pasolini's Moroccan setting is the drought-stricken aftermath of the Oedipal cut (rendered by the cut in the temporality of the film's montage) and a traumatic sequel to the preconscious blank(et) of the maternal body in the idyll of the Italian *alba pratalia*. If the philological parallel is a disputed early ninth-century example of writing in Italian (*pareba boves*) in the white field margins of a land contract, it is merely a spatial metaphor here for the writing of subjectivity and sexual difference through the cut of language. The second filmic cut after the arid yet decadent dream (which, to be sure, is no more than a *fantasy* of castration) leaves Oedipus blinded in Bologna but knowing the powers of poetic sublimation. Pasolini repeatedly refers in interviews (for example, see Rivolta [n.d.]) to the violence of his father as the source of his detestation of political violence and defers to Freud's account of filial rejection (see Stack 1970 and Schwartz 1992, 512). Contini writes eloquently of Pasolini's high-priced contest with his 'paranoiac' father and concludes that we should 'respect our friend in his solitude of challenger and struggler, paying ... the highest price' ('rispettiamo il nostro amico nella sua solitudine di sfidatore e lottatore col Padre, pagando ... il prezzo più alto') (1982, 15). In contrast, in the 1964 poem 'Prayer to My Mother,' Pasolini's image of his mother is an agonizing one of an irreplaceable love that dooms him to solitude: 'So I must tell you something terrible to know: / From within your kindness my anguish grew' ('per questo devo dirti ciò ch'è orrendo conoscere: / è dentro la tua grazia che nasce la mia angoscia') (1982, 108–9). In *Oedipus Rex*, Pasolini fulfils his dream of making love to 'a woman of stone' (in a direct allusion to Dante's *rime petrose*), and he is to be *driven* up the endless flights of (vaginal) stairs to replay the petrifying scene of maternal incest in even more vivid erotic detail in *Petrolio* (1992 [1975]), a detour round the law that would allow Pasolini (and which would explain Naldini's reading) to come closer to a resolution of his hatred for his father (Pasolini 1971a, 10; and see Stone 1992; Schwartz 1992, 511). The appendage of the flute is an indication of Pasolini's homosexual and fetishistic response to what Hans Loëwald insists is the 'waning,' rather than the 'resolution' of the child's Oedipal complex.

If the question 'Where do babies come from?' is the first poll a child takes, Pasolini was an obsessive poll-taker (I am referring to his sexual *sondaggio* – *Comizi d'amore* – the film in which he compulsively tries to get the Italian populace to speak about their attitude to sex and homosexuality while not letting them take him for what he is). The way Pasolini refers back to the paternal figures, Cesare Musatti and Alberto

Moravia, who play cameo roles, is both childish and endearing – in a relay of the words of Oedipus' father, Laius: 'you are here to take my place in the world and to rob me of all I have' ('tu sei qui per prendere il mio posto al mondo e di rubarmi di tutto quello che ho'). The psychoanalyst, Musatti, explains that the hostile responses Pasolini has culled are defences which indicate fear (a standard Freudian perception), while Moravia is more sardonic and states that only the opinions of half of Italy are heard here. One wishes almost out of embarrassment that Pasolini might have taken his swollen-footed quest (*piedini gonfi*, in Greek, *Oedipus*) inside himself and gone into analysis as had Bernardo Bertolucci and Zanzotto. To cull information or even to dispense it per se constitutes a 'wild' analysis which I discuss in relation to Gramsci (1984), and Pasolini's sexual empiricism only proves Freud correct that, as in the case of medical doctors who study psychoanalysis in the University, 'the medical student will never learn psychoanalysis proper' or its actual practice but, like Pasolini in his Oedipal quest, 'it will be enough if he learns something *about* psychoanalysis and something *from* it' (173). Nevertheless, Pasolini drafts the structure of the structure of an analysis in his self-analysis in the film, *Oedipus Rex*, in which he focuses on the Sphinx in all of us – the riddle and abyss within. How vivid is Oedipus' cinematic gesture of externalization – to cast the Sphinx into the abyss – a metaphor for the splitting of the ego in the process of defence: 'it's useless: the abyss into which you cast me is within you!' ('È inutile: l'abisso in cui mi spingi è dentro di te'). Pasolini remarks on this comic gesture: 'He knew that by pushing it back into the abyss he would be able to marry his mother: we thus have here an audio-visual case of displacement' (1971a, 9). Pasolini knew that the only knowledge that counted was the production of anti-knowledge (and compare the blind but insightful Tiresias' lament: 'Ah! How terrible it is to know, when this knowledge is of no use to its bearer' ('Ah com'è terribile sapere quando il sapere non serve proprio nulla a chi sa') (1971a, 68). Pasolini's tactics should not be confused with 'misology' – Plato's end to discussion. In Pasolini's system of contraries, knowledge and anti-knowledge are one and the same, just as in his prophetic and humorous meditation in *The Earth Seen from the Moon* (*La terra vista dalla luna*) (1965), on the Indian philosophical saying that death and life are the identical thing. *Oedipus Rex* closes with a shot that returns to the edenic *alba pratalia* of the beginning; 'life ends where it begins' ('la vita finisce dove comincia').

References

Contini, G. *Schedario di scrittori italiani moderni e contemporanei*. Florence: Sansoni, 1978
– 'Testimonianza per Pier Paolo Pasolini.' In A. Panicali and S. Sestini, eds., *Pier Paolo Pasolini: Testimonianze*. Florence: Salani, 1982
Dante. *Vita Nuova*. Translated by M. Musa. New York: Oxford University Press, 1992
De Mauro, T. 'Pasolini critico di linguaggi.' *Galleria*, XXXV, nos. 1–4 (1985): 7–20
Enzensberger, H. *Politische Brosamen*. Frankfurt: Suhrkamp Verlag, 1983
Golino, E. *Pasolini: il sogno di una cosa*. Bologna: Mulino, 1985
Haller, H.W. *The Hidden Italy: A Bilingual Edition of Italian Dialect Poetry*. Detroit: Wayne State University Press, 1986
Lepschy, A.L., and G. Lepschy. *The Italian Language Today*. London: Hutchinson, 1988 [1977]
Macciocchi, M.-A. 'Pasolini: Murder of a Dissident.' In A. Michelson et al., eds., *October: The First Decade, 1976–1986*, 139–50. 1987a [1978]
– *Di là dalle porte di bronzo: viaggio intellettuale di una donna in Europa*. Milan: Mondadori, 1987b
Pasolini, P.P. 'Dal diario di un insegnante.' In *Il mattino del popolo* (29 February 1948)
– 'Why That of Oedipus Is a Story.' In *Oedipus Rex*. London: Lorimer, 1971a [1967]
– 'La Beltà di Andrea Zanzotto.' *Nuovi argomenti* 21 (1971b)
– *Il padre selvaggio* (from *Cinema e film*, nos. 3–4). Turin: Einaudi, 1975 [1967]
– *Poems*. Selected and translated by N. MacAfee with L. Martinengo. New York: Vintage, 1982a
– *Lutheran Letters*. Translated by Stuart Hood. Manchester: Carcanet New Press, 1983 [1976]
– 'L'avventura della poesia.' (From *Rinascita* 51: 20–1) Reprinted in *Dialogo con Pasolini: Scritti 1957–84*. Edited by A. Cadioli. Rome: Mondadori, 1985
– *Pasolini: Lettere 1940–54* (vol. 1) & *Lettere 1955–75*, vol. 2). Edited by N. Naldini. Turin: Einaudi, 1986
– *Heretical Empiricism*. Edited by L.K. Barnett. Translated by B. Lawton and L.K. Barnett. Bloomington: Indiana University Press, 1988 [1972]
– *Petrolio*. Turin: Einaudi, 1992 [1975]
– *Pasolini: Inchiesta su una vita*. Edited by Carlo Rivolta (undated tape)
Schwartz, B.D. *Pasolini Requiem*. New York: Pantheon, 1992
Stack, O. *Pasolini on Pasolini*. London: BFI, 1970

Stone, J. 'Italian Freud: Gramsci, Giulia Schucht, and Wild Analysis.' *October* 28 (1984): 105–24.

– 'A Psychoanalytic Bestiary: The Wolff Woman, The Leopard, and The Siren.' *American Imago* 49, no. 1 (1992): 117–52

Zanzotto, A. 'Infanzie, poesie, scuoletta (appunti).' *Strumenti critici* 20 (1973)

– *Selected Poetry of Andrea Zanzotto*. Edited and translated by Ruth Feldman and B. Swann. Princeton: Princeton University Press, 1975

– 'Per una pedagogia.' In 'Omaggio a Pasolini.' *Nuovi argomenti* 49 (1976): 47–51

Pasolini's 'Second Victory'

WALTER SITI

'There are more things in Heaven, though, my Lord, than are dreamed of in Your philosophy.' – Bertrand Russell

In his essay Walter Siti examines Pasolini's poetic and narrative writings of the 1970s, an area that has been largely neglected by North American Pasolini scholarship up to now. By way of a psychoanalytic approach, Siti describes how Pasolini's work comes full circle when in 1975 he publishes *La nuova gioventù*, a book in which Pasolini collects his own previously published Friulian poems (written between 1941 and 1953) along with new Friulian ones (written in 1974), which represent poetic and often bitter reworkings of those original verses. For Siti, these poems offer insights into how Pasolini looked upon his own earlier writing (produced during the important Friulian period, which Naldini's essay in this volume helps to understand) as well as his thoughts concerning cultural politics and the nature of human desire and subjectivity in a society dominated by what Pasolini refers to as the new consumerist power. Such themes became insistent in all of Pasolini's writing and films of the 1970s, and led him to begin writing the novel *Petrolio* in 1973. This text marks a return to the genre he had abandoned after the 'Roman novels' of the late 1950s, and it rehearses many of the scandalous themes found in Pasolini's last film *Salò*. Projected by Pasolini to be two thousand pages in length, the book was left unfinished at his death and remained unpublished until 1992.

For Pier Paolo Pasolini, the name St. Paul was important as far back as the period when he was writing the poems for *L'Usignolo della Chiesa cattolica* (1958). Pasolini identifies with this name – but it is also a name bearing reproof. In the crucial year of 1968 it took him only a few days to produce an outline for a film about Saint Paul, *Abbozzo di sceneggiatura per un film su San Paolo (sotto forma di appunti per un direttore di produzione)* (Pasolini, *San Paolo*). The film scenario explores the character's dramatic ambiguity – as a scandalous, anti-conformist homosexual and founding father of churches. Crucial to the Pauline theology is *agape*, whose revelation foreshadows a mystical and ecstatic itinerary, and is also a sign of a love that is independent of human desires and justifications, a love attainable through praxis, not through knowledge. If the Kingdom of God consists in the progressive self-realization of history, history in turn cannot be but the self-actualization of this love, which is paradoxical and outside human subjectivity. In the poem 'The Enigma of Pius XII' (Pasolini, *Trasumanar e organizzar*, 15–22) Pasolini has the Pope cite the famous Pauline passage concerning *agape*, contained in the first letter to the Corinthians, to proclaim that 'institutions are pathetic' ('le istituzioni sono commoventi') and to justify Hitler's policy on historical grounds, taking the side of peasant farmers, imbued with *charitas*, against the Jewish bourgeoisie, which had no need of *charitas*. Thus, if one associates St. Paul with Hegel, a combination that is anything but surprising in twentieth-century theology and utopianism (see the work of Jurgen Moltmann and Ernst Bloch in this regard), *agape* is inseparable from the objectivity of historical epochs.

Soon after 1968, however, Pasolini begins to speak of a new event of incalculable importance: a consumerist Power has carried out a revolution that renders all other revolutions impossible. It has done so by utilizing the infinite nature of desire. As Pasolini says, 'the bourgeoisie is in entropy' (Maingois 1974, 21), using Freud's term 'entropy' in order to indicate the chaotic point of arrival of the pleasure principle.

'Vincenzo Rizzi believed that the fulfillment of a dream (that of spending the night with a woman) – so difficult to fulfill in his old culture – was miraculously possible in the culture of the modern world' (Pasolini, *Lettere luterane*, 106). By confronting men with the brutal and cynical fulfillment of their desires, consumer society suddenly toppled a thousand-year-old culture based on repression. But there is more: if it is true (again, in Freudian terms) that the mechanism of substitution, which originates with the denial of satisfaction of desire, constitutes the symbolic order, then the easy satisfactions of consumer society would seem to deny the very possibility of structuring our social existence symbolically. When dreams flatten against and merge with reality, then the laws that govern dreams no longer have any reason to function. Metaphor and, in the final analysis, *meaning* itself, come to be abolished.[1] Every struggle to change the world is at once crushed between absolute hyper-realism (where everything is put on the same plane, every thing drained of any figural connotation) and total de-realization.

Faced with this new situation, it seems to Pasolini that the Hegelian dialectic is no longer tenable; as he declares, 'I am against Hegel ... my dialectic is no longer ternary but binary. There are only oppositions' (Pasolini, 'Ancora,' 130). And in his unfinished novel, entitled *Petrolio* (with the alternate title *Vas*), Pasolini writes: 'Naturally, Hegel made a mistake, albeit a divine one. The only true infinity is that which he calls "bad infinity".'[2] Thus, for Pasolini, a philosophy of history is no longer possible because, by now, a totalistic hierarchy of the real has been rendered impossible. However, neither is the 'heretical empiricism' that Pasolini opposes to the dialectic found within a general critique of Totality so that we can begin theorizing the construction of partial hierarchies. As often happens to empiricisms that cannot see the forest for the trees, the particular is invested with absolute responsibilities, and is involved in an infinite series of oppositions. Pasolini's criticism of Hegel ends up resolving itself by substituting one religion for another: a dualistic type of religion based on cyclical time, as opposed to a Christian (Pauline) religion, founded on the irreversibility of history. Again in *Petrolio*, he writes:

what was invoked was the possibility (largely lost) of a 'dyadic' logic, in which everything coexisted and was not 'superseded,' and in which contradictions were nothing but oppositions. In such a case, history would no longer have been a unilinear and successive history born, as we know, of the Reformist exegesis of the Old and New Testaments, in addition the interpretations of St. Paul's Letters. All of modern Western rationalism had been founded on this basis, precisely during the time when science was demonstrating that time had never been founded on unilinearity and succession, and indeed did not even exist, given that everything is co-present – this in keeping with what the dravidi religions had already taught.

si invoca la possibilità del resto perduta di una logica 'duadica,' in cui tutto restasse coesistente e non 'superato,' e le contraddizioni non fossero che opposizioni: in tal caso la storia non sarebbe stata più la storia unilineare e successiva, nata, com'è noto, dall'esegesi riformistica del Vecchio e del Nuovo Testamento, oltre che dalle Lettere di San Paolo. Su ciò si era fondato tutto il razionalismo occidentale moderno, proprio mentre la scienza dimostrava che il tempo non era affatto fondato su unilinearità e successività, e anzi addirittura non esisteva, tutto essendo compresente (come già avevano insegnato le religioni dravidiche).' (Pasolini, *Petrolio*, 523)

By accentuating the infinite nature of desire (always insatiable), consumer society reasserts a traditionally metaphysical problem, in itself a healthy jolt for every overly self-satisfied historicism. However, the metaphysical problem is then immediately translated into a mixture of pragmatism and mysticism, and herein lies the root of the deception. The Absolute is made to coincide with the infinite and with hidden complications of the mechanisms of economic production. Any contact with Being is said to be reached by abandoning oneself to the 'realism' of Capital.

In order to escape from metaphysics in a less deceptive way, it is necessary to begin with a *criticism of the infinite* in the following ways: (1) in logical-mathematical terms, through playing with the paradoxes of transfinities, and learning that 'infinity contains more things than God can imagine'; (2) in psychological terms, by viewing infinity as one of the (imperfect) ways in which the unconscious unfolds itself into consciousness (see Matte-Blanco 1981, 439); (3) in physical-biological terms, by transforming every mystical ineffability into simple 'unimaginability,' which is linked to limitations of categories of perception and to the traditional understanding of space and time.

That is, in its demonstration that time does not exist, contemporary science is not at all allied with religion. On the contrary, science states that today, more than ever, criticism of religion is necessary when understood as criticism of the Absolute. Only if Infinity is a normal operative concept can Reason find itself freed from both the astonished contemplation of necessity and from any hope in the Spirit.

Pasolini instead appears powerless before the appearance of mystical Totality that consumerism adopts. The almost religious mystery of consumeristic 'apparitions' (and this quality makes them competitors threatening the Church) can be compared to the 'behaviourism' that Pasolini notes in Indian religions (Pasolini, *Descrizioni di descrizioni*, 176–80). That is, we have yet to emerge from the mysticism-pragmatism mixture.

However, the cause of Pasolini's powerlessness is also historical and cultural in character: it stems from his own exclusively humanistic education. Perhaps a more interesting explanation, however, is linked to Pasolini's 'existential project,' in which the basis of the symbolic – as well as the objectivity of the Law – depend on the phantasm of the Father. The St. Paul–Hegel binomial belongs to that historical, paternal 'severity' or 'sternness' that founds the sense of guilt and, in its turn, this sense of guilt structures the ego. If the new consumerist Power now renders that binomial ineffectual and seems to abolish the very figure of the Father in a society of Sons, then it is as if narcissistic Infinity, which constitutes the other pole of the psychological system, discovered that it had won without a fight, and furthermore, that it had done so as mandated by Authority. Thus consumerist Power appears at once fascinating and demonic because it is secretly and horrendously right. The sense of guilt remains non-saturated, and the disappearance of psychological polarity leads to a terrorizing sensation of psychological nullification.

What happens within the logic of consumerism is that desire, with its psychological infinity, opens itself to an infinite, material extension, and is reduced to a desperate metonymic slippage, which is just what Pasolini's notion of 'bad infinity' emphasizes. The loss of symbolic depth leads to eruptions of violence. But later, even Pasolini's youthful eroticism (arising from an ancient matrix of a type of atheistic mysticism) revealed, with the economic well-being that came with maturity, its own destructive nature:

Repeat to infinity the word 'sex': what sense will it make in the end? Sex, sex, sex, sex, sex, sex, sex, sex, sex, sex, sex, sex, sex, sex . . . The world becomes the object of sexual desire, and it is no longer the world, but the locus of a single sentiment. This sentiment reproduces itself, and with itself it reproduces the world, until it gathers such strength that it is annulled.

Ripeti all'infinito la parola sesso: che senso avrà alla fine? Sesso, sesso, sesso, sesso, sesso, sesso, sesso, sesso sesso, sesso, sesso, sesso, sesso, sesso, sesso . . . Il mondo diventa oggetto di desiderio di sesso, non è più mondo, ma luogo di un solo sentimento. Questo sentimento si ripete, e con sé ripete il mondo, finché accumulandosi si annulla. (Pasolini, *La divina mimesis*, 18)

The God of eros is Nothingness: Pasolini's long fidelity to Leopardi is unleashed without pity upon Sade. Consumerist Power has annulled the repressive structures around which the ego had constructed its own Oedipal myth. And it was this myth that was the originating locus of knowledge. From there came the anxiety of knowledge, of the 'coming to know.' As Pasolini writes:

I am
condemned to understand. But my understanding
reckons with Duty.

Io sono
condannato a capire. Ma il mio capire
fa i conti col Dovere.[3]

To Pasolini, therefore, consumerism not only seems to be the negative
of his passion but also appears as something capable of subtracting
any heuristic and cognitive possibilities from his passion – by 'hyper-
realizing' it. As Pasolini writes in a 'self-review' of his book of poems
entitled *Trasumanar e organizzar*, 'Pasolini does not love truth: love for
truth destroys everything, because nothing is true' (Pasolini, 'Autorecensione,' 4). The criticized object is also the frightening, but certainly
liberating, image of a possible disarticulation of the criticizing subject.
The epistemological weakness of which we spoke is born here, at perhaps its deepest level. Despite Pasolini's courageous, open-minded, and
often incisive use of such methodologies as linguistics and semiology,
there is an apocalyptic and deeply disturbing gaze that is cast over everything, a gaze entirely dominated, in spite of itself, by the mystical
'novelty' and 'naturalness' of Power.

In 1972, Pasolini writes the program notes to an exhibition of the
art of Lorenzo Tornabuoni, in which are figured monumental and frag-
mented male bodies, athletic and decorative. These are art works em-
ploying the Soviet collage technique of the 1920s, over which pop-art
motifs have been superimposed in a rather mischievous manner. In
his program notes, Pasolini underlines how the desire tied to those
bodies, through the myth of Health and Fitness, offers an ambiguous
link between the period of revolutionary populism between the two
world wars and the advertisement culture of contemporary consumer
society. He detects an association between the Heroes of the Revolution and the Heroes of Integration. Pasolini denounces this association,
as intolerably contradictory: 'There is no one who does not see how
this [Tornabuoni's] work is truly a tangle of references and allusions,
through which, in practice, everything is evaded and discredited' (Pasolini, 'Breve studio,' 4). His reaction is dictated by a love of clarity, but
also, I would suggest, by the impossibility of admitting that there may
be a deep affinity between the body, permeated with perverse desire,
and consumerism.

Both perversion and consumerism are centred around the dynamic of frustration. For both of these, the confrontation with the phantasm comes without mediation, and ecstasy can turn into desperation in an instant. Both give the illusion of an infinite expansion while they follow obsessively enforced rules that are determined externally. Both tend to decontextualize the object of desire, to the point of making all of reality into a fetish.

The beautiful body presumes the suspension of time. Recovering the physical perfection of one's own body (in the gym, or with sports) involves a turning back of the clock. In the poem 'Il poeta delle ceneri,' Pasolini writes:

> So I am forty-four years old, I wear them well
> (only yesterday two or three soldiers, in a little grove of
> whores, said I looked only twenty-four – poor guys
> who mistook a baby for one their own age).

> Ho dunque quarantaquattro anni, che porto bene
> (soltanto ieri due o tre soldati, in un boschetto di
> puttane, me ne hanno attribuiti ventiquattro, – poveri
> ragazzi che hanno preso un bambino per un loro coetaneo).
> (Pasolini, 'Il poeta delle ceneri,' 3)

In the author's corrected manuscript of this poem, one can read the word 'monster' ('mostro') crossed out and replaced by the word 'baby' ('bambino').[4] The trauma found at the origin of perversion impedes the movement of time. Yet, in the final analysis, that trauma can lead to a 'double bind' situation – that is, to a logical contradiction that governs any analytical operations involving infinity (see Bateson 1976 and Radice 1981, 84–7). Consumerism also plays at confusing various types of infinity, and favours the time-suspension trick. Moreover, consumerism also celebrates the perfect surface of the body.

In a cynical vein, I would suggest that the revelation of formal or structural similarities between an intimate and all-consuming eros and the hated consumer society would perhaps have led Pasolini to an analysis of the historical roots (both personal and social) of the theory of pleasure.[5] It would have led him to a verification of both the arbitrariness and the 'bad manners' of desire in the moment of its greatest ineluctability and innocence. It would have led him to articulate an epistemology less restrained by the old mythic influences.

Instead Pasolini's solution is to underline the difference between eros and consumerism by relying on a cultural tradition that identifies beauty with non-corruption and the natural. In this way Pasolini 'justifies' desire, and fascination with the body becomes a symbol of a marginal and vital world repressed and killed by consumer civilization. The suspension of time splits ambiguously into cyclical time (good eternity) and empty time (bad eternity).

One must wait for the 'Abiura dalla *Trilogia della vita*' (the 'Abjuration of the *Trilogy of Life*') to get Pasolini's confession that the myth of purity and popular innocence was nothing but a reassuring substitute formation. By now the coincidence of eroticism and commodification, as revealed in Pasolini's last film, *Salò*, can no longer become a clear (even if tortured) intellectual patrimony. Their coincidence must remain a dark threat, a paralysing linkage, and the word that Pasolini uses to describe it is once again a mystical word (albeit black and melancholy): 'informe accidia,' or 'shapeless torpor' (Pasolini, 'Abiura,' 72).

Transfiguring itself in cultural and civil passion, eros certainly acquires an extraordinary sentimental force, but it loses its own name. Thus, when it finds itself confronted with time, work, and death, eros may undergo one of the most useless of sufferings, and one that doesn't have even the comfort of lucidity. For Pasolini, all of this is expressed in the face and laughter of Ninetto.[6]

> That you were lacking in charity, Pius XII told you:
> and he was not all wrong. He quoted Paul:
> Nunì dè ménei pìstis, elpìs, agàpe,
> ta tria tàuta: méizon dè touton e agàpe.
>
> Che tu mancassi di carità, te lo diceva Pio XII:
> e non aveva tutti i torti. Citava Paolo:
> Nunì dè ménei pìstis, elpìs, agàpe,
> ta tria tàuta: méizon dè touton e agàpe. (Pasolini,
> *Trasumanar e organizzar*)

In his review of Elsa Morante's *Il mondo salvato dai ragazzini*, written in verse-form (31–47), Pasolini accuses Morante of lacking charity because she suggests that institutions are only negative and because she is gifted with a sort of humour that Pasolini considers to be a quality of the élite. But Morante's mysterious 'grace' consists precisely in the transformation of humour into a quality of the people, in the transvaluation of her own bourgeois anarchy by means of poetry: 'how much charity there is in your lack of charity' ('quanta carità nella tua mancanza di carità') (38). Humour as *charitas* is the objective love for another class; it is represented by the character Pazzariello in Morante's book. But for Pasolini Ninetto represents it most of all:

> the idea of Ninetto, which for you is owed ...
> owed, I say, to the objectification of that Grace
> which is humor made into charity through the work of
> the intellect,
> is superior to Pazzariello.

> l'idea di Ninetto a te dovuta ...
> dovuta, dico, all'oggettivazione di quella Grazia
> in quanto umorismo fattosi carità per opera
> d'intelletto,
> è superiore al Pazzariello. (40)

In Pasolini's psyche, Ninetto represents the paradoxical union of *eros* and *agape*, of desire and affection.

In 1971, however, while they are filming *The Canterbury Tales*, Ninetto decides to get married, and this becomes a source of great pain for Pasolini: unthinking, blind pain, as expressed in *L'Hobby del sonetto*.[7] The objective misery of the other class, represented by Ninetto, turns out to be conformism as well, and a surrendering to time, expressed in the humble instinct to procreate, which is found in adult love. 'Manual labor. Time that enters the body. Through work the human being becomes material like Christ through the Eucharist. Work is like death' (Weil 1948, 206). Eros, by exalting a body completely outside of time,[8] is, in reality, extraneous to the body *that works*. The true vitality of the people – that is, the mortal, conformistic vitality – is not reachable through perverse desire:

Then I think that that apartment could serve two newlyweds extremely well. And thus I see the future life, organized, in a time in which dying is my obligation. A life naturally very friendly with the heavens, with the usual smile, humble and not servile but owed to something else, in an infinite light.

Poi penso che quell'appartamento potrebbe servire benissimo a due sposi. E così vedo la vita futura, organizzata, in un tempo in cui morire è mio obbligo.

Una vita naturalmente molto amica al cielo, con il solito riso umile e non servile ma dovuto ad altro, in una luce infinita. (Pasolini, *L'Hobby*, 16)

Here Pasolini's conscious will clashes with the compulsion to repeat that comes from deep down, with the resulting impossibility of radically restructuring his own psychological make-up. To follow *agape* entails the complete deprivation of one's own eros; it is a deprivation of one's motivation to live. And thus is born Pasolini's rebellion, against destiny and against Elsa Morante, who, with inhuman consistency, proposes love as a sacrifice, which results (at the extreme limit) in the erasure of the self:

> By applying the morals
> that Elsa expected from me . . .
> I would even have been able to accept,
> certainly, that girl who 'took you away,'
> thinking that, if I loved you
> you would stay the same.
> The fact is that the universe slowly
> moved beneath my feet.

> Applicando la morale
> che Elsa pretendeva da me . . .
> avrei potuto accettare
> certo, anche quella ragazza che 'ti portava via,'
> pensando che, se ti amavo, tu restavi uguale.
> Il fatto è che lentamente l'universo
> si è mosso sotto i miei piedi. (90)

The abandonment of Ninetto drives him back to his position as *letterato*, as writer – indeed, he writes sonnets. The impossibility of his accepting adult love is also the inability to accept the conformism of the popular classes:

> like the great hero I laughed about human things
> that I called, rightly, in any case,
> bourgeois: and conjugal fidelity
> was the height of that just disdain of mine.

> da bravo eroe io risi delle cose umane
> che chiamavo, a ragione, del resto,

borghesi: e una fedeltà coniugale
era il colmo di quel mio giusto disprezzo. (68)

Pasolini identified the people as 'beautiful nature,' as a mythical continent, and this allowed him to express his nostalgia for the infinite without risking a total fracture with reality and without jeopardizing his own self-image.[9] In consumer society, conformism functions as an agent of the 'historical revelation' of the need for purity. And the contempt that befalls the poor, that destroys myth, instead of being the sign of moral superiority, indicates that nostalgia for the infinite is unable to translate itself into a cognitive force able to withstand abrupt historical changes. Just as Pasolini's affection for Ninetto represented his love for an entire social class, so the crisis of that love topples the very idea of class division, or at least the 'visibility' of such a division. Infinite desire is unable to conceive of the Other as independent and autonomous; desire is therefore completely beyond mediation. So, it is logical that this desire expands during those periods when the laws of objective mediation show themselves to be in crisis. Throughout history, the security of laws – through the certainty of class struggle – allowed the people to experience their misery with pride. Similarly, the insuperable distance between the people and the intellectual became, for the intellectual, a source of great regret. These days the intellectual cannot have anything but words of agonized pity for the conformism of the people:

You talk to me of your trips through the little book of
Enpals, and I also intuit that you both are watching
television. I connect this to a phrase about 'some
money' to put aside (in this way you tried to justify
yourself to her, in order to get permission to leave).

mi dici dei tuoi giri per il libretto dell'Enpals,
e intuisco anche che state vedendo la televisione.
Ricollego questo a una frase su 'qualche soldino'
da metter da parte (così cercavi di giustificarti
presso di lei, per avere il permesso di partire). (104)

From now on, the people are only able to experience their own misery with humiliation – a misery perceived as a passive residue of consumerist desire.

In extending itself over the entire social system, the potential infinity of pleasure has created victims resembling executioners. The inability to conceive of love as *charitas* leads to the inability to think of life as being determined and constructed, and this is even more the case during a time when social distinctions are masked. Objective love for another class is no longer possible; nor can the nostalgia for the infinite take form in anything that could limit it and make it concrete: it remains pure annihilation. Monstrously transformed by consumerism into a technique of domination, eros leads the people to the loss of self. Even deeper than Pasolini's pain of abandonment, is the pain of not knowing how to save Ninetto, because the way one loves him is the same way one loses him.

The final period of Pasolini's production shows the reappearance of some gnostic allusions:

> I am Valentino who scorned Christ's earthly body
> – or the subtle African heretic leader
> Sabellio who maintained that the Father
> was the Son of Himself.

> io sono Valentino che spregiava il corpo terreno
> di Cristo – o il sottile eresiarco
> africano Sabellio che sosteneva che
> il Padre era Figlio di Se Stesso.[10]

And in the 1974 additions to the screenplay *San Paolo* there is a false Luke who in reality is a messenger of the Devil, with a message that recalls certain Manichean texts (the *Interrogatio Johannis*, for example).

However, it is a gnosticism that no longer has anything opposing it, and thus it becomes meaningless. In a review of P.J. Jouve's book *Il mondo deserto*, in which the author stages the moral torments of a homosexual, Pasolini writes: 'Jacques's spiritual crisis and his struggle against guilt, in the name of a bankrupt pagan ideology and terror, is, I say loud and clear, a real pain in the ass' (Pasolini, *Descrizioni di descrizioni*, 391). Infinite desire, which at one time could be considered a spiritual (even if cursed) privilege, has now spread by sad contagion, deforming itself and those subject to it. During an interview with Furio Colombo, Pasolini draws the following analogy: 'What is cancer? It is something that changes *all* cells, something that makes them *all* grow in a crazy manner, outside of any known logic' (Colombo 1975,

2–3). The stern Father who blocked pleasure also possessed a hierarchy of reality. But now the poles have been perversely conjoined in the viscosity of daily life,[11] in the horror of a seemingly intact body, but a body whose tissues have been emptied from the inside, becoming other tissues. The 'bad infinity,' in which Pasolini says he recognizes the only real infinity, is Tantalus' torment of perversion.[12] The Hegelian dialectical infinity that Pasolini repressed takes its revenge: free of the awareness of conflict and of becoming, the Other reappears as a vampire.

Obsessive frustration tried to justify itself intellectually, and in so doing it discovered previously unknown perspectives. But just when it believes it has become completely objective, and knowledge has freed itself from bias, at precisely that moment its truth loses weight and depth, and it becomes, itself, intellectual obsession: an obsession with the nonexistence of History, and an obsession with Totality. Between *eros* and *agape*, between mysticism and law, no tragic opposition whatsoever is possible any longer, nor is any dramatic scission that might constitute the nucleus of a heroic individuality. St. Paul's sublime 'anachronism' has by now become anachronistic.[13]

In the novel *Petrolio*, whose alternate title was *Vas*, the protagonist Carlo (Pasolini's father's name and therefore, in Lacanian terms, the Name of the Father) is a hollowed-out St. Paul. He is not *vas electionis* (the chosen vessel), according to New Testament and Dantesque diction, but rather, in accordance with the suggestion that comes from the protagonist of Pasolini's *La divina mimesis* (1975), he is 'vas di riduzione' ('the vessel of reduction').[14] Carlo splits into the two 'souls' of St. Paul – the mystical one (translated into a disordering of the senses) and the organizing, managerial one (with a career at the ENI).[15] But the tragic opposition (based on the literary expedient of doubling) no longer has any reason to exist: 'This is the poem of the obsession of identity, and, also, of its shattering' (Pasolini, *Petrolio*, 156). The two Carlos unite in a single, banal, 'tepid' character.

Petrolio links up with *La divina mimesis* to form a comprehensive imitation-emulation of Dante's *Divine Comedy*. The novel is almost a derisive, consumer Paradise following upon the Inferno of this earlier text. With the obscuring of charity, however, history has also lost direction and meaning. The absolute, instead of integrating itself with history and thereby gaining strength from it, remains suspended and befuddled:

this inscription ... a) foresees or prefigures a 'mystical' act that will take place at the end of this novel – and it will be a resolving, vital, totally positive and orgiastic act, which will re-establish the serenity of life and the return of the course of history; b) actually positions itself as an epigraph of the entire present work ... but in that case its meaning is diametrically opposed to that mentioned above. This one is in fact mocking, corrosive, delusive (but not therefore less sacred!): *I erected this statue in order to laugh.*

questa iscrizione ... a) prevede o prefigura un atto 'mistico' che accadrà alla fine di questo romanzo: e si tratterà di un atto risolutore, vitale, pienamente positivo e orgiastico: esso ristabilirà la serenità della vita e la ripresa del corso della storia; b) si pone addirittura come epigrafe di tutta intera la presente opera ... ma il suo senso è in tal caso diametralmente opposto a quello qui sopra accennato: esso infatti è irridente, corrosivo, delusorio (ma non, per questo, meno sacro!): *ho eretto questa statua per ridere.* (386)

The playful attitude is a final heroic glimmer, under disguise as senile irresponsibility, with which Pasolini faces the total loss of reference points, and which is also the consequence of the 'end of the symbolic.' As Pasolini remarks: 'Okay: the disobedience of the young. But the disobedience of the old? The former is based substantially on obedience ... the latter is based substantially on 'play' ... With the total loss of faith (in history, that is) I rediscovered a happiness, yes, a happiness I had never had' (Bellezza 1970). This is the equivalent of saying that play is not reliable or aggressive; it does not open upon analytical activity, but is rather the result of desperation and adaptation;[16] it is the residue of a totalizing but empty ambition.

It is known that Gogol thought of *Dead Souls* as an 'inferno' that would have been followed by a 'purgatory' and a 'paradise,' in a Dantesque imitation that appears very similar to what Pasolini imagined in *Petrolio*. Drawing a parallel between Dante and Gogol himself, Pasolini points out that both authors highlight the moment of the writing, such that the reader is never allowed to forget 'the rules of the game' (Pasolini, *Descrizioni di descrizioni*, 226–8). However, while for Dante the personal moment of writing is inserted into a comprehensive figural and theological event, for Gogol (with whose position Pasolini evidently identifies), the stress is placed on the arbitrariness of the representation, on the fact that the writer 'is free to do whatever he wants,' free to describe for the pure pleasure of describing. The young man in white pants minutely described on the first page of *Dead Souls*, who later will not play any part in the novel, has no essential *meaning*: 'He is, precisely, purely arbitrary. Therefore the description of this figure cannot have any other meaning than that of demonstrating that Gogol is, at that moment, writing' (228).

In *Petrolio* medieval allegory is absorbed into a structure derived from twentieth-century formalism (Victor Schklovsky's chaotic 'swarming novel'), which leads to certain conclusions concerning the insignificance of the work of art – an insignificance coincident with its autonomy. The work means nothing other than itself; it is a dense object in which every dialectic and every infinite opposition of values is tautologically annulled. A short story inserted in the novel (entitled *Prima favola sul potere*, or *First Fable about Power*) presents us with a man who sees God transform Himself into the Devil, and then back into God, and continues thus forever, in an insane dualism. In the end the man is transformed into a rock fallen from the sky:

and still today that stone remains a complete enigma. The infinite variety of its subtle colors corresponds to an infinite variety of materials, but none of these was ever actually identified, because every mineral presents contradictory properties, both in relation to itself and in relation to the other minerals with which it is amalgamated and composed.

E ancor oggi quella pietra resta un puro enigma. L'infinita varietà dei suoi soavi colori corrisponde a un'infinita varietà di materie, ma nessuna di esse è stata realmente individuata, perché ogni minerale presenta caratteri contraddittori, sia in rapporto a se stesso che in rapporto agli altri minerali con cui è amalgamato e composto. (Pasolini, *Petrolio*, 136)

From an epistemological and logical point of view, there is no interest in utilizing any metaphorical density here. There is, rather, a mimetic adhesion: the world of the undifferentiated and of the continuous, in which metaphor is found, imitates the indistinct Totality of the present, the continuity of daily life. 'Play' is not used to settle the score with the culture of infinites, and thus to prefigure new, articulate hypotheses about history. In the Pasolinian 'system,' the new consumerist Power derives its terrifying force from the fact of its having become indistinguishable from life itself, and from the fact that it conflates knowing and being, and joins past and present with the same naturalness of a single body.

The changes necessitated by consumerist Power may be the same as those required by revolutionary ideology, yet they are perniciously different and longer lasting (the end of nationality was obtained not with political internationalism, but with the commercial multinationals).[17] The precarious position of the revolutionaries results from their desire to distinguish between plan (*progetto*) and reality, between what actually happens and what could or should happen. In *Petrolio*, the protagonist adapts to Power, and this occurs when he abandons himself to the flow of his unconscious life, that deep life, far below traumas and dramatic schisms:

he could not even have said what the real novelty was – that novelty experienced in the immensity of his unconscious life: 'the Tao that can be voiced is not the eternal Tao.'

non avrebbe potuto neanche dire qual'era la novità *vera*, quella cioè sperimentata nell'immensità della sua vita inconscia: 'Il tao che si può dire non è l'eterno tao.' (Pasolini, *Petrolio*, 507)

If, for the last time, we use a formula from *La divina mimesis*, the novel *Petrolio*

will have both the magmatic form and the progressive form of reality (which doesn't erase anything, which makes the past coexist with the present, etc.).

avrà insieme la forma magmatica e la forma progressiva della realtà (che non cancella nulla, che fa coesistere il passato con il presente ecc.). (Pasolini, *La divina mimesis*, 57)

The part of the quotation in parentheses could be a good Freudian definition of the unconscious.

An identical viscosity joins the literary work, the unconscious, and Power all together. The relationships between infinite dispersion and limit-form mix themselves invisibly in the immediacy of the unthinkable. But if Power coincides with and actualizes the unconscious, it also means that Power dispossesses the individual of his own unconscious, transferring the psychological need for unity and coherence into an unspeakable Openness.

In the poem 'Aneddoto dei Vecchi re,' Pasolini tells of a hero who in his youth killed a monster, and who unexpectedly manages to conquer another monster in his old age. However,

> it was an unhappy victory:
> even if there were two monsters and two victories,
> a man enjoys but a single victory in life!

> è stata una vittoria infelice:
> anche se i mostri sono stati due, e due le vittorie,
> un uomo non gode che una sola vittoria nella vita. (Pasolini,
> 'Aneddoto dei Vecchi re,' 22)

The repressive Law was defeated; with old age and success, the repressed vital instincts experience a strange joy in living, a freedom
from responsibilities. But the economic system that has allowed this
liberation has rendered those instincts unrecognizable, parodying them
horribly, and has transformed the victory into the most cruel of de-
feats. The victory over that which allowed one to orient oneself and
take form is not a happy victory. One's own, extremely private, and
oft-noted 'guilt for feeling innocent' has become a dangerous and intolerable collective irresponsibility. Imperceptibly, parasitically, something
has entered life's continuity, rendering it monstrous. In the later years
of his life, Pasolini's imagination is obsessed with the phantasm of a
generalized impulse to kill (as a result of the hypertrophy of pleasure
and the demise of the symbolic) that is hidden under apparently innocent forms: murderers wearing the faces of friends, friendly smiles
deformed by latent smirks. As Pasolini remarks: 'It is the same rainwa-
ter of so many infantile poems, little tunes about 'singing in the rain.'
But the water rises and drowns you' (Colombo 1975). Here the acute-
ness of Pasolini's sociological prophecy is made possible – but is also
distorted – by an extreme psychological projection through which any
understanding of external novelty or change is nothing more than an
exaggerated extroversion of a fear of annihilation that has been forever
hidden inside the Self.

It is often suggested that the work of art is also involved in this
ambiguous viscosity of the unconscious and Power, but in that case the
work of art will also become the locus of this parasitic invasion. With
true lyrical genius, Pasolini realized this intuition in 'La seconda forma
della Meglio gioventù,' when he writes of the 'body within a body':
'cuàrp drenti un cuàrp' (Pasolini, La nuova gioventù, 162). Chia, Pasolini's
home away from Rome, is a sort of Friuli that has been emptied and
turned upside down; the tree of Play casts a shadow on the same place
as the tree of Passion; the pure lexemes of his youth are invaded from

within by other syllables, both similar and different. As seen in the verses of 'Dansa de Narcìs,' the polarity that had allowed the ego to appropriate the Friulian world by now no longer exists:

> Saint Paul
> was the great disaster
> of this little world.
> To liberate oneself
> means
> to liberate oneself from his embrace:
> but alas with him
> disappear also
> the prayers of the boys ...
>
> San Pauli
> al è stat la gran disgrassia
> di chistu pìssul mond.
> Liberassi
> a vòul dizi
> liberassi dal so abràs:
> ma ah cun lui
> a sparìssin encia
> li prejeris dai fantàs ... (219)

The world lives in the unmanageable mixture of the Infinite and the Law, and brings together Necessity with the absolute lack of any structuration of history. As he writes in the poem 'Ciants di un muàrt,' 'the second form of time is without end' ('la seconda forma del timp a è sensa fin') (206). By emptying itself of its objects, the ego also empties itself. The theory of the pleasure principle no longer serves to offer an identity: the Other is no longer something on the outside, but the ego is itself that Other that no longer exists in time. We are no longer discussing a form of anxiety born of conflicts, but rather that more radical anxiety of a human subject that no longer recognizes the categories that gave rise to those conflicts, and knows only his own exclusion from reality, because he never knew how 'to die and to become':

> the days have moved
> towards a labor that has ruined
> the sanctity of its heart:

the grain is not dead
and he remains alone.

i dis a son passàs
a un lavoru ch'al à ruvinàt
la santitàt dal so còur:
il gragnèl a no'l è muàrt
e lui al è restàt bessòul. (227)

In the final analysis, the vision of the new consumerist Power is nothing but the testimony of an inability to conceive of life outside those values that are, in any case, no longer feasible. Extreme sincerity consists in dying before life begins again:

it means to die
inside it before it [the world] dies
and is reborn.

a vòul dizi murì
in lui prin che lui al mori
e ch'al torni a nassi. (184)

   In existential terms (as seen in the final stanzas of his last collection of poems, *La nuova gioventù*), Pasolini's intellectual regression (that is, his critique of the dialectic, which is actually a failure to take the dialectic into account at all) translates into an act of radical abdication – the ego does not know how to carry the weight of life any longer. In his 'last poem in Friulian' (255), Pasolini places this weight on the shoulders of a young man, a twenty- or twenty-one-year-old fascist described as still being able to counter 'what is' with 'what should be'; able, that is, to counter the horrifying and necessary fluidity of material life with a Rule. In 'Saluto e augurio,' Pasolini describes this figure as a 'boy carrying the Book without the Word' ('fantàt cun in man il Libri sensa la Peràula' [259]). Pasolini entrusts this 'burden' ('chistu zèit plen') to a young fascist, and Pasolini's stricken ego returns to that fork in the road where he once chose to heal his abnormality with an ideology whose failure causes him so much suffering today:

You, the boy who hates me, you take this burden:
you take it. It shines from the heart. And I will walk

lightly, going ahead, forever choosing
life, youth.

Ciàpiti su chistu pèis, fantàt ch'i ti mi odiis:
puàrtilu tu. Al lus tal còur. E jo i caminarai
lizèir, zint avant, sielzìnt par sempri
la vita, la zoventùt.' (259)

Translated by Adrienne Ward

Notes

1 Any direct influence of the work of Jean Baudrillard on Pasolini is not
  demonstrable, but certainly some of the ideas found in Pasolini's later
  writing (especially, as we will see in our discussion of the novel *Petrolio*,
  the connection between the end of the symbolic dimension and Pasolini's
  ideas concerning 'play') recall Baudrillard's *La société des consommations*
  (Paris: Gallimard, 1970).
2 'Hegel naturalmente si è, sia pur divinamente, sbagliato. L'unica vera
  infinità è quella che egli chiama "cattiva infinità" ' (Pasolini, *Petrolio*, 410).
3 From a poem dedicated to Giovanni Comisso (Pasolini, 'Appunti con una
  romanza,' 1974). Like the poet Sandro Penna, Commiso represented for
  Pasolini the hypothesis of a cognitive happiness without the Father; yet
  this hypothesis is contradicted by the obsessive stylistic perfectionism of
  these very poets.
4 The author's corrections to 'Il poeta delle ceneri' are found in the manuscript at the Fondo Pier Paolo Pasolini (Rome).
5 At most Pasolini sees such a connection as a wretched, objective convergence in the moment of the reception of his works, or as the instrumen-
  talization of his work by Power: 'I am sorry if my films should ever have
  a liberating influence on the sexual customs of Italian society' (Pasolini,
  'Tetis,' 102).
6 The actor-character Ninetto Davoli, found in nearly every film after 1966
  (and intended to have one of the lead roles, along with Eduardo De Filippo,
  in the film that was to follow *Salò*, entitled *Porno-Teo-Kolossal*).
7 A collection of over one hundred sonnets, not all finished, found in two
  versions at the Fondo Pier Paolo Pasolini in Rome. My citations are from
  the later, typewritten version, and the page numbering corresponds to that
  found on the manuscript pages.

8 The erotism of 'typical' bodies is not an exception, since through them tradition serves precisely as a protection against time.

9 'But perfection cannot be attributed to them [to natural beings] as a reward, since it is the fruit of their choice. They allow us, therefore, to experience the very special pleasure of recognizing them as our models without being humiliated by them' (Schiller 1981, 23).

10 From a preliminary version of Pasolini's poem 'La baia di Kingstown,' kept at the Fondo Pier Paolo Pasolini (Rome); the final version is in *Trasumanar e organizzar*, 177–9.

11 'Daily life is not representable, because it is the shadow of life' (Pasolini, *San Paolo*, 36).

12 'In an analogous way, Tantalus in Hell is tormented by an inextinguishable, infinite thirst, and Sisyphus, laboring in vain, is forced repeatedly to push a boulder upwards, but which repeatedly rolls back down. These punishments, like the Titanic powers themselves, are in themselves unmeasurable, bad infinity' (Hegel 1976, 524).

13 'The 'questions' that the evangelized people will pose to St. Paul will be the questions of modern men ... formulated in the typical language of our own time; instead, St. Paul's 'answers' will be what they are: that is, exclusively religious, and for the most part formulated in the typical language of St. Paul, universal and eternal, but anachronistic' (Pasolini, *San Paolo*, 7).

14 *La divina mimesis*, composed in the mid-1960s but published only in 1975, held immense importance for Pasolini. It is a text that has, as we shall see, so much in common with *Petrolio* that it virtually constitutes a necessary antecedent to the novel.

15 The Ente Nazionale Idrocarburi (ENI) is a government agency that, since 1953, has been responsible for overseeing national petrochemical and nuclear industries.

16 'Therefore, it is time to confront the problem: where does the "Abiura dalla *Trilogia della vita*" take me? It takes me towards adaptation' (Pasolini, 'Abiura,' 75).

17 Included among the documents attached to the manuscript of *Petrolio* is Cefis' famous speech (given at the Modena Military Academy on 23 February 1972) on the end of nationality (see Cefis 1972).

References

Bateson, G. *Per un'ecologia della mente*. Milan: Adelphi, 1976

Baudrillard, Jean. *La société des consommations*. Paris: Denoel, 1970

Bellezza, Dario. Interview with Pasolini. *L'Espresso* 47 (22 November 1970): 18–22

Cecchi, Emilio. *I grandi romantici inglesi*. Milan: Adelphi, 1981

Cefis, Eugenio. 'La mia patria si chiama multinazionale.' *L'erba voglio* 6 (1972): 3–21

Colombo, Furio. Interview with Pasolini. *Tuttolibri* (8 November 1975): 2–3

Gogol, Nikolai Vasilevich. *Dead Souls*. New York: Norton, 1971

Hegel, G.W.F. *Estetica*. Turin: Einaudi, 1976

Maingois, Michel. 'Entretien avec Pasolini.' *Zoom* 26 (1974)

Matte-Blanco, I. 'L'infinito è qui per restare.' *L'inconscio come insiemi infiniti*. Turin: Einaudi, 1981

Pasolini, Pier Paolo. *L'Usignolo della Chiesa cattolica*. Milan: Longanesi, 1958

– *Trasumanar e organizzar*. Milan: Garzanti, 1971

– 'Ancora il linguaggio della realtà.' *Filmcritica* 214 (1971)

– 'Aneddoto dei vecchi re.' *Sipario* 300 (1971): 22

– 'Autorecensione a *Trasumanar e organizzar*.' *Il Giorno* (3 June 1971): 4

– 'Tetis.' In V. Boarini, ed., *Erotismo, eversione, merce*. Bologna: Cappelli, 1974

– 'Appunti con una romanza.' *Il Mondo* (31 January 1974): 17

– 'Breve studio sulla pittura di L. Tornabuoni.' Exhibition Catalogue, Galleria Forni, Rome (22 April–5 May 1972)

– *La nuova gioventù*. Turin: Einaudi, 1975

– *La divina mimesis*. Turin: Einaudi, 1975

– 'Abiura dalla *Trilogia della vita*.' In *Lettere luterane*, 71–6 Turin: Einaudi, 1976

– 'Soggetto per un film su una guardia di PS.' *Il Mondo* (7 August 1975). Reprinted in Pasolini, *Lettere luterane*, 99–106. Turin: Einaudi, 1976

– *San Paolo*. Turin: Einaudi, 1977

– *Descrizioni di descrizioni*. Turin: Einaudi, 1979

– 'Il poeta delle ceneri.' *Nuovi argomenti* 67–68 (1980): 3

– *Petrolio*. Turin: Einaudi, 1992 [1975]

Radice, L. Lombardo. *L'infinito*. Rome: Editori Riuniti, 1981

Schiller, F. *Sulla poesia ingenua e sentimentale*. Rome: Il Melograno, 1981

Weil, Simone. *La pesanteur et la grâce*. Paris: Plon, 1948

Free/Indirect/Discourse

PAOLO FABBRI

In this essay, Paolo Fabbri addresses Pasolini's often unorthodox ideas concerning the semiotics of film. During the late sixties and early seventies, debates in film semiotics focused on the possibility of drawing analogies between literary and cinematic narrative models, and on the appropriateness of applying analytical paradigms derived from linguistics to the study of film. Fabbri takes as his starting point the argument between Pasolini, Umberto Eco, and Christian Metz concerning whether or not there was a 'double articulation' in film language, basing themselves largely on André Martinet's Saussurean analysis of the double articulation in spoken-written language. From this discussion Fabbri examines Pasolini's formulations concerning free indirect discourse (otherwise known as *oratio obliqua* or reported speech), and its importance for an understanding of Pasolini's approach to montage. Fabbri asserts that for Pasolini what motivated the montage or editing of his films was not narrative clarity, as in the classical style of Hollywood filmmaking, and its continuity system of narrative time or space. Rather, Pasolini was moved by a desire for a 'poetic' editing style designed to provoke an ambivalent reaction in the spectator.

During the late sixties, I recall attending a conference at Pesaro, in Urbino, and I remember a debate between Pasolini, Christian Metz, and Umberto Eco concerning the attempt to discover the cinematic equivalent of second articulation of language. That is, language can be divided into morphemes (or 'monemes'), units of meaning that form the 'first articulation.' These units can then be broken down into smaller but meaningless units of sound, or 'phonemes,' that form the 'second articulation.' It will be necessary to return to this issue in a moment.

This conference in Pesaro was held during a period that witnessed theoretical attempts to draw certain analogies between spoken-written language and the language of film, using semiotic methods derived from the work of the linguist Ferdinand de Saussure. One of the questions under debate concerning semiotic's 'linguistic metaphor' was whether or not film was a language at all, or whether film was always necessarily a *langage* (language) or *parole* (speech) lacking the equivalent of a *langue* (or language system). One of the most noted results of these inquiries was Metz's categorization of the basic syntagmatic structures of narrative cinema (see Metz 1974a). In Pasolini's 1966 essay, 'The Written Language of Reality,' he responds to an article Metz (1964) published in *Communications* ('Le cinéma: langue ou langage?'). The response takes the form of Pasolini's articulation of his own stylistic grammar of the language of cinema, and his application of this grammar in an analysis of two films by Ermanno Olmi and Bernardo Bertolucci (Pasolini, *Empirismo eretico*, 202–30; *Heretical Empiricism*, 197–222). However, while the wider debate among these theorists is itself of great interest, I will focus upon a few details in Pasolini's theoretical approach.

Pasolini worked in semiotics, or what he called semiotics, for almost ten years, from 1965 until his death in 1975. Most of his essays concerning semiotics were collected in the volume entitled *Empirismo eretico* (*Heretical Empiricism*). Pasolini's reflections upon semiotics were very close to his film work in this period.

There is no way to return to the debates of this period today unless you can find within them some problem useful for the analysis of the present, and this is what I will do here, by taking up the problem of prophecy. There are two kinds of prophetic attitudes. One, according to Maurice Blanchot, suggests that there is a voice speaking behind you, in your past, passing through you and going into the future. The present would be simply a point crossed by this language. There is another strategy of prophecy: the past is there to give space to the present, and the knowledge of the present is possible only in a simple way. You go to the future, you come back to the past because you do not read the past from the present (because you don't know the present). You need a hypothesis about your future, you read the past from the future, and from the past you come back to the present. That is, you have to return to the present from the future. What I am suggesting now is that the notion of free indirect discourse, so crucial for Pasolini, provides a way to try to understand what is going on in the present, by thinking about strategies of signification in texts today.

Well this may be very banal but, finally, if along the path you meet the monster Chimera and experience witchcraft, it would probably be most amusing – and this is what we will try to do.

Free, Indirect, *Discourse*

First, let us invert the order of the formulation 'free indirect discourse.' Begin with discourse, or speech. What was interesting and crucial in Pasolini was the complete refusal of Roland Barthes's idea that semiotics was a sort of 'trans-linguistics.' In this period, Barthes insists that we must extend to semiotics the strategy of linguistics. Metz argues that it was not possible to make this kind of extension in the case of cinema because a filmed image is always an *énoncé*, a large utterance that does not analytically dissolve into smaller units comparable to linguistic units, like monemes or phonemes. In his semiotics, Pasolini argues that the relation between film and the world is a relation of translation. I do not know if the idea of the semiology of reality (*semiologia della realtà*), as he called it, is a good one. Nonetheless, the fundamental idea is that, in a certain way, the signification – the meaning we receive from a film – is not based on reality, in the sense that you can count and name the objects reproduced in the image. This sort of analysis, based on Pasolini's formulation in *Empirismo eretico* concerning 'cinemes' (*cinemi*: the individual elements within the frame, which Pasolini asserted as the filmic equivalents of phonemes) and the second articulation, was common in this period. Indeed, I know some Pasolini scholars working in order to find all the objects inside the frame. This is amusing because they are what I would call the main victims of language. That is, by trying to escape from language you become the victim of language because what you can see in the picture, in the frame, is only what you can give a name to. You say: well this is a horse, this is a house, and so on. While trying to escape from the linguistic model by looking directly at the picture, at the frame, and while pretending that in that moment you are looking at objects, in the end you only see the objects for which you have names. You become a victim of what can only be called linguistic superstition.

More interesting was Pasolini's refusal of the metaphorical model. In the essay entitled 'Cinema of Poetry,' Pasolini very clearly denounced the naïve quality of all metaphor in the cinema. The idea of refusing to look in the traditional linguistic way, refusing the model of metaphor, and posing the question of translation, is, in my opinion, an interesting way to approach the problem of meaning in a film.

Free, *Indirect,* **Discourse**

However, there is more than this in Pasolini's work (although in part implicit and in part explicit). I will now take into account the notion of 'indirection': discourse, *indirect* and free. The indirection in Pasolini's work is extremely interesting, because it is not, he would insist, involved only in metaphor. Pasolini was formed in a very traditional philological framework in Italy. Regarding free indirect discourse in particular, Pasolini drew freely from Herczeg's book *Stile indiretto libero* (indeed there are many direct quotations of this philologist's work in Pasolini's essays). What is interesting about indirection is the idea that in indirect discourse one is speaking unspeakable sentences. This kind of discourse does not take into account the objects or the words or the images, but rather the relationship between images. Implicitly one is indirectly producing an impossible viewer.

Let us consider an example, originally offered by Pasolini, of free indirect discourse: 'They arrived in front of the plane. They look at the plane. How beautiful.' Who is speaking? You don't know if the speaker is the actor (the character inside the story) or if it is the narrator. You are unable to assign a single point of view. The fact is that there is no complete theory in linguistics about the many speaking positions in the special kind of stylistic moment we call free indirect discourse. The very term free indirect discourse is a great problem for literature because it poses the question of unspeakable sentences: unspeakable in the sense that we do not know who is speaking.

And finally, what is the effect of free indirect discourse? The indirection takes off from the literal definition, the referential definition, exactly in the same way in which the metaphor is supposed to take off from the denotational and the referential feature of language. From a certain point of view, free indirect discourse has a metaphorical quality, but it is not a metaphor of a sign. Rather it is a metaphor of a speaker or of a viewer inside the text itself. This is not a discovery. You can find it clearly explicit in Weinrich's (1971) book about the *tempus*. He says very clearly that when you pass from one sentence to another sentence and you cannot locate who is the speaker speaking in the second sentence, you can suppose that you have a metaphorical process, though in a very broad sense of metaphor. Here metaphor should not to be taken in the sense of a sign substituting another sign (a man is a lion, and so on) but an impossible though necessary substitution in the sense of *meta - phor*, in the sense of 'after moving,' in which you cannot make a clear demarcation of who is speaking. The metaphor falls between the sentences, not inside the sentence itself. From this point of view, in cinema, the indirection of discourse poses the crucial question of *who is seeing*? In Pasolini's example, found in his 1971 essay on the edit or cut between shots, entitled 'Il rema' ('The Rheme') (Pasolini, *Empirismo eretico*, 293–301; *Heretical Empiricism*, 288–92), he speaks about presenting a shot of a woman looking at a plane followed by a subjective shot. He raises some questions about the relationship between the first image and the second one: what is going on? who moved there? and so on. Well, this is precisely the problem of indirection. In the first case, you have semiosis (which is not just translinguistics). In the second you have the problem of indirection: the fact is that you can produce metaphors of enunciation, and not only metaphors of images.

Free, Indirect, Discourse

We arrive now at the third problem, what I would call the problem of freedom (*free* indirect discourse). Most of us remember that in the beginning of the sixties Eco wrote a very influential essay about the open work or *opera aperta* (Eco 1962). Eco insists that there is a sort of tyrannical hold of the reader able to attack the open work from everywhere and to construct or execute for himself the final meaning of the work. This is not Pasolini's position, and furthermore this is not Eco's current position on the matter (see Eco, *The Limits of Interpretation* and *Interpretation and Overinterpretation*), and his novels (*The Name of the Rose* and *Foucault's Pendulum*) differ from his earlier notion of an open work. In this period, Pasolini was seeking another kind of freedom: the freedom inside the text itself. He asks himself: how to build the text? He was able to introduce, inside the text itself, a simulacrum of Eco's freedom of interpretation. How is it possible to give voice, to give the answer, to the addressee, to the reader inside the text itself? He answered: by way of the *cinema di poesia* (cinema of poetry). He asserted that the cinema of poetry is like a Persian carpet (the analogy is Pasolini's) in which the soul of the author and the soul of the character blend. The problem can be confronted through a description of the form of knots. Perhaps the soul can blend but what is the form of knots? The knot takes on many forms. The *oratio obliqua*, which is in fact the old name of free indirect discourse, permits different kinds of strategies. Irony for example – violent irony – is one of the effects of *oratio obliqua* (see Pasolini, *Empirismo eretico*, 98; *Heretical Empiricism*, 91).

How is 'violent irony' possible for Pasolini? Pasolini took the idea of linguistic contamination very seriously, but in this period the problem of contamination, as in all periods, was difficult to make explicit. In Gilles Deleuze as well you will find a great idea which is very modernistic: the idea of the 'purity' of the image. An image is pure as a substance of expression having its own quality. But there was also, during this same period, what we will call the 'De Mauro obsession' (see De Mauro 1985). Tullio De Mauro was a strong and very faithful member of the Italian Communist Party, and in this period he had very strong attitudes concerning the question of regional dialects (the old Gramscian hypothesis). But, in fact, what Pasolini did through the contamination of dialects in his writing gives an idea of the direction in which modern Italy is going today. The Italian individual today is constituted by a contamination of dialects, certainly not by a purity of dialect. Pasolini's idea is interesting insofar as freedom, for him, is ensured by the various linguistic levels mixed together; by the chaotic motion between levels of discourse which is not just a level of language. But this chaotic motion, which I will call the indirect unspeakable motion, using a temporal metaphor, is a kind of mixing of contamination, not just a contamination of Italian and different kinds of languages. This is what the novelist Carlo Emilio Gadda did so well, and certainly did better than Pasolini. I would assert this notion of indirection is the key to understanding the problem. In fact I would change slightly the order of the terms, and suggest that it is *indirect*, free discourse with which I am mainly concerned.

But what is the quality of this 'precious form of contamination,' this chaotic movement of languages? The idea is an aesthetic one. Pasolini writes,

On such material is enacted a violent and brutal laceration, a cut, from which erupts the *other* material which composes the objectivity, the real fabric of things which escaped the intellectual poet and also escaped, by and large, man.' (Pasolini, *Empirismo eretico*, 99, my translation; *Heretical Empiricism*, 92)

And further:

the language is no longer that of the *character* but that of the addressee. The quotation of the laceration indifferent to this language – which is monstrous with respect to the work.' (ibid.; my translation)

I announced that we were looking for monsters. The monster is coming.

What about this idea of laceration? Generally the aesthetic experience can be defined as follows: you have to work until you arrive at the shifting moment, the splitting moment, in which a new kind of reality appears (Heidegger calls it *der Stoss*). What is interesting here are two points. The first one is that Pasolini does *not* insist that there is a reality to reproduce in a film, but that it is necessary to work on the image until the reality appears. All around us we have no reality; this is simulation, we are 'fabrics' – we create reality. Reality can appear sometimes with the Medusa face, the Gorgon face. This is the reality Pasolini saw, appearing as a brutal laceration having the traditional definition of the aesthetic experience. The reality appears (though not all the time), yet we do not see reality; and we don't see appearances, since we are used to them. When you look at reality there is a brutal laceration of the world and the reality appears and disappears immediately (fortunately for us, but also unbearably for us). In this moment of laceration, what is the reality, for Pasolini? The reality of the addressee (see Pasolini, *Empirismo eretico* 99; *Heretical Empiricism*, 92).

Theoretically, this is very interesting during a period in which the avant-garde, working on reality, does not attempt at all to make the addressee appear in its own discourse. Let us recall how it was possible, during the sixties, simultaneously to disrupt traditional language and yet at the same time also make the audience adhere to your discourse. For Pasolini, the real problem was how to produce the monster of the addressee. The real addressee, not just the empirical one (which is, exactly like reality, a product of statistical definitions). For Pasolini the problem becomes: how is it possible to produce an addressee, a Medusa face, speaking to you?

This is a huge problem, but you cannot obtain the desired result through poetry. Poetry in the double sense of the word: poetry speaks about something and also speaks about more than that. A very simple definition of poetry could be something like this: a man or woman says to you I like you, I love you, I love you, I love you, I am dying, I am dying, I am dying. But by the same means, and at the same time, you are saying other things to another addressee. With a minimal level of ambiguity, poetry produces a split between the subject speaking, something speaking inside us, and something speaking to another addressee. The point is that poetry is not just a doubled language presupposing a split in the doubled sender and a split in the doubled receiver. The problem of poetry is to make this receiver appear. We have to look to the split addressee. In Italian I would say, hopefully in a funny way (recalling Freud's metaphor), the *super-tu* ('super-you') and not just the *super-io* ('super-ego'). In my opinion, what is interesting in the psychoanalytic metaphor of transference is the idea that finally there is a real poetic quality in the psychoanalytical relationship between analyst and analysand. From the sender (analysand) you have a 'floating speaking,' an indirect speaking. The psychoanalyst will never believe in the surface level of the analysand's discourse, but the analyst uses a sort of indirect free way of hearing the analysand. There is a poetic communication in the pre-transferred activity, which is very close to Pasolini's ideas as quoted above. That is, not only is the subject free and indirect, but also the space is free and indirect in cinematic representation. Moreover, time is really indirect and free. Let me give an example from Pasolini. In 'Observation on the Sequence Shot,' written in 1967, he speaks about the multiplication of the 'presents' in montage (Pasolini, *Empirismo eretico*, 241–5; *Heretical Empiricism*, 233–7). Pasolini asserts that the 'multiplication of the 'presents' in reality abolishes the present' (242; 234). What is necessary for us is to look to the coordination or the relation between sentences or sequences (segments if you prefer), the coordination that 'renders the present past' (243; 235). According to Pasolini, the narrator transforms the present into the past,

a past that, for reasons immanent in the cinematographic medium, and not because of an aesthetic choice, always has the qualities of the present (it is, in other words, a historical present). (244; 236)

The historical present is the absolutely crucial feature created by the montage, by what Weinrich in linguistics would call the metaphorical mode of time.

Let me give an example of free indirect time. I will quote from a Sicilian story, which goes as follows. The Normans arrived in Palermo (*arrivarono*, using the preterite form) in the twelfth century and their king will be the best king of Sicily (*will be*). This narrative raises a series of questions. 'Will be' until when? Until you speaking now? 'Will be' in the immediate future in this past of this past? Up until the period when the Normans disappeared from Sicily? Or 'will be' forever, passing through my present until forever? As you can see, we cannot make a decision there. This is the strict internal ambiguity of the montage between the time 'they arrived' and the time when the king 'will be.' This is specific free indirect discourse. This is specifically a metaphor of time.

One of the great strengths of Pasolini is to point, by way of the idea of free indirect discourse, to this monstrous combination, the Chimera, possessing different qualities of time. He speaks about the 'rhythmeme' (*ritmema*), a unity of rhythm, and he suggests that it is a sort of monster of amphibious nature, of space and time, producing non-existent meaning. This is a quality in Pasolini's work that is useful for our present.

I agree, along with many others, that for us Pasolini is part of a very distant past. What is incredible for an Italian today is how much the world of Pasolini, the Roman *borgata* (the subproletarian ghettos as found in *Accattone* and *Mamma Roma*), is really a prehistoric experience. Italians today look upon this historical moment as they do the *Risorgimento* (the period of nineteenth-century Italian unification struggles) – that is, as a distant period of our history. From this point of view, Pasolini is for us part of a very, very distant past. Also part of the past is the idea of a semiology of reality (*semiologia della realtà*). However, the crucial idea of the semiosis of the unspeakable sentence, of out-of-sight segments, and the project of freely creating, inside the discourse, the effect of a future addressee, is an aesthetic project that is not concluded or closed. It remains open for us.

This is why Pasolini is not just a medium, in the sense that, by his own genius, he chose the medium of film, before many others, because of the internal quality of modern language. Rather, he was a medium in the sense that the medium is a sort of witchcraft evocation. (I promised monsters and witchcraft, and they have arrived.) I think there is a quality of the medium speaking to our present in the right way of prophecy: going to the future, using the hope of the future for reading the present, coming back to the past, in order to return again to an ambiguous present.

References

Deleuze, Gilles. *Cinema 1: The Movement Image.* Translated by H. Tomlinson and B. Habberjam. Minneapolis: University of Minnesota Press, 1986
– *Cinema 2: The Time Image.* Translated by H. Tomlinson and B. Habberjam. Minneapolis: University of Minnesota Press, 1989

De Mauro, Tullio. 'Pasolini linguista.' *The Italianist* 5 (1985): 66–76

Eco, Umberto. *L'Opera aperta*. Milan: Bompiani, 1962. English trans., *The Open Work*. Translated by A. Cancogni. Cambridge, MA: Harvard University Press, 1989

– *The Limits of Interpretation*. Bloomington: Indiana University Press, 1990

Eco, Umberto, et al. *Interpretation and Overinterpretation*. New York: Cambridge University Press, 1992

Herczeg, Giulio. *Lo stile indiretto libero in italiano*. Florence: Sansoni, 1963

Martinet, André. *Elements of General Linguistics*. Translated by E. Palmer. Chicago: 1964

Metz, Christian. 'Le cinéma: langue ou langage?' *Communications* 4 (1964): 52–90. Translated in his *Film Language*, 31–91. New York: Oxford University Press, 1974a

– *Language and Cinema*. Hague: Mouton, 1974b

Pasolini, Pier Paolo. *Empirismo eretico*. Milan: Garzanti, 1972. English trans., *Heretical Empiricism*. Translated by B. Lawton and L. Barnett. Bloomington: Indiana University Press, 1988

Weinrich, Harald. *Tempus. Besprochene und erzählte Welt*. Stuttgart: Kohlhammer, 1971. Italian trans., *Tempus. Le funzioni dei tempi nel testo*. Bologna: Il Mulino, 1978

The Body of Pasolini's Semiotics: A Sequel Twenty Years Later

GIULIANA BRUNO

> And I devour and devour ... How will it end, I do not know.
> – Pier Paolo Pasolini

Far too few of Pasolini's enormous volume of essays and articles have been translated for English readers to recognize how Pasolini allowed the different disciplinary orders of investigation to 'contaminate' each other in the body of his writing. In this wide-ranging and suggestive essay Giuliana Bruno first briefly catalogues the great range of Pasolini's essays and then addresses his singular ambition, that semiology might become a 'philosophy.' Pasolini's first forays into a film semiotics during the mid-1960s arose from an epistemological desire to bring reality and cinema closer. This effort, at the height of the 'structuralist' moment of semiology, drew harsh criticism, bordering on dismissal, to Pasolini's proposals. Now that moment has passed, argues Bruno, and we can see that Pasolini's semiology was really ahead of its time and that it has important points of contact with contemporary poststructuralist theory. Bruno's rereading of Pasolini's film semiology locates his anti-nominalism, contending that the real is a language, not made by language but brought to consciousness through the interactive bond of the social interpretant. Pasolini's theory was not, then, a brand of cinema ontology, as his critics claimed, but instanced a practice of interpretation. From this fundamental revision of the dimensions of the body of his semiotics, Bruno surveys Pasolini's foresight into the psychoanalytic, feminist, and postmodern developments of contemporary theory, proposing what she rightly terms a 'sequel twenty years later.'

This essay offers a critical reconsideration of Pier Paolo Pasolini's theoretical writings on film, showing their links to current developments in critical theory. Though heavily criticized by his contemporaries, Pasolini appears today to have anticipated some of the crucial issues of post-structuralist thinking and of the condition of postmodernity. Showing these links, my essay aims to reassess the work of one of the most important intellectual and artistic figures of our times, one whose contribution has yet to be acknowledged fully in North America. In fact, only a very small portion of Pasolini's 'volcanic' production has ever been translated into English. Even when translated, Pasolini's work has not made a real impact on the American cultural landscape, while for Italian, as well as French and German, culture, it holds a position of central importance. The recent translation of *Heretical Empiricism*, one of his many books of collected essays, published in Italy almost twenty years ago, is a step toward the entry of Pasolini's critical theory into the realm of American culture.[1] Finally available to English readers, this book enables a reconsideration by offering a sample of the range of Pasolini's cultural input and the expanse of his intellectual horizon.

A true Renaissance man, Pasolini wrote extensively on a variety of topics and in diverse fields, and practised in many different creative media. His *engagement* in critical theory claimed 'theory' as a practice of 'writing.' To anyone who asked him whether he was a novelist, a theorist, a filmmaker, a critic, a polemicist, a playwright, a poet writing in dialect or in standard Italian language, he would answer, 'I am a writer, just as it says on my official ID.' In any of its forms, the *body* of writing is the centre of Pasolini's research. His multifaceted and eclectic creative trajectory was marked by civil activism, just as his position as a 'writer' was characterized by a passionate *engagement* in the cultural and political debates of his time. Practising a form of utopian thinking, Pasolini incessantly intervened with his 'scandalous' work in sociocultural praxis, and let his transgressive curiosity contaminate the separate areas and modes of 'professional' writing.

Outlined in the following pages are a few aspects of Pasolini's wide-ranging practice of writing. Over the years, as a critic and theorist, he collaborated with various cultural publications such as *Fiera letteraria*, *Paragone*, and *Nuovi argomenti* (which from 1966, he codirected with writer Alberto Moravia), and wrote for publications affiliated with left-wing parties, such as *Rinascita* and *Botteghe oscure*. From 1948 to 1958, Pasolini was involved in a critical and theoretical activity mostly concerned with literature and literary analysis (as well as the analysis of language and dialects) that took the form of essays appearing in *Officina* and other publications. In 1960, he published a selection of his essays with the title *Passione e ideologia* ('Passion and Ideology'). From 1960 to

1965, he wrote for *Vie nuove*, and maintained a cultural and political dialogue with its readers, answering a variety of letters. A collection of these essays was published in 1977 with the title *Le belle bandiere* ('The Beautiful Flags'). From 1965 on, he wrote on film in magazines such as *Filmcritica*, *Bianco e nero*, *Cinema nuovo*, *Cinema e film*, and participated in the pioneering panels and seminars aimed at founding a film semiotics, organized by the Mostra Internazionale del Nuovo Cinema at Pesaro. Some of these writings are collected in *Heretical Empiricism*, together with critical essays on language and literature. In the years of the *autunno caldo* (the 'hot autumn' of 1968–70), the turbulent years of political struggle of the Left, Pasolini chose to write for a weekly, *Tempo*, and named his own column *Caos* ('Chaos'). In 1974–75 he was responsible for a column in a leading daily newspaper *Il corriere della sera*, and for a column in the magazine *Il mondo*. In the last year of his life, from the pages of these journals, he engaged in a reflective polemical chronicle of Italian cultural and sociopolitical life in its making. Observing and criticizing anthropological and sociological, as well as political, changes in Italy, never tiring of fighting his own famous battle against petit-bourgeois values, Pasolini wrote very controversial articles on such topics as abortion, television, education, crime, police, consumerism, fascism, left-wing politics, and intellectual life. These articles were collected in books with the significant titles of *Scritti corsari* (1975) ('Pirate Writings'), and *Lettere luterane* (1976) ('Lutheran Letters').[2] Other books of collected essays, published posthumously, include *Il caos* (1979) ('Chaos'), and two anthologies of literary criticism, *Descrizioni di descrizioni* (1979) ('Descriptions of Descriptions'), and *Il portico della morte* (1988) ('The Arcade of Death').

Pasolini holds a particular place in cultural history, not only for how interesting he was but also because his ideas, insofar as they were heretical, they were not readily accepted or acceptable. During his life, Pasolini was criticized, misunderstood, and often marginalized not only in North America but also in Europe. As far as his semiotic work is concerned, in the midst of the polemics surrounding his position, Pasolini wrote in 1967 in the cultural journal of the Communist party *Rinascita*: 'Semiology ... has not taken the step which would lead it to become a Philosophy ... This, Christian Metz told me, is a dream of mine. An Italian linguist would tell me that is a foolishness of mine. In conclusion, I find myself isolated.'[3]

The majority of the criticism directed against Pasolini concerned the way in which he posited the relation between cinema and reality. The motivation of such criticism was the belief that his semiotic project intended to collapse the notion of reality onto cinema and reintroduce a neo-Bazinian reverence for reality. Among others, Stephen Heath criticized Pasolini in his essay 'Film/Cinetext/Text,' contending that the

occultation of the work of film has a whole history in the development of thinking cinema . . . It represents . . . the *natural attitude* to cinema. In the context of a cinesemiotics it can only lead to the denial of cinema as semiotic system: cinema becomes not process of the articulation of meaning, but direct duplication of some Reality; it represents 'reality' with 'reality.' Certain ideas of Pasolini will perhaps have been recognized at this point. (Heath 1973, 109)

There could be nothing worse, in a moment when the semiotics of film was trying to gain a new status, than being labelled a partisan of reality. Many critics expressed a negative opinion of Pasolini's 'semiological heresy' and considered it unusable for the development of semiotics.[4] Early film semiotics, concerned with mediumistic specificity, and engaged in structuring, categorizing, and systematizing discourse, was itself constructing a rigid systemic language that Pasolini's approach did not share. Considered threatening to the legitimation of 'scientific' semiotics, his work was looked at as if through a screen, one that did not enable critics to accept the importance of critical 'dissemination,' the fascination of 'intertextual' cultural theory, and the nuances of theoretical 'pastiche,' nor to see beyond that notorious question of reality. As a result, a complex, multifaceted intellectual was taken for an imprecise thinker.

Writing 'a sequel twenty years later,' it may now be possible to overcome the position that Pasolini himself challenged as the reality-phobia in a text of 1967 entitled 'The Fear of Naturalism' (*Heretical Empiricism*, 244–6). As the question of 'scientific' semiotics is today no longer an issue, the discussion of Pasolini's work can finally avoid the judgment impending on it in the past. Pasolini's position was not understood insofar as it was much ahead of its time. Furthermore, his semiological heresy is intriguing in its very aspect of heresy, as an act of transgression. Reconsidering the criticism addressed to Pasolini's semiotic work, I will suggest a few points of contact with recent theoretical developments, and place his discourse in the context of the politics of theory and its apparatus. Pasolini's position seems prophetic today not only in relation to the development of semiotics but also in terms of poststructuralist theory and the ideological implications of the postmodern condition. The work of an eternal dissident, Pasolini's controversial discourse presents a series of questions and issues in the domain of critical theory that anticipate the direction of 'cultural studies.'

Addressing Pasolini's investigation of reality, Teresa de Lauretis has called for a reconsideration of Pasolini's semiotics, revealing its attempt to expand the very range of the discipline. Reconsidering Pasolini's position in the debates of his time, de Lauretis suggests points of contact between Pasolini's ideas and the development of Umberto Eco's semiotics.[5] Pasolini's notion of the sign, proposed in 1965, anticipates Eco's notion of sign-function. Moreover, Pasolini's 'scandalous' attempt to define the reader's collaboration in the *sceno-testo* – the screenplay as text in movement, as diachronic structure – is very close to Eco's formulations of the open text. As de Lauretis aptly puts it in her book, *Alice Doesn't*:

In light of the developments within semiotics and especially of Eco's critique of iconism, it is interesting to reread Pasolini's essays on cinema, written in the mid-sixties and at the time quickly dismissed as un-semiotic, theoretically unsophisticated, or even reactionary. Ironically, from where we now stand, his views on the relation of cinema to reality appear to have addressed perhaps the central issue of cinematic theory. In particular, his observation that cinematic images inscribe reality as representation and his insistence on the 'audio-visuality' of cinema . . . bear directly on the role that cinema's imaging has in the production of social reality. (de Lauretis 1984, 48–9)

In fact, rereading Pasolini's well-known 1965 essay, 'The Cinema of Poetry' (*Heretical Empiricism*, 167–86), without the banner of the reality-phobia, we now realize that the relation he established between reality and the cinema is much more complex than the simple collapse of reality onto cinema. Reality itself is not a monolithic, unitary, ontological entity. Rather, it is a site that inhabits the dynamics of social negotiation, contradiction, and communication. In the 1966 essay, 'The Written Language of Reality' (*Heretical Empiricism*, 197–222). Pasolini speaks of both cinema and the real as modes of communication and, as such, interrelated. He suggests that one investigate the text(ure)s of these two instances, and the two-way impact between reality – 'the language of action' – and cinema. Pasolini's theoretical attachment to the real is to be understood as the inscription of cultural productions, and of theoretical discourse itself, into the realm of praxis. His 'reality' is social practice – the site of interaction of historicity and the social text with the language of film.

For Pasolini, it is not a question of positing a realistic cinema or viewing cinema as the reproduction of reality, but rather reversing the terms of classic realism. Pasolini conceives of reality as the 'discourse of things' that cinema renarrates. The cinematic sign becomes a meta-linguistic sign, a vehicle, an interpretant for another sign. As he writes in an epistolary interview, 'What does the "sign" make of the "signified": does it "signify" it? It's a tautology... In reality there is no "signified": *because the signified is also a sign.*'[6] This approaches a position that many theorists now adopt as a result of Jacques Lacan's famous notion that 'a signifier represents a subject for another signifier' (Lacan 1966, 840).

Conceived in these terms, reality is viewed by Pasolini as a participant in the process of imaging. Considering cinema 'the written language of reality,' Pasolini speaks of the real as cinematic. Rather than seek the impression of reality in the language of film, this position pursues the cinematic trace of the real, as Pasolini establishes a relation between the real and cinema based on their status as 'spectacle.' This view, expressed in 1967 in the essay 'Is Being Natural?' (*Heretical Empiricism*, (238–43) is a direction of thought that has been largely explored in postmodernism. It is by now a common assumption that we live in a 'society of spectacle.' As for the loss of a traditional notion of the environment, and the way in which the real is represented, reality ends up becoming that which is always already reproduced.[7]

'Res sunt nomina' ('the real is a language'), Pasolini argues, reversing a nominalism based on the assumption that 'nomina sunt res' ('language is a reality').[8] *Res* are recognized as signs, and the relation of subject to objects is the instantiation of a language. Suggesting that language is the structuring system of the real, Pasolini foreshadows post-structuralist concerns. This view is not so scandalous any more if we place it against the assumption that even the unconscious is structured as a language (Lacan 1966).

Pasolini's formulation of cinema as 'the written language of reality' assumes, on the one hand, that the real itself be considered a language (the discourse of action), and, on the other hand, that cinema be considered as *scrittura*,[9] in a sense that approaches the now widely used notion of *écriture*, writing.[10] Conceiving of the real and cinema as systems of signs, inhabited by the trace of other signs, Pasolini inscribes them in a process that eludes definition, and affirms endless textuality. Based on polysemic signification, his semiotics enacts the play of contamination and intertextuality. As expressed in the article 'L'ambiguità' (1974) ('Ambivalence'), his semiotic research does not seek to establish codes or to categorize, but rather to venture into the polyphony of an all-encompassing signification.

Pasolini's semiotics suggests ways to overcome the strict adherence to linguistics; intertextually questions the monopoly of linguistics in accounting for the codes of cinema. Instead of collapsing, for example, the sign of Saussurian linguistics onto the cinematic sign, Pasolini recognizes cinema's iconic and metonymic nature. He invents a word, '*imsegno*,' literally 'image-sign', to account for the complex function of the cinematic sign, which involves iconic resemblance and metonymic bond to *res*. The notion of *imsegno* can be reconsidered in light of the rediscovered work of another heretical intellect: Charles Sanders Peirce.[11] Pasolini's *imsegno* can be acknowledged as sharing the theoretical direction of Peirce's triad of signs: iconic, indexical, and symbolic. According to Peirce, only one type of sign, the symbolic, has characteristics similar to the Saussurian sign, while the icon and the index are signs that have an iconic or metonymic relation to *res*. Like Peirce's sign, Pasolini's *imsegno* demands to be decoded in its interactive bond to the social referent. The relation of Pasolini's semiotic project with Peirce's extends to Peirce's notion of the Dynamic Object – that which determines the formation of a sign. This, in Pasolini's words, is the interaction of *res* with *nomina*. For both Peirce and Pasolini, objects are functions, results of the dynamics of experience. When Pasolini says that *res sunt nomina* he speaks of *res* as texts that trigger 'semiosis,' as semiotic systems that demand deciphering. The attitude that Pasolini's critics generally mistook for an ontology, on the contrary is aligned with Peirce's approach to interpretation as grounded in praxis.

Theorizing cinema as 'the written language of reality,' Pasolini furthermore states that 'the processes of dream and memory, both involuntary and, above all, voluntary, are the primordial outlines of a film language.'[12] 'The world of memory and of dreams' (*Heretical Empiricism,* 168) is the dimension of the real that he often relates to the cinema. This view foreshadows not only Christian Metz's notion of 'imaginary signifier' (Metz 1982) but also anticipates Jean-Louis Baudry's view of the *dispositif* (apparatus). Building an argument from the connotations of the Italian linguistic sign for the movie-camera, *macchina da presa* – a machine to capture, enrapture, devour – Pasolini calls cinema a 'voracious devourer' and renames the 'kino-eye' 'occhio-bocca,' 'eye-mouth.' In 1967, he suggests that the cinematic apparatus has an oral function as a machine of reproduction and perception (*Heretical Empiricism*, 255). As Baudry later wrote, 'Desire which constitutes the cine-effect is rooted in the oral structure of the subject. The conditions of projection do evoke the dialectics ... swallowing/swallowed, eating/being eaten, which is characteristic of what is being structured in the oral phase' (Baudry, 317–18).

Foreshadowing poststructuralist concerns, Pasolini's semiotics puts a stress on notions such as 'discourse,' 'process,' and writing. In an interview, he states, 'Barthes, who has so widened the concept of "writing," should be profoundly jealous of my idea of cinema as "writing"' (*Heretical Empiricism*, 231). Pasolini proposes *discourse* as a way to bridge the gap between his own work and Christian Metz' (*Heretical Empiricism*, 199). He theorizes *process* in a 1965 text significantly titled 'The Screenplay as a "Structure that Wants to Be Another Structure"' (*Heretical Empiricism*, 187–96). Here, Pasolini seeks to define the language of film in terms other than the semiotician's static *syntagmatique* or structure. He insists on a notion of structure in motion and text-in-progress. Pasolini's interest in a dynamic form striving to be another form recalls the Brechtian concept of change of function, insofar as the task of intellectual endeavour is to transform the form of production into work-in-progress.

The body itself of Pasolini's semiotics is work-in-progress, and produces a similar notion of the cinematic sign. Cinema's impact as a signifying practice is a result of its constitution as 'the written language of pragma.' Filmic 'writing' is grounded in a sociohistorical terrain: it is the enactment of the historical moment of the sign, as writing enables the modification and increase of the historicity of language.[13] In 1965, Pasolini already spoke of the historicity of the sign, an issue of great interest that only recently has been addressed by later thinkers. He seeks a semiotic language that may account for the work of the film-*parole*, and not only for cinema as a *langue*, as well as accounting for the transformation of the real into narrative.[14] For Pasolini, it is editing, as it fragments, selects, and links in coordination, that performs this operation, transforming the ideal long take of the cinema-*langue* into the film-*parole*. A process of fragmentation, juxtaposition, and deconstruction, epitomized by montage, enacts historicity for cinema: montage interrupts the continuous present of cinema and life, and changes it into the 'historical present' of film and death. A culture of death emerges from Pasolini's reflections on the historicity of writing. Film, a devouring machine, a 'reality eater,' is positioned on the brink of death and history. Not a Bazinian recapturing of the continuum with the long take, but the working of montage is the link between reality and film – a discourse of fragments that dialectically corresponds to the language of pragma.

Pasolini's interest in, and account of, social structures extends to the dynamics of readership and spectatorship. In the introduction to his book *Scritti corsari* ('Pirate Writings'), Pasolini writes:

> The reconstruction of this book is left to the reader. It is the reader who must put together the fragments of an incomplete and dispersed opus. It is he/she who must find a connection between passages far away from each other but nonetheless linked. It is he/she who must organize the contradictory moments and research their substantial unity. It is he/she who must fill in the possible incoherences, that is, the abandoned research projects or hypotheses. It is he/she who must substitute repetitions with variants or rather understand repetition as passionate anaphora. (Pasolini 1975a, 1)

As this extract testifies, Pasolini's critical theory values and foregrounds the issue of reception.[15] He considers the reader/spectator an active participant in the cultural productions, since a text depends on the reader's contribution, and its signification is made possible by his/her involvement in the activity and freedom of writing. Pasolini's 'scandalously' unprofessional, eclectic, and passionate semiological predicaments resemble recent developments toward a theory of readership. Theorizing the reader has now become a central issue at an international level, as the proliferation of work on film spectatorship testifies. Recent film theory dwells on the idea that the text signals the presence of the spectator, and assigns him/her a place, and potential interpretative itineraries. The notion and practice of deconstruction also foregrounds the initiative of the reader, privileging the function of the (de)construction of a text performed by the interpreter.

Pasolini's work also offers a contribution to the present debate on film spectatorship insofar as he reclaimed an interesting notion of 'empiricism.' The issue of the empirical level has come to the fore in current American theorizations of film spectatorship, including feminist ones. Pasolini's 'empiricism' offers an alternative to the dichotomy between *spectatorship* and *audience* – that is between, on the one hand, spectatorship conceived as an address, a position, a function of discourse and, on the other hand, the treatment of an actual audience response. Pasolini's tendency is far from expressing an interest in individual responses to cinema or in the empirical spectator. His 'heretical empiricism' is articulation of film language as well as theoretical discourse itself. As de Lauretis claims, Pasolini's work

points to a current notion of spectatorship as a site of productive relations, of the engagement of subjectivity in meaning, values, and imaging. It therefore suggests that ... cinema's binding of fantasy to images institutes, *for* the spectator, forms of subjectivity which are themselves, unequivocally, social. (de Lauretis 1984, 51)

The empiricism that Pasolini proposes is the foregrounding of subjectivity as a social production, the interplay of signifying practices with affects, the 'engagement' of fantasy in cinematic 'imaging.'

Attempting to overcome the limitations of semiotics, Pasolini intended to incorporate semiotic research within a larger perspective. His film semiotics hinted toward today's cultural studies, placed as it was within a vast project of inquiry that extended to 'other cultural systems (those which, for example, put into play usable objects, as happens with architecture or industrial design).'[16] A system of signs that triggers a play with objects, cinema shares its cultural 'constructions' with other arts of spatial and tactile appropriation. *Res* are operational descriptions of the multiformity and polyphony of experience – objects and semiotic signifiers, inscribed in a process of unlimited interpretation and recodings, determined and overdetermined by the instantiation of a readership. Voicing a need for a semiotics of *res*, Pasolini anticipates a contemporary cultural concern for the image-object and for the semiotics of everyday objects. By linking cinema to other cultural productions, such as architecture and design – practices concerned with usable spaces and forms – Pasolini has initiated the semiotics of everyday life.

The centre for this communication process between cultural productions and the real, that is social practice, is the body. Pasolini writes: 'Reality is a language ... As pragmatic dialogue between us and objects (including our body), nothing is ever rigidly monosemic; on the contrary almost everything is enigmatic because it is potentially polysemic' (*Heretical Empiricism*, 258). A concern for the body, like that recently brought to the fore by contemporary critical theory and, in particular, feminist investigation, already informs Pasolini's theory as well as his filmic practice.

This concern could not be completely understood by Pasolini's contemporaries because it was a heresy that anticipated 'things to come.'

In 1967, Eco blacklisted Pasolini's semiotic work arguing that 'Pasolini's idea ... contrasts with the most elementary aim of semiotics, which is to reduce the facts of nature to cultural phenomena and not to retrace the facts of culture to natural phenomena' (Eco 1967, 142). To this attack, Pasolini responded in a fictional epistolary form:

A blond young man, my dear Eco, advances toward you. You do not smell him. Perhaps because he has no smell, or because he is far away, or because other odours form a barrier between him and you, or perhaps because you have a cold. Strange, because he should have a certain odour on him ... Dear Eco, things are exactly the opposite of how you interpret them ... All my chaotic pages on this topic (the code of cinema equal to the code of reality in the context of a General Semiology) *tend to bring Semiology to the definite transformation of nature into culture* ... I would like to plumb the depths. I would not want to stop on the brink of the abyss on which you stop ... the dogma of semiology. (*Heretical Empiricism*, 276–8)

The dogma of early semiology was to name as off-limits the realm of the social body and of corporeal experience, including sexuality and sexual difference. Pasolini's theoretical filmic writings acknowledge such domains. As he says, semioticians were insensitive to them; they could not smell because of a temporary cold or, in some cases, a permanent dis/ease. Suffering from a physical inhibition, semiotics could not touch the realm of the body. To this blockage Pasolini responded with an attempt to found a semiotics that would treat the 'reality' of the body, grasp its semiotic interplay, and explore the relation of the body of the viewer to the world of narrative signs, to the fiction of the real, to that fiction that is the real.

Pasolini's writings make room for grasping ideology in the context of experience and the material world. Ideology is ingrained in the realm of the corporeal as, for example, Pasolini's book of collected essays, *Passione e ideologia* (*Passion and Ideology*), suggests. His work enters a territory that post-1968 culture was to bring to the fore. I am intrigued by a connection between Pasolini's concerns and feminist inquiry. Unlike other semiological projects of his time, Pasolini's questions and practices sexual difference, the discourse of the body, of 'passion and ideology.' In so doing, he ventures onto a terrain that feminist theorists may recognize as our own concern. His emphasis on the nexus of 'affects, passions, feelings and ideas' is not unrelated to a notion of subjectivity, as conceived and practised by Italian feminism. It is a notion that acknowledges a collective dimension of subjectivity as shared psychic formation as well as social function. Pasolini's work reaches into 'the ethics of passions,' a topic that has become central especially to Italian and French feminist research.[17] Aware of formulating a 'heresy,' I would claim that rereading Pasolini's work from this specific viewpoint affirms his potential contribution, complex and controversial as it may be, to feminist research.

Pasolini's heresy corrodes the very borders of semiotics and approaches a site that semio-psychoanalytic studies have later appropriated. As Maurizio Viano has put it in his account of 'passion according to Pasolini,' Pasolini's 'empire of signs is the empire of passion' (Viano 1987 and 1987–8). In Pasolini's film theory, passion signals his understanding of the bodily effects of signs. His subject of language is not a transcendental, disembodied subject. Rather it is the body that is the 'scene of writing.' The body constitutes a reserve, an archive that informs the decoding of images – the locus where signification makes its mark, embodying the social process and historicity. Such is, for Pasolini, the site of the sign's impact. Communication is ingrained in a social process where signs and object-signs are shaped by, and shape, the social geography.

Cinema's relation to the real is the expression of a social text – the physical quality of cinematic forms. Like his writings, Pasolini's films are populated by corporeal signifiers. His cinema refigures the politics of the body, and reclaims the inscription of the subproletariat physiognomy and the homosexual gaze in the filmic landscape.[18] Both his cinematic and theoretical work are informed by 'fisicità,' a physical pregnancy, as Pasolini practices writing's visibility. In the dialogue between the subject and *res*, the position of the subject is defined in relation to the corporeal 'smell' – the imprint of sex, class, race, and the geopolitics of physiognomy. This imprint is marked on the subject's body as well as on the body of things, on their system of use and exchange values. The pragmatic and proxemic relation between *res* and *nomina* (i.e., social practice and language), as mediated by the body, is the territory of definition of ideology.

In this respect, the form, as well as the content, of Pasolini's theoretical writing needs to be considered insofar as part of its novelty and interest emerges in the form of the writing itself, and the context of its production and circulation. Pasolini's is a theory-in-the-making, constituted by a constellation of suggestive predicaments and passionate interventions, expressed in different forms, formats, and mediums.[19]

His semiology of film was developed from 1965 on in the form of essays, conference reports, and panel discussions, but also as a proliferation of magazine and newspaper articles, oral interventions, interviews, notes to screenplays, letters, introductions to records, and so on. The circulation of Pasolini's semiotics as well as its object are moulded in historicity and praxis. Emerging from a multiform, constant, and passionate research-in-progress attentive to and involved in the current sociopolitical, artistic, and cultural debate, Pasolini's intellectual venture questions, and seeks to expand, its own theoretical range and grasp of actuality. His work does not separate intellectual/artistic, theory/praxis, political/militant. Like the majority of Italian intellectuals who develop and carry on the theoretical work from the columns of newspapers and weekly magazines as well as academic journals, Pasolini especially conceived of theorizing as such an *engagement*.

It is in this aspect of the *apparatus of theory*, and not only in its text, that Pasolini's theory is political, for, to bear a political dimension is not merely a question of choosing the appropriate methodology and object. It is also a question of tackling the politics of theory and the relation of power to knowledge. Pasolini's political dimension is articulated in the form of writing as well as in the modes and channels of circulation of discourse. Michel Foucault's question: 'Where does discourse come from; how is it circulated; who controls it?'(Foucault 1977, 138) is central to Pasolini. With his practice of heretical writing and dissemination, he addressed the positioning of discursive practices. He visualized Foucauldian concerns with an architectural metaphor, the *Palazzo* (literally the 'palace'), a metaphor that stands for a wide-range notion of 'institution.' The expression refers to the network of transactions created by and within dominant discourse. In a famous newspaper article, precisely titled 'Fuori dal palazzo' ('Outside the Palace'), he analysed and denounced the strategies of intellectual life, questioning discourse in regard to its modalities and its placement 'fuori dal palazzo' or 'dentro il palazzo,' outside or inside the horizon of the hegemonic nexus.[20]

It is only against this contextual background that Pasolini's semiotics of film can take full shape in interpretation, and the misunderstandings be clarified. Pasolini did not construct a theoretical system but rather affirmed a theoretical writing. His notion of theory did not seek the truth of a system or an uncontradictory argumentation but rather the dissemination of writing. A strength of his work resides in its being a theory of praxis, a praxis dense in theoretical implications and investigations. In this respect, when he discusses reality as 'the language of action' or 'a pragmatic dialogue between us and the objects, including our body,' when he speaks of the cinematic language as 'the written language of reality,' 'imsegno,' 'voice-desire,' 'kino-mouth,' 'writing,' these terms have to be understood as a semiotic opening up to historicity and to the realm of the body rather than as the terms of a retrograde realism.

Pasolini's immediate, inventive, ironic, and polemic semiotics is attentive to the logic of the cultural mode of production, as evident, for example, in the essay 'The End of the Avant-Garde (Notes on a Sentence by Goldmann, on Two Verses of an Avant-Garde Text and an Interview with Barthes).'[21] In 1966, Pasolini questioned the relation of narrative structures to social and economic structures, and related cinema to what he named, with two illuminating definitions, 'the obscene health of neo-capitalism,' and 'the industrial puritanism.' He remarks that the heroes of contemporary films are no longer the filmic transmutation of the figures of popular bourgeois literature, that is, the heroes of production. They 'represent instead a subtle instance of technological interclassism' (*Heretical Empiricism*, 124), a narrative figuration of the technocratic levelling of class conflicts. Pasolini names filmic heroes 'heroes of the leisure time,' as their morphology corresponds to the 'industrial puritanism' – the new leisure-time world view, a common imaginary shared by both the ruling class and subaltern social strata. Certainly, when we consider the 'cultural logic of late capitalism,'[22] in a time such as this, where the 'industrial puritanism' rewrites sexuality; a time dominated by the yuppie emphasis on spare-time (trivial) pursuits; a time of 'obscene health of neo-capitalism,' where the Jane Fonda/Arnold Schwarzenegger syndrome, and other less explicit cases of 'heroes of leisure time,' literalize the link between the health club and culture; a time in which for eight years, the American president, Ronald Reagan, was one such 'spare-time hero,' Pasolini's words sound like a prophecy.

Pasolini's ideas, however, were strongly criticized at the time he expressed them. His polemics against the cultural logic of late capitalism were generally taken as nostalgia for an archaic world. Attacking the levelling of conflicts and the superficial unified picture resulting from the 'industrial puritanism' of consumer society, he called attention to regional cultures and historical peculiarities. Rather than a conservative call for traditional values, this interest in geographical and historical specificity can today be understood, in the context of postmodernism, as the denunciation of the end of history in the postmodern era. Pasolini was one of the first intellectuals to voice it, and to articulate the implications of the eclipse of history. Today Pasolini's call for a discursive reinscription of the past, and for the re-enactment of historicity in cultural practices seems very contemporary. Also current are Pasolini's intertextual practice and his passion for quotations, which informs his writings as well as his cinema, filled by citations and remakes of literary texts, as well as visual remakes of the masters of Renaissance and Mannerism, from Giotto to Pontormo to Mantegna. Very appropriate to our era is Pasolini's 'unfinished,' an expression of what Fredric Jameson calls 'the learning process,' the didactic practice of postmodernism (Jameson 1988). Very contemporary is Pasolini's practice of the contamination of forms and objects of the artistic expression. Bricolage and pastiche are finally understood, not as the mark of theoretical imprecision, but of cultural inventiveness.

Pasolini's intertextual practice, his transgressive semiotics-in-progress, which investigates codes in a heretical empiricism, attempt with dissemination to grasp through writing the physical pregnancy of the body and the historical praxis that, inevitably, as he knows, will remain elusive and unattainable. This is the 'reality' of which he obsessively wrote, which he fetishized and challenged – and dreamt. When Eco stated that early structuralists were driven by a dream, Pasolini replied 'Why have you allowed yourself to be awakened from this dream? Are you afraid of dreams? And why, if the structuralist can permit himself dreams, cannot the semiologist do so?' (*Heretical Empiricism*, 280). It is with great pleasure that theorists can now finally share Pasolini's dream, and write cultural theory embodying a materiality of writing – a Pasolinian corpo*reality*.

Notes

1 See Pasolini, *Heretical Empiricism*. Two recent conferences have promoted a reconsideration of Pasolini's work, in conjunction with the retrospective of his films held at the Museum of Modern Art in New York, 27 April–29 May 1990. 'Pasolini: The Aesthetics of Transgression' was held at New York University, 11–12 May 1990, and co-sponsored by the Associazione 'Fondo Pier Paolo Pasolini' (Rome, Italy), the Italian Cultural Institute of New York, and the Italian Ministero del Turismo e dello Spettacolo. 'Pier Paolo Pasolini: Heretical Imperatives' was held at the University of Toronto, 8–9 June 1990, co-sponsored by the Italian Cultural Institute (Toronto), the Art

Gallery of Ontario, Innis College, and the university's Department of Italian Studies and Cinema Studies Programme.

2 Pasolini's position on sociopolitical issues was so controversial that he was, and still is, attacked and reclaimed by both the Left and the Right.

3 Pasolini, 'Living Signs and Dead Poets' (1967), in *Heretical Empiricism*, 247

4 See, for example, Antonio Costa, 'The Semiological Heresy of Pier Paolo Pasolini.' Pasolini's work was found unacceptable by professional semioticians including, among others, Umberto Eco, Stephen Heath, Christian Metz, Emilio Garroni, and Gianfranco Bettetini.

5 See Teresa de Lauretis, 'Language, Representation, Practice: Re-reading Pasolini's Essays on Cinema.' The whole issue is dedicated to rereading Pasolini's work.

6 Pasolini, 'The Nonverbal as Another Verbality' (1971), in *Heretical Empiricism*, 262

7 On this subject, see, among others, Jean Baudrillard, *Simulations* and 'The Ecstasy of Communication'; and Guy Debord, *The Society of the Spectacle*

8 See Pasolini, 'Res sunt Nomina' (1971), in *Heretical Empiricism*, 255–60

9 See, for example, Pasolini, 'Quips on the Cinema' (1966), in *Heretical Empiricism*, 223–31

10 This commonly employed notion is derived from the work of Jacques Derrida. See *Of Grammatology* and *Writing and Difference*

11 See Charles Sanders Peirce, *Collected Papers.*

12 Pasolini, 'The Written Language of Reality' (1966), in *Heretical Empiricism*, 204

13 See, for example, Pasolini, 'The Cinema of Poetry,' in *Heretical Empiricism*, 169.

14 See Pasolini, 'Observation on the Sequence Shot' (1967), in *Heretical Empiricism*, 233–37. The title of this essay may be more appropriately translated as 'Observations on the Long Take.'

15 See, for example, Pasolini, 'The Unpopular Cinema' (1970), and 'The Screenplay as a "Structure That Wants to Be Another Structure"' (1965) in *Heretical Empiricism*, 267–75, 187–96

16 Pasolini, 'The Code of Codes' (1967–71), in *Heretical Empiricism*, 280

17 Italian feminist theorists such as, most notably, Lea Melandri have been exploring this terrain as a development of earlier discourse on/of 'il personale' (the personal as political). See, for example, Lea Melandri, *Come nasce il sogno d'amore: L'estasi, il gelo e la mestissima libertà* (1988a). An excerpt from this work is published in English: see Melandri, 'Ecstasy, Coldness, and the Sadness Which Is Freedom' (1988b).

From a different perspective, the work of Luce Irigaray on the ethics of sexual difference is also conceived in the realm of 'the ethics of passions' (Irigaray 1985).
18 Think of *Accattone* (1961), *Mamma Roma* (1962), *Il vangelo secondo Matteo/The Gospel according to St. Matthew* (1964) and *Uccellacci e uccellini/Hawks and Sparrows* (1966), among others.
19 The 'pedagogic' aspect of Pasolini's intellectual enterprise is discussed by Enzo Golino in his book *Pasolini: Il sogno di una cosa*.
20 Pasolini, 'Fuori dal palazzo.' See also Pasolini's use of the *Palazzo* in his last film *Salò* (1975).
21 *Heretical Empiricism*, 121–41. See also, Pasolini, 'What Is Neo-Zhdanovism and What Isn't' (1968), in *Heretical Empiricism*, 159–63.
22 The expression is borrowed from Fredric Jameson's work (see Jameson 1984, 11–25)

References

Baudrillard, Jean. *Simulations*. New York: Semiotext(e), 1983a
– 'The Ecstasy of Communication.' In Hal Foster, ed., *The Anti-Aesthetic: Essays on Post-Modern Culture*. Port Townsend: Bay Press, 1983b
Baudry, Jean-Louis. 'The Apparatus: Metapsychological Approaches to the Impression of Reality in the Cinema.' In P. Rosen, ed., *Narrative, Apparatus, Ideology*. New York: Columbia University Press, 1986
Costa, Antonio. 'The Semiological Heresy of Pier Paolo Pasolini.' In Paul Willemen, ed., *Pier Paolo Pasolini*. London: British Film Institute, 1977
Debord, Guy. *The Society of Spectacle*. Detroit: Black and Red Press, 1983
de Lauretis, Teresa. 'Language, Representation, Practice: Re-reading Pasolini's Essays on Cinema.' *Italian Quarterly*, nos. 82–3 (Fall/Winter 1981)
– *Alice Doesn't: Feminism, Semiotics, Cinema*. Bloomington: Indiana University Press, 1984
Derrida, Jacques. *Of Grammatology*. Baltimore: Johns Hopkins University Press, 1976
– *Writing and Difference*. Chicago: University of Chicago Press, 1978
Eco, Umberto. *Appunti per una semiologia delle communicazioni visive*. Milan: Bompiani, 1967
Foucault, Michel. 'What Is an Author?' In D.F. Bouchard, ed., *Language, Counter-Memory, Practice*. Ithaca: Cornell University Press, 1977
Golino, Enzo. *Pasolini: Il sogno di una cosa. Pedagogia, eros, letteratura, dal mito del popolo alla società di massa*. Bologna: Il Mulino, 1985

Heath, Stephen. 'Film/Cinetext/Text.' *Screen* 14, 1–2 (Spring/Summer 1973)

Irigaray, Luce. *Éthique de la différence sexuelle*. Paris: Les Éditions de Minuit, 1985

Jameson, Frederic. 'Postmodernism or the Cultural Logic of Late Capitalism.' *New Left Review*, no. 146 (July-August 1984): 111–25

– 'Postmodernism and the Didactic.' Unpublished paper, presented at 'Symposium: The Work of Alexander Kluge,' CUNY Graduate Center, New York, 28 October 1988

Lacan, Jacques. *Écrits*. Paris: Seuil, 1966

Melandri, Lea. *Come nasce il sogno d'amore: L'estasi, il gelo e la mestissima libertà*. Milan: Rizzoli, 1988a

– 'Ecstasy, Coldness, and the Sadness Which is Freedom.' In G. Bruno and M. Nadotti, eds., *Off Screen: Women and Film in Italy*. London and New York: Routledge, 1988b

Metz, Christian. *The Imaginary Signifier: Psychoanalysis and the Cinema*. Bloomington: Indiana University Press, 1982

Pasolini, Pier Paolo. *Passione e ideologia*. Milan: Garzanti, 1960

– 'L'ambiguità.' *Filmcritica*, no. 248 (October 1974)

– *Scritti corsari*. Milan: Garzanti, 1975a

– 'Fuori dal palazzo.' *Corriere della sera* (1 August 1975)

– *Lettere luterane*. Turin: Einaudi, 1976

– *Le belle bandiere*. Edited by G.C. Ferretti. Rome: Editori Riuniti, 1977

– *Descrizioni di descrizioni*. Turin: Einaudi, 1979a

– *Il caos*. Rome: Editori Riuniti, 1979b

– *Il portico della morte*. Edited by C. Segre. Rome: Associazione 'Fondo Pier Paolo Pasolini,' 1988a

– *Heretical Empiricism*. Edited by L.K. Barnett. Translated by L.K. Barnett and B. Lawton. Bloomington: Indiana University Press, 1988b

Peirce, Charles Sanders. *Collected Papers*. Boston: Harvard University Press, 1931–58

Viano, Maurizio. 'The Left According to the Ashes of Gramsci.' *Social Text*, no. 18 (Winter 1987–8): 51–60

– 'Passion According to Pasolini.' Unpublished paper, presented at the Society for Cinema Studies Conference, Montreal, 1987

Toward a Materialist Linguistics: Pasolini's Theory of Language

SILVESTRA MARINIELLO

From his first efforts as a young poet through to the end of his career as a essayist and filmmaker, the question of language remained absolutely critical to Pasolini's thinking. He devoted many efforts toward formulating a theory to meet his concerns and his diverse artistic activities, efforts pursued within often politically charged debates about language. In this essay, Silvestra Mariniello proposes to set out a theoretical bridge between a Marxist understanding of ideology and the methods of structuralist linguistics associated with Ferdinand de Saussure. She analyses Pasolini's linguistic theories through an approach suggested by the work of Bakhtin, Medvedev, Gramsci, McLuhan, and others, concerning oral traditions (and related issues of regional dialects) and the cultural/ideological impact of printing technology. She suggests that for Pasolini the ideological significance of film is analogous to that of the printing press. For Pasolini, just as any natural relationship between language and thought or things is made problematic with the advent of writing (or 'literacy'), so with film will our relationships with the world, that is, the way we relate to people and the things that surround us, stand revealed as ideological relationships. Through the development of a 'non-instrumental' theory of language, that is, a language no longer conceived as merely a vehicle for mental thoughts and objective meanings, Pasolini conceives of language as a 'productive' and potentially 'renovating' material practice of active mediation between reality and understanding. Ultimately, Pasolini's linguistic and cinematic preoccupations (seen in theory in *Heretical Empiricism*, in practice in the screenplay *Il padre selvaggio*) concern his attempt to render what had been considered merely 'physical' relationships with reality into 'cultural' relationships, open to renegotiation.

In his work, Pasolini was constantly concerned with language, with understanding and defining its nature. In particular he attempted to understand the relationship between language, thought, and the outside world. Deeply influenced by his reading of Antonio Gramsci, Pasolini's thinking arrived at a theory of language as mediation and agency, a theory recognizing a dialectic between language and ideology.

'From the Laboratory (Notes *en poète* for a Marxist Linguistics),' an essay that appeared in 1965 (in Pasolini, *Heretical Empiricism*, 50–76; hereafter indicated by *HE*), represents the moment when within Pasolini's discourse he offers his central premises on language. This essay outlines a theory that does not match any linguistic orthodoxy; it allows for rethinking the notions of ideology and agency and, therefore, political commitment in the setting of what Pasolini was, by then, persistently calling 'neocapitalistic society.'

By the time the essay appeared, Pasolini had already made several films – the two inaugural features, *Accattone* (1961) and *Mamma Roma* (1962); the short films *La ricotta* (1962), *La rabbia* (1962), and *Comizi d'amore* (1964); a documentary travelogue, *Sopralluoghi in Palestina* (1964); and the film that brought him international recognition as a director, *Il Vangelo secondo Matteo* (1964). At the same time, Pasolini had also drawn the first elements of his film theory. The well-known statement, 'Cinema of Poetry' ('Il cinema di poesia'), presented at the 1965 Pesaro Film Festival, dates from this period (Pasolini, *HE*, 167–86). It is necessary to stress the link between film and language in order to understand Pasolini's theory because his film work significantly influenced his linguistic theory. Both were in turn closely connected with his studies of the state and the neocapitalistic revolution. In fact, it was precisely by working on two levels, the cinematographic and literary-linguistic, that Pasolini came to his non-instrumental concept of medium and language.

I want to distinguish two phases – although these do not always correspond to a chronological 'before' and 'after' in Pasolini's writings – that deal with the relationship between language and ideology. In the first phase, Pasolini establishes a dependency between ideology and the means of expression and communication. This dependency subtends the instrumental aspect of both the means of expression and the referential aspect of expressed reality. Language is not yet for Pasolini the *active* mediation between reality and understanding; rather, language appears as an instrument that ideology uses to shape our grasp of the real. In the second phase, Pasolini comes to understand the relationship between language, ideology, and reality in terms of exchange and interaction. Action – that is, the primordial expression of human being – articulates such exchange.

In a 1966 essay, 'The Written Language of Reality,' Pasolini asserts,

The advent of audiovisual techniques, as languages ... puts in question the concept which probably each of us, by force of habit, had of an identification between poetry – or message – and language. Probably, instead – as audiovisual techniques lead us rather brutally to think – every poem is translinguistic. It is an *action* 'placed' in a system of symbols, as in a vehicle, which becomes *action* once again in the addressee, while the symbols are nothing more than Pavlovian bells. (Pasolini, *HE*, 198)

What is this identification between 'poetry – or message – and language' that Pasolini refers to here? It is the transparency of language vis-à-vis the message, its instrumentality, its distance from the material object and from the way of conceiving of and feeling the object. Why does the advent of audiovisual techniques put in question such transparency, instrumentality and distance? Audiovisual techniques – and Pasolini insists on the fact that film operates precisely this way as audiovisual technique – produce a language that is scandalous from the perspective of Saussurian structural linguistics. The reason is that because, with these techniques, 'reality remains' and it is now impossible to separate reality from language. In this way, audiovisual techniques contradict the concept of message as a construction built from a system of arbitrary codes, the concept that subtends Saussurian structural linguistics as a whole.

It already appears that audiovisual techniques bring us close to the global experience of what Pasolini terms 'orality.' How? On the one hand, film makes us aware of the fact that reality can be analysed in terms of a language – the language of action. Just as writing makes us aware of oral language, film makes us aware of 'reality' in its 'oral' stage. At the same time, however, the language of action discloses reality to be what Pasolini calls 'cinema in nature.' Film refers back to cinema (i.e., to a process of the disclosure of reality), whereas a language refers back to another language, (i.e., *langue*, a system of codes). In language, the referent itself does not – cannot – appear, for there we are in a discursive universe that does not allow for the appearance of the real per se. In contrast, audiovisual techniques, like film, because of their nature, generate reproductions that make use of the very material to be reproduced (bodies, gestural expressiveness, objects, space ...). By reproducing action, these techniques produce in us the consciousness of action. In other words, audiovisual techniques do not cause separation from the object (from the world they interact with); they form an organic relationship with the reality from which they have drawn their materials.

Pasolini's second phase of theorizing is characterized by the intuition of film as the 'written language of reality' and by the corresponding definition of reality as 'cinema in nature.' However, Pasolini's ideas concerning cinematic representations are not entirely consistent. At times his views are paradoxical, even contradictory, especially in statements made during the initial period of his filmmaking. What are the factors that cohere in Pasolini's theorizing?

In a 1961 interview for the Italian journal *Cinema nuovo*, Pasolini remarks apropos *Accattone*: 'The wish to express myself with film falls within my need to adopt a new technique, a renewing technique' (Pasolini, 'Intervista'). Then, answering the question, 'Do you think it possible to express in film something more and different than what already expressed in literary forms?' he replies, 'No, I don't think so. I think that only with poetry can we arrive at infinite variations, the maximum of vibrancy. Film and poetry are two totally different forms.' There is, he suggests, a world of thoughts, feelings, facts to be expressed and communicated, and an author resorts to one technique or another to give voice to this world. The contents are the same, Pasolini seems to imply, and while the means to express them change, they do so without altering the contents. Pasolini also describes film as a 'new technique, a renewing technique.' However, like literary language, film is just another technique to give form to the same contents even if 'contamination' involved in using the new technique is already operative. Paradoxically, Pasolini also says in his reply that poetry is the exception, that it is 'totally different from film' and affords 'infinite variations,' 'the maximum of vibrancy.'

What does this exceptional status for poetry mean? While poetry enjoys a special status in Pasolini's theory, it is important to recognize that, in the later essays, poetry will come to share its special status with audiovisual techniques and that the gap between film and poetry, so forcefully asserted here, will be closed. The special condition of poetry leads us back to the word's etymology: poetry comes from the Greek *poieo*, meaning 'to make,' 'to do,' 'to act.' Poetry makes reality, it is translinguistic and it endlessly creates manifold relations between addresser and addressee, orality and literacy, history and prehistory, but without fixing them.

In 1962, a year after the *Cinema nuovo* interview, in a debate organized by another Italian film journal, *Filmcritica*, Pasolini expresses an attitude toward cinema that is already more complex than the instrumental view just reviewed:

To address an issue explicitly it is necessary to master the technique fully; otherwise it remains mere issue, bare structure, so I did not dare in this first film [i.e., *Accattone*] to deal explicitly with a social issue. Of course, by choosing the film subject, in treating and adapting it, I knew that I couldn't even vaguely deal with a question like that of *A Violent Life* [*Una vita violenta*] that is, with the choice of which political party to join and fight for; I was afraid that technically I wouldn't have the necessary strength to go beyond the issue and turn it into poetry or at least literature ... I was afraid [technique] would remain instrumental. (Pasolini, 'Incontro con Pier Paolo Pasolini')

The question of poetry comes up again in these comments: Pasolini says that to turn a social issue into poetry it is necessary 'to master technique.' In poetry, technique is not instrumental; it becomes part of real life experience and, in this process, turns into action. Nonetheless, something has changed with regard to the earlier statement. Here Pasolini is saying that, contrary to other techniques, cinema is not an objective instrument for expressing pre-existent contents but is defined in terms of the subject who uses it. It is the author's lack of experience that makes the technique instrumental and so the possibility of a different subjectivity begins to take shape. Pasolini implies that technique produces the subject and is not a mere instrument in the artist's hands.

Nonetheless, as these interviews given prior to the essay 'From the Laboratory' indicate, Pasolini still regards film as basically a different technique, a new means of expression. As such, it stands in contrast to poetry, which, despite representing a moment of total control of the medium, film already anticipates by suggesting a non-instrumental understanding of medium and hence a non-instrumental theory of mediation. Pasolini's 1963 screenplay, *Il padre selvaggio*, which was never produced, is possibly the text that bears Pasolini's clearest definition of the 'translinguistic' nature of poetry, and it is here that the relationship, or rather the identification, between poetry and cinema begins to emerge. In this script, the gap between the world of traditional, essentially written, literary culture and the world of African oral tribal culture is bridged by poetic action. Through the agency of the script's protagonist, an African boy, poetry draws together prehistory and history and brings orality to consciousness through writing. Poetry is a dynamic moment, a force that moves things; like film, it sets things into motion, and connects what is separate. Poetry is mediation. However, the lively, pragmatic moment in the boy's experience of writing a poem is threatened by institutionalization and reification; the motion begun will be stopped, destroyed, and it will have to occur again. When the African boy's poem is evaluated through the aesthetic categories of the white teacher who plans to publish it in a European journal, the script puts us at the edge between two worlds' contamination/mediation, and at the end of one of them – the tribal, oral culture. Pasolini will always be extremely lucid about the destructive necessity of this mediation process and his awareness will bring him to renew his 'poetry' throughout his life.

At this moment in Pasolini's thinking, the author, mastering or not mastering technique, seems to be the central figure in his theory. Later, as he progressively comes to understand film as a medium, as language rather than just another technique, and when the idea of a 'spoken-written language' takes shape in his thinking, it offers a possible answer to the question about the relationship between Marxism and structural linguistics. The author's mastery or non-mastery becomes secondary when compared with the dynamics arising between various forces and different moments, including subjectivity. The statements on *Accattone* examined above already start to disclose the premises of Pasolini's discourse on language as mediation. Let us look closer at passages in which the *instrument* he is using turns, for Pasolini, into a new *language* intended as 'intermediary' between thought and 'reality.'

The *Filmcritica* interviewer insists on the pessimism of *Accattone*, and emphasizes the film's lack of a positive resolution. He even suggests to Pasolini that he could and probably should have followed the example of Giuseppe De Santis' 'popular realism.'[1] Pasolini responds that the meaning of his film should be mapped onto two coordinates: language and the historical moment to which the film belongs. He rejects the model of 'popular realism' along with the intentionality it implies. An author's outlook on the world, as a specific historical product, is not independent from the means of expression; it is not at the origin of such expression, but rather it enters into a relationship with the medium. These remarks anticipate the central concern of 'From the Laboratory (Notes *en poète* for a Marxist Linguistics),' where film will be seen to present all the features of language and where Pasolini will argue that language and thought are inseparable. 'By renewing technique I renewed inspiration,' Pasolini says. He tries to explain this relationship in a 1964 interview in *Bianco e nero*:

If, let's suppose, I succeeded in offering what I wanted to offer in *Accattone*, that is, the epic-religious stature of these miserable fellows, if I succeeded in producing it through the stylistic elements of my film, through the narrative rhythm, the way I move them, the atmosphere in which I immerse them, the light, the sun, the surroundings, if I succeeded in giving this image of them it means I love them, if, though, I failed it means that my love is a false love ... in style lies redemption ... if I failed stylistically, that is if I didn't reach a stylistic result it means that my love is false, it means that I will try to love more. (Pasolini, 'Una visione del mondo epico religioso')

In this passage Pasolini implies that a more or less faithful representation of a pre-existent reality is not at stake. Neither is it a question of whether the medium has been used adequately to express someone's love. Instead, this very love is put into question in the event that language was not able to express it. Representation is not at stake here, but mediation between a linguistic (non-psychological) subject and the world in which she or he operates. Language becomes such mediation. In other words, the inadequacy of a representation puts into question not the medium but the relationship between the subject and the world. On the other hand, as in the following passage, Pasolini sometimes reverses his argument and claims that 'expressive perfection' presupposes 'ideological perfection':

But I will tell you something; when a movie is good it is also popular! And by saying good I do not refer to some aesthetic value, but to an expressive perfection that necessarily implies, even if the artist is not completely aware of it, an ideological perfection. All set courses are always wrong: films that are supposed to correspond to certain definitions always fail. (Pasolini, 'Incontro con Pier Paolo Pasolini')

In such passages as these, Pasolini specifies and defines the concept of film language. Film language, he says, happens in the interaction of the various specific languages, and of reality that 'remains' in them – in cinematography (light and atmosphere), set design (the environment surrounding the characters), acting (the way characters move) and narration (the story's rhythm) which organizes the action. That is, in a film, language coincides with the moment of dynamic encounter between many different languages, including reality, which condition and transform each other. Film language is always mediation between many possibilities and, as such, it calls into question the separation between rationality and passion, ideology and art, theory and practice. It creates instead a global space for the interaction of various discourses; it connects 'existential' oral language with 'historical' written language, to anticipate the hypotheses of the 'From the Laboratory.'

The first part of this essay consists in an analysis of Gramsci's language. Gramsci provides not just the pretext, the concrete example, for arguing the relationship between language and ideology – Gramsci is also the inspiring source of Pasolini's linguistic and political theory. In her study, 'Pasolini, Gramsci: lecture d'une marginalità' (1980), Catherine Buci-Glucksmann analyses the relationship between the Friulian poet and the political leader from Sardinia, so close with regard to their life experience and political analysis, yet so tragically distant in history. 'I strayed from Gramsci,' explains Pasolini, 'because objectively I was not facing the same world as Gramsci: there are no more people to tell stories to' (257). Buci-Glucksmann's reading of their relationship casts a new light on both authors. She introduces us to a non-orthodox Gramsci going against the current of the Italian Communist Party (PCI), a Gramsci who rejects the separation, peculiar to modern Western culture, between rationality and irrationality. She also introduces us to an innocent, imprisoned Gramsci

who will think not only against fascism, in a permanent hand-to-hand struggle, but also against the current of the Third International, against the current of the P.C.I.'s strategy of class versus class, showing that political thought develops against any orthodoxy and Stalinistic and/or reformist statolatry. (255)

Language becomes the crux of this controversial analysis, 'as symptom of politics and historical processes and the place of their operation' (254). Pasolini works on the same wavelength as this unorthodox Gramsci – 'and it is precisely on this point [the theory of language] that Pasolini's debt to Gramsci becomes more profound' (254). In particular, in 'From the Laboratory,' Pasolini works on Gramsci's own language – where Sardinian dialect contaminates the Italian language learned in Turin and vice versa – and Pasolini reconstructs the very process of the struggle between subaltern culture and official culture that has been a privileged object of Gramscian analysis.

Pasolini's analytical procedure is peculiar. Instead of starting from the theoretical discussion of Gramsci's texts, he starts from the personal linguistic experience of the political leader. It is not Gramsci's psychological biography that is of interest to Pasolini, but the linguistic background, at the same time individual and social, and Pasolini elaborates his theoretical account on this linguistic base. He moves from theory (Gramsci's political thought presented in the *Prison Notebooks*) to life (Gramsci's actual language) and then back to theory. By proceeding in this way, Pasolini creates a totality where the unsimplifiable, irreducible link between theory and life produces a new form of materialism that integrates rationality and irrationality with the process of getting to know reality which is action. Pasolini's filmmaking experience, which brings to his consciousness the 'language of action,' a global language including the 'spoken-written language,' informs this essay. In a certain perspective, 'From the Laboratory' represents the systematization of what both theoretical reflection and creative activity have engendered within Pasolini's linguistics. Film is no longer a mere technique but now becomes a language that 'allows [us] to express reality with reality' (Pasolini, *HE*, 225), a language showing the register of both prose and of poetry.

Before a closer examination of 'From the Laboratory,' let us open a brief parenthesis on a text Pasolini published a year before, in 1964, 'New Linguistic Questions.' (Pasolini, *HE*, 3–22) An intense debate was provoked by this essay, one that continues and will likely continue into the foreseeable future. Pasolini puts forth a thesis here that has become an object of sharp polemics from both the Right and the Left. His thesis is that Italian was born as a national language for the first time in contemporary neocapitalistic Italy. Inspired by Gramsci's analysis of an Italian bourgeoisie incapable, for historical reasons, of achieving a sociopolitical hegemony, and whose language consequently remained limited as a literary phenomenon, Pasolini understands, with an acumen that once again isolates him within the political-intellectual milieu, the dramatically new features of the contemporary historical conjuncture. For the first time, Italy is now united. This has not been accomplished from above, as in 1870, through a series of governmental decisions and accords, but through a revolution spreading from the northern factories and business offices that involves all the layers of society, from The north to the south, from the subproletariat to the bourgeoisie. This is the neocapitalistic revolution, and it is a technological revolution: a homologating process radically transforming society. This revolution spells the end of humanistic culture. Today, factories and business firms replace universities in spreading culture and a new, completely different, society is coming to life. From this perspective, the opposition between standard Italian and dialect, constantly the object of linguistic debate in the past, is no longer pertinent. Dialect is a holdover now, not a living reality.

If the Right refuses to accept the Gramscian hypothesis of a bourgeoisie without hegemony, rejects as well the notion of a merely literary national language, and therefore denies Pasolini's analysis of neocapitalism, the Left does not want to acknowledge the risk of hegemonic vacuum resulting from the new economic and political situation. It is necessary, Pasolini argues, to renew Marxism, to invent a new form of engagement. Such a renewal cannot be construed as 'a return to the origins,' by which he means some appeal to the authority of sacred texts.

If that were possible, a renewal of Marxism would be presented analogously as one of the many returns to the gospel in the history of the Church, and one knows that all such returns are made part of the glory of the Church. It is certainly necessary to reread Marx and Lenin, but not as one rereads the gospel (Pasolini, *HE*, 37–8). The contemporary situation has no precedent in the past, so it must be faced with new means and we have to redefine the notion of political commitment. Language is still a central question in this struggle:

But on the specific problem of language ... the PCI could attempt a criticism of itself and a verification of its own revolutionary relationship to an evolving reality. (48)

Two weeks before his death, during a debate published posthumously under the title *Volgar'eloquio* (1987) with teachers and students in Lecce, Pasolini argued precisely against a Left that intends to reclaim regional dialects and local cultures while refusing to acknowledge the cultural genocide perpetrated by consumer culture and failing to redefine political intervention. This 'clerical-progressive' Left often used the argument of nostalgia against Pasolini, claiming that his critique of consumer society and his analysis of cultural genocide manifested a desire to return to the past. Dismissing Pasolini's putative nostalgia allowed the Left to keep intact its categories (the party, the proletarian state, classes, the subject, and the mass) and its value system (emancipation, progress, historical development) while also permitting them to ignore the extremely difficult task imposed by a changed reality. For over a decade Pasolini complained

Marxism doesn't know, or knows badly, how to insert itself in this 'scandalously dialectical' relationship between the petit-bourgeois rural irrationalism of the Third World (the Italian South is included here) and liberal capitalistic rationalism. (47)

The recent reduction of the PCI to the Democratic Party of the Left, bereft of a program, becomes easier to understand if one keeps in mind the terms of this debate.

But let us go back to the essay 'From the Laboratory,' that, as I said, represents a central moment within Pasolini's discourse, and let us try to see how, in fact, Pasolini managed to enter, with a new form of commitment, this 'scandalously dialectical relationship.' Writing about the young Gramsci, Pasolini remarks that 'his language is only capable of grasping the sentimental or passionate moment in its ideas' (50). Such an extreme statement reveals the meaning that language assumes for Pasolini as an active element in the production of thought. On this basis, it reveals the nature of the relationship between language and ideology. A little later, he says,

It is only with *New Order*, that is, with the first maturation of an original Gramscian thought through experiences lived as his own ... that his language first begins to become possible, then in some way absolute.[2] (51)

One might express whatever ideas one's language grasps, but, nonetheless, the development of these ideas acts upon language and changes it; the terms of the relationship become reversed. The continuation of this passage is worth quoting at length because it expands on the manifold aspects of the problem we are considering.

Gramsci had conquered the irrationality of the literary language adopted from the Italian bourgeoisie along with unity by means of a long and almost religious apprenticeship to rationality, so that every time he had to express a thought, language vanished and the thought shone through ... [The] functionality [of language] makes it in some way absolute. When instead a remnant of the old irrationality, compressed and subdued, is discovered, Gramsci – who had not trained himself to dominate it linguistically – became its prey, and his language falls again into the casualness and emphasis of his first schoolboys pages. Only in the letters from prison, toward the end of his life, does he succeed in bringing together irrationality and the exercise of reason; but still it isn't a question of the irrationality that haloes or follows the reason of political thought as through a sentimental impulse or polemic rage. Because in such a case irrationality always hides ideological insufficiency, the lack of a deductive connection. *And in fact from his youth Gramsci hid the gaps of political inexperience, or, more precisely, the gaps in the socialism to which he adhered, within the expressive casualness of his Italian.* It's a question, rather, toward the end of his life, of giving voice to a tale or evocation of even the most humble or casual facts of life, to just that amount of the mysterious and irrational that every life has in abundance and which is the 'natural poetic quality' of life. (51–2; emphasis in original)

Rationality exercises control over language, turning it into a functional language that is 'somewhat absolute.' The resurfacing of irrationality brings back in Gramsci's pages the emphasis of the language learned in school, but not only that: Gramsci becomes prey of irrationality precisely because his language is not able to master it. Language in its 'expressive casualness' reveals the immaturity of thought. In the ultimate balance of expressiveness and functionality; language, in the end, mirrors the equilibrium between rational and irrational in Gramsci's late writing.

Does language only mirror the balance between rational and irrational elements in Gramsci's thought, or does it actively participate in establishing such a balance? Questions such as this, and the way Pasolini deals with them, refer back to a complex theoretical context whose origins are not always obvious. The reference to two ideological trends that are already institutionalized seems apparent: Marxism and structural linguistics. But Pasolini makes the reference in a way that it brings to light precisely what the process of institutionalization of these doctrines had to repress: Marxist identification of language with 'real consciousness' and Saussure's 'philosophy' respectively. Moreover, Pasolini's text undeniably echoes the discussions on orality and 'media.' It is these very years of the early sixties, in fact, that saw the appearance of a series of works that concerned the difference between oral culture and literacy. Albert Lord's *The Singer of Tales* (1960), Eric Havelock's *Preface to Plato* (1963), and H. Marshall McLuhan's *The Gutenberg Galaxy* (1962) and his *Understanding Media: The Extension of Man* (1964) are among the best known. All of them emphasize the restructuring of thought produced by writing and they – especially McLuhan's books – draw a parallel between the rise of contemporary audiovisual techniques and oral, 'primitive' culture.

In 'From the Laboratory' Pasolini suggests that he initiated the essay as a polemic against Stalin's theory of linguistics. According to

Stalin, language, on a par with the means of production, turns out to be merely a record of the results of thinking and 'an instrument with the help of which people communicate with one another' (Stalin 1972, 20). Marx, in *The German Ideology*, however, defined language in terms of 'practical, real consciousness that exists for other men as well, and only therefore does it also exist for me' (Marx and Engels 1976, 49), a formulation in which the notion of consciousness excludes the idea of mere passive instrumentality that one infers from Stalin's words. If a Marxist perspective constitutes a fundamental reference in Pasolini's theory, his linguistic point of view leads him to reconsider the nature of language in depth. What is most interesting is not Pasolini's references to Saussurian structural linguistics instanced, for example, in his use of specialized semiological terminology, but his implicit references to the philosophy informing Saussurian theory. According to Saussure,

Without language, thought is a vague, uncharted nebula. There are no pre-existing ideas, and nothing is distinct before the appearance of language ... The characteristic role of language with respect to thought is not to create a material phonic means of expressing ideas but to serve as a link between thought and sound, under conditions that of necessity bring about the reciprocal delimitations of units. Thought, chaotic by nature, has to become ordered in the process of its decomposition. (Saussure 1966, 112)

Saussure's philosophy of linguistic value informs all of Pasolini's analyses of film language; it is a theoretical orientation that cannot but be confirmed over and over again in examining his film writings. On the one hand, Pasolini posits that film (as language-medium) is the active mediation between 'the shapeless mass of sounds and images' (reality) and the 'shapeless mass of jumbled ideas' (Pasolini, *HE*, 68).

In the second part of 'From the Laboratory' Pasolini explicitly deals with the question of the relationship between Marxism and structural linguistics, following a path in many ways similar to that of Mikhail Bakhtin and his circle. According to Bakhtin and Medvedev (1985) in *The Formal Method in Literary Scholarship*, formalists (early heirs of Saussure's theory) separate meaning from poetic form when, instead, it was necessary to find an element in the literary work that simultaneously participates in both aspects: the technical one of the artistic construction and the ideological one of making meaning. They argue that this element 'would serve as a medium joining the depth of generality of meaning with the uniqueness of the articulated sound' (Bakhtin and

Medvedev 1985, 118). According to Bakhtin, the element that joins the material presence of the work with its meaning is the medium itself. It makes of sign and meaning an organic, non-abstract unity; in other words, the medium is intended as the whole of evaluations, comments, feelings constituting an utterance, an image, an object in the concrete interchange between two or more people.

> The organic connection of meaning and sign cannot become lexical, grammatically stable, and fixed in identical and reproducible forms, i.e., cannot in itself become a sign or a constant element of a sign, cannot become grammaticalized. This connection is created only to be destroyed, to be reformed again, but in new forms under the conditions of a new utterance. (121)

Bakhtin's medium, 'this organic connection, created only to be destroyed and reformed again,' is a dynamic principle, a system of relationships, and the social aspect of any phenomenon.

The medium Pasolini is theorizing in 'From the Laboratory' bears a striking resemblance to this dynamic principle as described by Bakhtin. Pasolini offers a distinction between 'spoken' language and 'spoken-written' language to replace two most common theoretical oppositions: (1) language of structure versus language of superstructure, as in Marxism; and (2) *langue* (language system) versus *parole* (speech), as in structuralist linguistics. Pasolini exercises caution and urges linguists to read his statements as those of a poet (of an outsider, then) and he tries to systematize his theory of language on an imaginary site between structuralism and Marxism. As if he were in a laboratory, Pasolini draws charts, separates and analyses the different concepts and categories of Saussurian linguistics; he tries to combine the scientific authority of structuralism with a materialistic understanding of reality. Despite his considerable efforts in this respect, these pages are less interesting for the linguistic system they outline than for the concept of oral language that emerges.

Significantly enough, criticism has never paid much attention to spoken language and its implications. Oral language, however, becomes central to Pasolini's linguistics and, more generally, to his theoretical thought. After introducing the distinction between 'spoken language' and 'spoken-written' language, Pasolini associates spoken-written language with a 'spoken/written/structural *langue*' and to a 'spoken/written/superstructural *parole*'; then he refers this 'spoken-written *langue*' back to an ideally written language and to an ideally spoken language (see Pasolini, *HE*, 58). In his attempt to hold the fundamental concepts and terminology of Marxism and linguistics together, Pasolini multiplies distinctions and categories so extensively that, at times, one loses track of them. Despite these complexities, the term 'spoken' (*orale* in Italian) remains a constant, and certain features characterizing orality begin to become manifest. Orality cannot be suppressed; it is a constant factor of contamination. If, for instance, one distinguishes language in use 'from the spoken-written *langue* downwards, and from the spoken-written *langue* upwards' (58), what we have is the following:

Downwards, the purely spoken language is found, and nothing else. Upwards, the languages of culture are found, the infinite *paroles*. (58–9)

Persisting alongside the spoken-written language, purely spoken language (orality) 'continually divides its nature: it continually represents an archaic historical period of the latter and at the same time its vital necessity and its type' (59). Features of oral language are continuity, materiality, and necessity, which are features of 'reality' as well. The film medium offers the opportunity to articulate the following equation: film is to written language what reality is to oral language; film is the written language of reality. Oral language unremittingly relates to spoken-written language; *langue*, as social institution, is in fact this very relation. *Langue* is constituted as circulation between these two linguistic levels. Reality does not exist without the consciousness of reality, that is without culture; meanwhile, culture is contaminated by the continuum of reality; it is forced constantly to split and to acknowledge the mediation that repeatedly produces it.

The persistence of orality forces us to adopt a new perspective, for Pasolini's concept of oral language leads us beyond such dialectics. In considering cinema, for instance, if it is the case that film is written language, with spoken language (i.e., reality) referring back to a written language (film), and so establishing film as distinct from reality, then this very relationship between film and reality is ambiguous. The separation between reality and thought is not obvious; reality does not let itself be reduced to an object. On the other hand, spoken-written language, necessarily comprising the metahistorical and absolute continuum of oral language, cannot represent it. To represent implies to separate, objectify, and distinguish. Language is mediation, the dynamic continuum of the thought-reality relationship. It is not an instrument of thought used to organize reality; language is a process that makes the separation and the objectifying knowledge of two polarities impossible. Knowledge becomes possible only as experience and action.

The script touched on above, *Il padre selvaggio*, articulates the theory advanced in 'From the Laboratory' in the filmic-literary mode of a screenplay. It is the same quest pursued on a different level, and I want to emphasize the selection of the verb 'articulate.' This screenplay does not illustrate, but it articulates, 'acts,' as it were. In the film Pasolini intended to shoot, poetry explodes, happens suddenly at the end of a sequence: '65. Then, suddenly, uttered by his inner voice, a word resonates' (Pasolini, *Il padre selvaggio*, 53). The text does not identify this word, but it refers us to the next sequence, to an image: '66. Forest bathed in sunshine. Exterior. Daytime.' Without interruption we read: 'It is the first word of a poem. At that utterance something starts moving in the forest' (53). Other images follow the first one, introduced by other words, words that are not written but only announced – 'another word . . . A third word' (53) – and immediately made into images. In the next scene (67) the oral poem is put into writing. The teacher assigns a composition in class, and the boy writes the poem that the previous night had risen to his lips. The poem becomes text, object, but also consciousness. Now the boy writes the poems that his inner voice dictates. He writes another one. Scene 69 concludes with these lines: 'And word by word, image by image, in the sweet, austere wave of Bach's sonata, here is his poem.' The next sequence follows whose title reads: '70. A, B, C, D, E, F, G, H, I. African settings poem. Exterior. Day time' (55). The screenplay tells us that it will not be a joyous poem, nor full of life, but critical: consciousness has evolved through writing – in the moment of mediation, of 'the written language of reality.' The text presents us with a list of images and then, at the bottom, in parentheses, the word 'POEM' (55). The poem as literary text is repeatedly announced while remaining absent; the poem (and poetry) is the event of the awareness of orality (of Africa); it is mediation, and film (even if here it is only evoked) is its materialization. Film seems to offer the opportunity of understanding the non-instrumentality of poetic mediation.

The problems Pasolini dealt with in these pages strongly recall the theoretical works on orality mentioned above. I am not so much interested here in establishing whether Pasolini knew McLuhan's or Havelock's writings, but in identifying and restoring his work's complex historical dimension. The sixties witnessed a deep change in Western culture produced by the extraordinary spread of television that during the 'economic boom' invaded all homes. In North America, the cradle of mass media, many tried to understand the meaning and the implications of this development. Pasolini, whose views are never constrained within the limits of national debate, takes part in this effort and, with great lucidity, makes a significant contribution to the investigation. Dwelling on some of the essential theoretical points will suffice to understand how his discourse on orality, so often ignored, addresses the question in its international context.

What are, then, the main questions animating international debate about spoken versus written language, about orality and literacy? With the advent of writing and even more so of print, words become concrete delimited units, susceptible of control, dead and lined up over a flat surface. Words turn from being events into things. Writing makes possible objective knowledge that separates the subject from its object. Time and space become knowable objects too, and one gains at least the illusion of manipulating them; calendars, maps, charts, story outlines serve this purpose. The sense of sight prevails, isolating and dissecting, over against the sense of hearing which harmonizes and connects. Writing marks the beginning of the modern era, where the world is turned into pictures for the human subject. In this context, rationality comes to be separated from irrationality, and rationality makes writing its dwelling, and shuns the voice. As we have seen, these are also the problems dealt with in the essay 'From the Laboratory,' and Pasolini's analysis affirms the impossibility of representation, as well as of an objective knowledge located in a subject. He claims the inseparability of rationality and irrationality.

For Pasolini, orality is doomed to produce writing; that is, it is doomed to produce the form of culture that exceeds it, that reduces it to a 'holdover.' And yet orality persists in writing, continues and contaminates that same culture that exceeds it. For, as Walter Ong (1982) argues,

writing can never dispense with orality ... Oral expression can exist and mostly has existed without any writing at all, writing never without orality. (7–8)

The implications of Pasolini's words quoted above now achieve wider force:

Downwards, the purely spoken language is found, and nothing else. Upwards, the languages of culture are found, the infinite 'paroles' (that are never, like spoken language, *only written and nothing other than written*: they always continue to be spoken also). (Pasolini, *HE*, 58–9; emphasis in original)

Writing has a positive function with regard to spoken language: it is through writing that we become aware of language. This argument is central to Pasolini's writings, including, as we have seen, to the screenplay *Il padre selvaggio*, as well as to the critical literature we have been addressing. Moreover, although oral language participates in our conscious life, it flows from the unconscious. The unconscious dimension of spoken language is repeatedly emphasized by Pasolini and finds confirmation in his film theory where unconscious language, like dreams, constitutes the oral language for which film is the written language. As Pasolini writes in 'The Cinema of Poetry,'

The linguistic instrument on which film is predicated is, therefore, of an irrational type: and this explains the deeply oneiric quality of the cinema, and also its concreteness as, let us say, object, which is both absolute and impossible to overlook. (169)

Poetry belongs to orality. The exclusion of poets from Plato's Republic, as Havelock (1963) argues, is mainly the rejection of the way of living and interacting typical of oral culture and that very exclusion becomes the founding act of modern Western thought.

Plato's exclusion of poets from his Republic was in fact Plato's rejection of the pristine aggregative, paratactic, oral-style thinking perpetrated in Homer in favour of the keen analysis or dissection of the world and of thought itself made possible by the interiorization of the alphabet in Greek psyche. (Ong 1982, 100)

As I have argued in this essay, poetry enjoys a special status in Pasolini's writings because it refers back to this oral dimension: poetry is able to re-produce that world in which words are not separate from the 'living present'; poetry produces the 'acoustic space,' to use McLuhan's words, 'boundless, directionless, horizonless' (McLuhan 1962, 48). Poetry rejoins audiovisual techniques in the creation of what McLuhan calls 'global village,' a not very dissimilar reality from Pasolini's *pragma*.

Ours is a brand new world of allatonceness. 'Time' has ceased, 'space' has vanished. We now live in a global village ... a simultaneous happening. We are back in acoustic space. We have begun again to structure the primordial feeling, the tribal emotions from which a few centuries of literacy divorced us. (63)

What happens to myth in a culture that has rejected orality? Oral language cannot be examined. It constitutes a continuity no longer amenable to analysis unless one is ready to alter it by dividing what is not separable: the dynamic parts of a whole. Studies of myth such as those conducted using the methods of structural anthropology alter it. As Ong (1982) reminds us,

Goody shows in detail how, when anthropologists display on a written or printed surface lists of various items found in oral myths (clans, regions of the earth, kinds of winds, and so on), they actually deform the mental world in which the myths have their own existence. (100)

The medium of film differs, perhaps. Pasolini's work on myth can be better understood if brought back to this context, safe from the questionable argument of nostalgia. McLuhan's words – 'our technology forces us to live mythically, but we continue to think fragmentarily, and on single, separate planes' (114) – could provide an interesting clue for the analysis of this aspect of Pasolini's work.

The last question that seems necessary to consider here underlies all the others. It is the question of the technological dimension of writing and mass media. How do we think about technology, and through which categories? Ong insists that writing is a technology and that only by comprehending this can we understand writing's relationship to the past, and so to orality. McLuhan speaks of television in terms of an entirely new technology, requiring different sensorial answers; but he also argues that the advent of electronic technology produces a sensorial world that resembles orality. Pasolini seems to respond by offering a form of action as a solution: technology becomes, for him, a way of being in the world.

Life is unquestionably drawing away from the classical humanistic ideas and is losing itself in pragmatics. The film (with the other audiovisual techniques) appears to be the written language of this pragmatism. But it may also be its salvation, precisely because it expresses it – and it expresses it from the inside, producing itself from itself and reproducing it. (Pasolini, HE, 205)

In orality a new kind of sociopolitical engagement is founded: audio-visual techniques allow us to act in the transformed reality that refuses to lend itself to any other form of knowledge. More than any other text by Pasolini, 'From the Laboratory' has a global character, which makes it all the more interesting. All the discourses that concerned him coalesce here, from linguistics to Marxism, to film, to the ethics of political commitment. Here they come to be jointly based on the association between reality and oral language and to share a materialism founded on the concept of orality. This is a materialism that calls into question the foundations of Western thought and especially the philosophy of knowledge fixed upon the appropriation of objects, upon instrumentality and representation, and upon the linear understanding of history. For Pasolini, a history of spoken language is not even possible

a) because past structures merge with present structures in a historical continuity which can no longer be reduced; b) because the spoken written language in the moment in which it settles in the oral structure, through the avenues of circulation established by the 'langue,' becomes merged there in a continuity no longer amenable to analysis. (60)

Pasolini's choice of film over the novel in the sixties was founded on the grounds of this materialism, and it is indissolubly connected to his understanding of the cultural genocide perpetrated by consumeristic civilization. By allowing for the expression of reality by reality and in effect never permitting a way out of reality, film seems to be the only language capable of knowing reality in a fashion adequate to the dramatic transformation that the real itself is undergoing.

Notes

1 De Santis belonged to the founding generation of neorealist film directors, having written for *Cinema* in the 1940s and worked with Visconti on *Ossessione* (1943). His first major film was *Caccia tragica* (1947) and he is best known for *Bitter Rice* (1948).
2 *Ordine nuovo* (*New Order*) is the title of the socialist weekly that Antonio Gramsci founded in 1919.

References

Bakhtin, M.M., and P.M. Medvedev. *The Formal Method in Literary Scholarship*. Cambridge, MA: Harvard University Press, 1985
Buci-Glucksmann, Catherine. 'Pasolini, Gramsci: Lecture d'une marginalité.' In Maria Antonietta Macciocchi, ed., *Pasolini*. Paris: Grasset, 1980

Gramsci, Antonio. *Prison Notebooks*. Translated and edited by Q. Hoare and
　G. Nowell-Smith. London: Lawrence and Wishart, 1971
Havelock, Eric A. *Preface to Plato*. Oxford: Basil Blackwell, 1963
Lord, Albert B. *The Singer of Tales*. Cambridge, MA: Harvard University Press,
　1960
Marx, Karl, and Friedrich Engels. *The German Ideology*. Moscow: Progressive
　Publishers, 1976
McLuhan, Marshall. *The Gutenberg Galaxy*. Toronto: University of Toronto Press,
　1962
– *Understanding Media*. New York: McGraw-Hill, 1964
– *The Medium Is the Message*. New York: Bantam, 1967
Ong, Walter. *Orality and Literacy*. New York: Methuen, 1982
Pasolini, Pier Paolo. 'Intervista.' Edited by Daisy Martini. *Cinema nuovo* 10, no.
　150 (March-April 1961)
– 'Incontro con Pier Paolo Pasolini.' Edited by B. Voglino. *Filmcritica* 116
　(January 1962)
– 'Una visione del mondo epico religioso.' *Bianco e nero* 25, no. 6 (June 1964)
– *Il padre selvaggio*. Turin: Einaudi, 1975
– *Volgar'eloquio*. Rome: Editori Riuniti, 1987
– *Heretical Empiricism*. Translated by L. Barnett and B. Lawton. Bloomington:
　Indiana University Press, 1988
Saussure, Ferdinand de. *Course in General Linguistics*. New York: McGraw-Hill,
　1966
Stalin, J.V. *Marxism and Problems of Linguistics*. Peking: Foreign Language Press,
　1972

A Genial Analytic Mind:
'Film' and 'Cinema' in Pier
Paolo Pasolini's Film Theory

DAVID WARD

David Ward's essay provides an important correction of the commonly held notion that Pasolini's film theory relied entirely on an idea of the 'unmediated' or realist reproductions of the 'long take.' This is perhaps true of the earlier (1966–7) film essays and especially of Pasolini's famous statement, 'Cinema of Poetry.' But, as Ward shows through close investigation of a wide range of his writings, Pasolini alternately privileges the 'cinema' of potentially infinite long takes and the 'film' with its editing and narrative structures. This makes *Heretical Empiricism* an 'unstable but nonetheless rich text.' The crux of the issue, to which Ward shows Pasolini returning again and again, is the problem of knowledge. The constructed character of conventional 'film' narratives, like verbal language, excludes the revelatory 'poetry' of reality; but the minimally constructed long-take, approximated for Pasolini by Andy Warhol's movies of the early sixties, yields only meaningless boredom, not knowledge. What is needed to gain representational knowledge is what Pasolini termed 'the genial analytical mind.' And yet ... In this recursive essay Ward follows Pasolini through his turns (backward, as well, to his literary reflections), and develops a far fuller portrait of the artist's film theory than we have known.

In the sixth episode of *Affabulazione* (1977),[1] probably the best-known and certainly the most performed of Pier Paolo Pasolini's verse trage- dies, the Shade of Sophocles makes the following remark: 'Man only became aware of reality once he had represented it' ('L'uomo si è ac- corto della realtà solo quando l'ha rappresentata,' 236). His reference to representation as the enabling condition for knowledge signals a return to the epistemological issues in Pasolini's thinking that had already come to light in the second half of the 'Cinema' section of his collec- tion of essays published under the title *Heretical Empiricism* (*Empirismo eretico* [1972]).[2] Up to the essays published in 1966 and early in 1967 the bulk of Pasolini's theoretical writings had made the case for a 'cinema of poetry' ('cinema di poesia'). Unlike its antagonist, the conventional narrative of the 'cinema of prose' ('cinema di prosa'), the former alerts us to the 'deep dream-like quality' ('profonda qualità onirica,' 173) that lies at the essence of reality and that films made according to Hollywood-style practices have almost completely ignored. Starting with 'Observations on the Long Take' ('Osservazioni sul piano-sequenza,' [1967]),[3] the picture begins to change as the limits of the 'cinema di poesia' become more apparent. At first, however, Pasolini assigns the 'cinema of poetry,' now renamed simply as 'cinema,' an accretive function: by reproducing the language of reality 'cinema' plays a central role in the formation of consciousness. 'Cinema' is now the name Pasolini gives to the process by which an unreflective consciousness develops into a reflective one:

As long as the language of reality was natural it remained outside our consciousness: now, through cinema, that it appears to us in 'written' form it demands a place in our consciousness. The written language of reality will enable us to know above all what the language of reality is. Finally, it will end up by modifying our thoughts about it and will turn our physical relations, at least with reality, into cultural relations.

Il linguaggio della realtà, fin che era naturale, era fuori della nostra coscienza: ora che ci appare 'scritto' attraverso il cinema, non può non richiedere una coscienza. Il linguaggio scritto della realtà ci farà sapere prima di tutto che cos'è il linguaggio della realtà; e finirà infine col modificare il nostro pensiero su di essa, facendo dei nostri rapporti fisici, almeno con la realtà, dei rapporti culturali. (239)

In other essays, however, this positive accretive function ascribed to 'cinema' is seen in a more negative light as its political and epistemological limits become clearer. In one of a series of shifts back and forth between competing terms, Pasolini abandons 'cinema' and goes back to the 'the cinema of prose,' the cinema of narrative and montage he previously disparaged, and which he now terms simply 'film.' Two of the most striking characteristics of *Heretical Empiricism* are, first, the variations that key terms like 'cinema of prose,' 'cinema of poetry,' 'film,' and 'cinema' undergo; and, second, the antagonistic relationship that obtains between them as, at different times, either cinema of prose/'film' or cinema of poetry/'cinema' becomes the privileged term. These two characteristics are merely the most outward signs of an instability that runs throughout *Heretical Empiricism* and that problematizes any interpretive attempt on the reader's part to recuperate the text in univocal terms. It is with the repercussions of Pasolini's shuttling to and fro between a theory of 'cinema' and a theory of 'film,' which turns *Heretical Empiricism* into an unstable but nonetheless rich text, that I will be concerned in what follows. But first, some definitions.

Whereas 'film' is the conventional artefact we see at movie theatres, 'cinema' for Pasolini means the reproduction of the entirety of the language of reality in 'written' but unedited form. It is the record of the entirety of our actions twenty-four hours a day made possible through the mediation of an all-encompassing number of cameras that film our every move from every conceivable angle. As it makes its first appearance in *Heretical Empiricism*, 'cinema' is an entirely hypothetical idea whose key element is an uninterrupted, infinite long take. 'Cinema,' then, as it follows the actions of our daily life, is

a virtual eye ... an invisible camera which won't miss any of those ... actions, even the smallest, and ideally will reproduce them – or will write them cinematographically. No matter how infinite and continuous reality is, an ideal camera will always be able to reproduce it in all its infinity and continuity. Cinema, then, as a primordial and archetypical notion, is *a continuous and infinite long take* ... a flowing, uninterrupted reproduction like reality, of reality.

Un occhio virtuale ... una invisibile macchina da presa, che non perderà una di quelle ... azioni, anche minime, e idealmente le riprodurrà – ossia le scriverà cinematograficamente. Per quanto infinita e continua sia la realtà, una macchina da presa ideale potrà sempre riprodurla, nella sua infinità e continuità. Il cinema è dunque, come nozione primordiale e archetipa, *un continuo e infinito piano-sequenza* ... una riproduzione, ininterrotta e fluente come la realtà, della realtà. (233–4)

Elsewhere the same idea is phrased like this:

Cinema is an infinite long take ... the ideal, virtual and infinite reproduction by means of an invisible machine that faithfully reproduces all a man's gestures, acts, words from his birth to his death.

Il cinema è un piano-sequenza infinito ... è l'ideale e virtuale riproduzione infinita dovuta a una macchina invisibile che riproduce tali e quali tutti i gesti, gli atti, le parole di un uomo da quando nasce a quando muore. (253)

Pasolini is initially drawn to 'cinema' because it seems to offer an antidote to the worn-out 'symbolic and arbitrary system of verbal signs. In order to "reproduce reality through its evocation" these signs are forced to interrupt it' ('sistema simbolico e arbitrario che è il sistema di linsegni. Che per "riprodurre la realtà attraverso la sua evocazione" deve per forza interromperla,' 233). Striving for what Stefano Agosti (1982) has called 'a total diction of reality' ('una dizione totale della realtà,' 135), Pasolini finds in 'cinema' a means of gaining immediate purchase on reality without the mediation that verbal signs or written language necessarily involve (see Agosti). In placing a kind of wall between reality and our access to it, verbal signs ('lin-segni') do little to approximate reality's life-affirming essence.[4] As his references to continuity and infinity suggest, Pasolini's real goal is to find a mode of representation that would match the immediacy he sees in reality itself. In 1966–7, when he writes 'Quips on the Cinema' ('Battute sul cinema'), 'cinema' would be his answer: 'Expressing myself through the language of cinema ... I always stay within the bounds of reality: I do not interrupt its continuity' ('Esprimendomi attraverso la lingua del cinema ... io resto sempre nell'ambito della realtà: non interrompo la sua continuità,' 233).

But here, even at the moment of one of its strongest formulations, the theory of 'cinema' begins to reveal its limits. Pasolini's realization of its inadequacies seems at least in part to have been occasioned by his encounter with the films Andy Warhol was making in New York. Although, by the way Pasolini describes 'cinema,' it is clear it cannot exist practically but only hypothetically, it approaches concrete form in the uninterrupted long take on which Warhol's cinema was based. In Warhol's marathon films of men sleeping, eating, getting a haircut, Pasolini came face to face with their 'long, senseless, illogical, measureless, unnatural, mute long take' ('lungo, insensato, smisurato, innaturale, muto piano-sequenza,' 249). And he saw, perhaps to his horror, an approximation of what his hypothetical 'cinema' might look like when turned into actual films. The picture of reality that Warhol's films offered was nothing like anything Pasolini had imagined his 'cinema' to be and performed none of the functions it was supposed to. Instead of triggering off a moment of enhanced possession of self, of greater and intensified perception of the vibrancy of reality, Warhol's cinema rendered it boring, insignificant, lifeless: the 'long take in its purest state would be made up of a series of extraordinarily boring things and meaningless actions' ('il piano-sequenza allo stato puro sarebbe costituito da un seguito straordinariamente noioso di cose e azioni insignificanti,' 248).

The boredom induced by Warhol's films is, however, just the outward sign of a deeper epistemological problem. Set up with the aim of reintroducing us to the phenomenological density of reality, 'cinema' in its practical form in Warhol's work turns reality into something that is not worth the effort to know. What comes out of 'cinema,' far from being vital and interesting, is now

something that has no interest or relevance whatsoever ... By representing it, the hypothetical and integral long take puts on display, the meaninglessness of life as life.

qualcosa di assolutamente privo di interesse: di una irrilevanza assoluta ... L'ipotetico piano-sequenza puro mette in vista, dunque, rappresentandola, l'insignificanza della vita in quanto vita. (248)

Pasolini's perception of the limits of 'cinema' is similar in many ways to the limits of the mimetic poetics he had outlined twenty years earlier in his essay on Italian dialect poetry, 'Twentieth Century Dialect Poetry' ('La poesia dialettale del novecento,' [1952]), that is now the opening essay in the collection *Passion and Ideology* (*Passione e ideologia* [1959]). The two moments are linked, for example, by the reliance on mirror metaphors to illustrate the enhanced perception of reality that mimetic poetics and 'cinema' were supposed to afford. Turning briefly to a section this essay dedicates to the nineteenth-century Italian novel, we find this parenthetical remark in which Pasolini takes issue with the realism of the Sicilian author Martoglio: 'as if the tape-recorder and not the mirror were the instrument the dialect author needs on his travels around the alleys of the casbah' ('quasi che il dittafono, anziché lo specchio, fosse il mezzo che il dialettale deve portare in giro per i vicoli della sua casbah,' 33). As off-handed as this comment might be, it bears directly on a question that will find strong echoes in Pasolini's later reflections on narrative where he develops a theory of realism based not on chronicling or copying but on enhanced repetition. Here the 'tape-recorder' stands for a realism that limits itself to recording the events of reality. In contrast, the mirror stands for a qualitatively different engagement with reality that aims at intensifying our perception of its essence. To use the tape-recorder and not the mirror as a means of mediating reality results in a desiccated replica of things, one in which essence, here identified as mystery, gets lost or misrepresented: a reality, then, 'deprived of the fantasy into which the mystery of life is translated' ('priva di quella fantasia in cui si traduce il mistero della vita,' 33). As the distinction suggests, Pasolini's championing of the mirror over the tape-recorder as a metaphor of representation bears on a notion of realism not as literal transcription but as reflectivity, specularity. Unlike the tape-recorder, the mirror does not limit itself to producing a double of reality. It can be considered a superior means of *re*production and *re*presentation only if we understand the prefix 're' of both terms to mean intensification of perception rather than mere copying.[5]

In the essay 'Quips on the Cinema,' Pasolini tells us that the turn from an oral culture to a written one had an effect entirely similar to that produced by the mirror. Opening up the possibility of a reflective consciousness, the advent of writing 'above all revealed to man what his oral language was. Certainly, this was the first step forward in a new, human, cultural consciousness' ('ha rivelato all'uomo cos'è la sua lingua orale, prima di tutto. Certamente è stato questo il primo scatto in avanti della nuova coscienza culturale umana,' 239). Pasolini seems originally to have envisaged a similar role for his hypothetical 'cinema': just as the move from oral to written culture opened up new horizons, so 'cinema' would lead to a heightened possession of both self and reality. In the same essay, he draws again on the mirror metaphor:

I found myself in the same position as someone doing research into the workings of the mirror. He stands in front of the mirror, he looks at it, examines it, takes notes. And what does he see? Himself. What does he notice? His own material and physical presence. The study of the mirror brings him back unfailingly to the study of himself.

This is what happens to those who study cinema. Because cinema reproduces reality, it brings us back to a study of reality. But in a new and special way, as if reality had been discovered through its reproduction, and some of its expressive mechanisms had become visible only in this new 'reflected' situation. By reproducing reality, cinema reveals its expressive qualities that we otherwise might have missed.

Mi è successo, insomma, quello che succederebbe a un tale che facesse delle ricerche sul funzionamento dello specchio. Egli si mette davanti allo specchio, e lo osserva, lo esamina, prende appunti: e infine cosa vede? Se stesso. Di che cosa si accorge? Della sua presenza materiale e fisica. Lo studio dello specchio lo riporta fatalmente allo studio di se stesso.

Così succede a chi studia il cinema: siccome il cinema riproduce la realtà, finisce col ricondurre allo studio della realtà. Ma in un modo nuovo e speciale, come se la realtà fosse stata scoperta attraverso la sua riproduzione, e certi suoi meccanismi espressivi fossero saltati fuori solo in questa nuova situazione 'riflessa.' Il cinema infatti, riproducendo la realtà, ne evidenzia la sua espressività, che ci poteva essere sfuggita. (236)

But when Pasolini goes on to develop this line of thinking in his cinema essays he soon discovers that the cognitive mode that corresponds most closely to the mirror is not 'cinema' but a new term, 'film.' Contrary to what his earlier writings may have suggested, Pasolini recognizes that the infinite, uninterrupted long take is of little use when we need to interpret reality. From a theory of 'cinema' Pasolini now makes a first turn toward a theory of 'film.' The tension that persists between these two terms is laid bare most explicitly in the essay 'Observations.' If 'Quips' tells us what Pasolini's unmediated 'cinema' might look like, 'Observations' offers us an insight not only into the strengths of 'film' but also its limits.

The initial concern of the essay is hermeneutical and concerns an event that was still topical at the time the essay was first published in 1966: namely, the assassination of John F. Kennedy at Dallas. The essay, in fact, attempts to tell us what must happen if we are to answer questions like: Who killed John F. Kennedy? What happened that day in Dallas? Suppose, Pasolini suggests, that we had not one but an infinite number of 16 mm films of Kennedy's assassination; suppose that the event was recorded as 'cinema,' that we had films that recorded the events of that day from every standpoint and not just from the single one of the tourist whose actual 16 mm film provides our sole record of the moment of the Kennedy shooting.[6] What would result is footage taken from every conceivable angle: from Kennedy's, his wife's, the assassin's, other spectators', the bodyguards', from the grassy knoll. Pasolini imagines a situation in which we as spectators find ourselves in a room surrounded by a number of screens onto which the footage filmed from all the different angles is simultaneously projected. If, then, we were to view all these bits of footage, which would make up as complete a record as possible of those events, would the truth of that day present itself to perception? Surprisingly perhaps, given all his groundwork, Pasolini says no. We would be faced with such a barrage of unprocessed raw events and happenings that we would not be able to make any immediate sense of them. Broaching the problem of the epistemological limits of 'cinema,' he says that to process the wealth of heterogeneous information we receive – these 'stunted and incomplete languages' ('linguaggi monchi e incompleti, praticamente incomprensibili,' 243) – we must call on the intervention of a narrator figure, an editor, a kind of super detective that he calls 'a genial analytic mind' ('una geniale mente analizzatrice,' 243). Pasolini does not provide a detailed description of what he means by such a figure, nor does he give any examples.

If I understand him correctly, however, he envisages something like a conventional omniscient narrator, a figure who quite literally takes control over a mass of heterogeneous information and works this material into coherent and plausible narrative form. It would be wrong, I think, to consider Pasolini's genial analytic mind as only a literary figure. Pasolini's apprehension of the necessity for such a figure is a response to the need we have to understand the causes and predict the consequences of the sometimes atrocious and scandalous events we encounter in the course of our everyday lives. The Kennedy assassination is one such event that even today, thirty years after it took place, and despite the efforts of the Warren Commission's report, the New Orleans' district attorney Jim Garrison's alternative version, and Oliver Stone's recent film *JFK* (1991) (which draws on Garrison's version), has yet to be fully explained and remains the object of intense speculation. All three of the above, in fact, serve very well as concrete examples of the kind of work that Pasolini delegates to the genial analytic mind. In Pasolini's terms, the task that all three set themselves is to coordinate the various events of that day, which he calls generically the language of action, into 'an order in relation to itself and the objective world' ('una sistemazione in rapporto a se stesso e al mondo oggettivo,' 243). In other words, the genial analytic mind's task involves a process of selection and combination that aims to weave the most crucial and significant moments of a given event into narrative form: 'Choosing the really significant moments of the various subjective long takes and finding, as a result, their actual order' ('Scegliendo i momenti veramente significativi, dei vari piani-sequenza soggettivi, e trovando, di conseguenza, la loro reale successività,' 243–4).[7] It is, then, in the narrated and segmented work of 'film,' and not in the uninterrupted long takes of 'cinema' that Pasolini locates the means by which the world can be made knowable in any certain sense. There is nothing very innovative about Pasolini's valorization of the epistemological necessity of the narrator figure. Indeed, the way he sets up the genial analytic mind as a principle of intelligibility, and the unperturbed way he seems to accept the security and authority of this knowing, masterful subject leads him into theoretical dilemmas. For example, an important political question attends the invention of the genial analytic mind: who chooses the events deemed significant and according to what criteria? There is some evidence to suggest that Pasolini thinks such events to be so self-evidently significant and outstanding that any rigorous justification of their choice is superfluous.[8] But reading Pasolini more generously, we could take this as a moment of hyperbole in a text written as a manifesto and say that Pasolini overstates his case for effect. Because he wants to sing the praises of the rigour of 'film,' what results may be less a theoretical dilemma than a by-product of a rhetorical ploy. At any rate, as we shall see, Pasolini later returns to the question of narrative order that 'film' raises and in a far more critical spirit. To leave the issue of narrative per se aside for a moment, what turns out to be new about 'Observations' is that his valorization of the narrator figure marks a considerable departure from the other linchpin of his theory, the uninterrupted long take.

A glance backwards at Pasolini's two 'Roman' novels reveals that the turn from 'cinema' to 'film' replays a turn that took place about a decade before, in the interval between *The Ragazzi* (*Ragazzi di vita* [1955]) and *A Violent Life* (*Una vita violenta* [1959]). The major difference between the two novels is in their narrative voices. *Ragazzi* is characterized by a narrative voice who, because he expresses himself in dialect, shares the same linguistic space as the characters. As a result, he is not an authoritative mediator between text and reader and does little to give coherence to the narrative. As a reader of *Ragazzi* as sophisticated as Italo Calvino has testified, it is often difficult to monitor time and follow the turns of the story line (see Calvino 1980). The later *A Violent Life*, on the other hand, has a configuration that conforms more fully to the demands of conventional narrative and makes it a far more accessible reading experience. It has, for example, a more familiar narrative voice, a central character whose attempts at self-improvement we can follow with little difficulty and a recognizable social and historical context (see Ferretti 1964; Asor Rosa 1965). Like 'film,' the second of Pasolini's

Roman novels is a far more coherent and stable text than *Ragazzi*, which is more like 'cinema.'

Pasolini's conversion to a more conventional narrative practice is, however, far from definitive. As soon as he completed *A Violent Life* he abandoned novel writing in favour of filmmaking. It is true that in his discussion of the merits of 'film' and 'cinema' in the mid- and late 1960s he develops in more formal terms some of the questions he had already raised in his novels. But if we examine essays like 'Observations' and 'Quips' we soon discover that Pasolini's return to the narrative practice he now calls 'film' is far from being his theoretical resting place.

As we read on in *Heretical Empiricism*, we find that in 'Observations,' the essay that had initially outlined the strengths of 'film,' he almost immediately attends to the constraints imposed by conventional narrative and soon goes back to a consideration of the merits of 'cinema.' At different phases of Pasolini's career one or the other seemed to offer a feasible answer. When he writes 'Observations' for example, when we need to know what happened that day in Dallas, 'film' seems to correct the shortcomings of 'cinema.' But, in a move that is characteristic of his theorizing, as soon as 'film' is posited, its flaws are immediately exposed.

It is important to underline, however, that the revisions in Pasolini's thought on narrative order are all internal. They come, that is, from within the body of Pasolini's own writings. One of the reasons I refrained above from pursuing the critique of the limits of the masterful subject, to which Pasolini's valorization of the genial analytic mind leaves him open, is that he develops the critique himself. In fact, he discovers that the underside of the epistemological certainty that conventional narrative would guarantee is the oppressive hold narrative structure takes over both our perception of the world and its potential for semiosis. We can follow this development in Pasolini's thought by noting, first, the kind of events over which Pasolini is willing to grant the narrator figure control; and second, how metaphors of death consistently punctuate Pasolini's references to narrative order.

Signs of discomfort with the textual stability and epistemological certainty afforded by the genial analytic mind are already present even in the essays that initially valorize 'film.' On closer inspection, these texts reveal that the only matter over which Pasolini is willing to grant the narrator figure control is that of past events: 'Only those events which have already taken place and are finished can be coordinated, and so acquire meaning' ('Soltanto i fatti accaduti e finiti sono co-ordinabili fra loro, e quindi acquistano un senso,' 243). Pasolini's examples make this clear. Once all the evidence is in on events such as Kennedy's death, Stalin's crimes, Lenin's 'great poem of action' (204), they can be entirely knowable. To be knowable an event must be finished and no longer subject to change. No late event – a conversion or a moment of genuine remorse, moments that are always possible as long as life goes on – can cast a new light on events and thus demand their reinterpretation.[9]

Concern with preserving the possibility of future signification within narrative structures bears directly on Pasolini's thinking about events still in progress. Given the inexhaustible potential for signification that inheres in reality, this possibility can never be discounted. Unknowable in any definitive sense while still in progress, these events resemble a chaos: 'an indecipherable, approximate, mythical and violently physical continuum which is at the same time ambiguous and duplicitous' ('un *continuum* indecifrabile, approssimativo, mitico e violentemente fisico insieme, ambiguo e menzognero,' 257). This is, however, far from saying that they are devoid of meaning. Before having any specific, single significance, events have a general sense of meaningfulness. 'Suspended and unrelated' ('Sospeso e irrelato,' 239), theirs is a meaning that gestures toward some future fulfilment. Events in progress, then, form the raw material of a project-toward-meaning whose aim is to interpret the meaningfulness inherent in the events and weave it into narrative form:

Every moment of the language of action is akin to *research*. But research into what? Into an order in relation to itself and the objective world. It is therefore a research into the relations between all the other languages of action with which the other languages, together with this one, express themselves.

Come ogni momento del linguaggio dell'azione esso è *una ricerca*. Ricerca di che cosa? Di una sistemazione in rapporto a se stesso e al mondo oggettivo; e quindi una ricerca di relazioni con tutti gli altri linguaggi dell'azione con cui gli altri, insieme ad esso, si esprimono. (243)

It is at this point that the repressive underbelly of the genial analytic mind becomes apparent. This leads to a new turn in Pasolini's thought, this time back to a consideration of 'cinema.' Pasolini's critique of 'cinema' started out by ascribing a positive role to the narrator figure as creator of order out of chaos. If, however, we attend to the metaphors of death that punctuate these pages, we find the beginnings of a new but no less hard-hitting critique, this time of 'film.' Whereas past events can be thought of as dead, events still in progress are alive. To discipline them into a narrative order is to bring foreclosure to their process of becoming. To bring narrative order to on-going events is, then, to bring a premature end to the possibility of future signification. Or, more bluntly, to bring narrative order is to kill events before they come to fulfilment.

Different from recent critiques of narrative, which have often been couched in metaphors of political repression – narrative as fascist, authoritarian[10] – Pasolini's critique, while never ignoring political concerns, centres on the ontological impoverishment narrative ordering forces on our perception of the world. Instead of perceiving what Pasolini elsewhere in *Heretical Empiricism* calls the 'natural poeticity of life' ('poeticità naturale della vita,' 57), narrative form imposes an external pre-formed order on the phenomena of the world. Rather than fulfilling its epistemological mission to gather up the potential for signification that inheres in the poeticity of things, narrative imposes an order of its own on the phenomena of reality. Narrative pre-interprets events by ordering them into a set of typifications according to which we expect the world to conform by virtue of repetition and familiarity. In so ordering events, a life-affirming heterogeneous present ('cinema'), whose potential remains untapped and also unknowable in any certain sense, is exchanged for a life-denying past ('film') which, in figuring the present according to the typifications of the past, denies it the possibility of autonomous semiosis.

As Pasolini's investigations into the strengths and limits of 'film' and 'cinema' develop, points of contrast with some of his earlier statements emerge. The discovery that both verbal and visual expression are tied to similar rules of narrative, for example, necessitates revisions in some of the earlier distinctions that had been made in 'The Cinema of Poetry' ('Il cinema di poesia' [1965]). (To the best of my knowledge, Pasolini himself does not draw attention to these contrasts, but they are, I believe, implicit in the later essays that discuss 'film' and 'cinema.') His initial move from the novel to cinema was founded on the qualitative difference he believed to exist between the linguistic sign (*lin-segno*) and the visual sign (*im-segno*). Unlike linguistic signs, which are dulled by convention and over-use, visual signs have a freshness and vitality that would open up new vistas of expression. However, the conclusion he comes to in 'Observations' is that narrative organization of both verbal and visual signifiers, as repressive as that ordering may be, is always necessary if we are to know the world, and this implies a reconsideration of the initial radical difference he claims exists between the two types of sign.

Pasolini's critique of narrative order leads him back to a consideration of the merits of 'cinema.' It should be underlined, however, that there is little sense of linear development in Pasolini's thought that leads from 'film' to 'cinema.' As I have suggested, we already find a decisive turn toward 'cinema' in 'Observations,' the 1967 essay that initially valorizes 'film.' It is here, for example, that we encounter the death metaphors that accompany Pasolini's comments on the narrative order the narrator figure makes possible: 'this narrator transforms the present into the past' ('questo narratore trasforma il presente in passato,' 244). Yet, for Pasolini, not even death can be given unequivocal meaning. As further proof of the lack of linear development in his thought, as we shall see shortly, Pasolini gives the death metaphor both positive and negative connotations.

As with the question of past events, at issue for Pasolini in his return to a consideration of the merits of 'cinema' is the question of safeguarding the possibility of future expression. Reality's potential for infinite semiosis is better safeguarded by the presentness of 'cinema' than by the ordered pastness of 'film.' The former is the privileged space of creativity, 'the mystery of the act of creation' ('il mistero dell'atto della creazione,' 231), while the latter is a space governed by reason where 'everything is defined coldly ... by the ordering powers of reason' ('tutto è definito freddamente ... dalla ragione ordinatrice,' 231). Against the ongoing life of 'cinema,' whose continuity is guaranteed by the absence of a narrator figure, 'film' is associated with pastness, history, and death: 'this is how *a life becomes history*' ('questo è il modo con cui *una vita diventa una storia*,' 258), As long as the long takes that form the basis of Pasolini's 'cinema' remain unprocessed, they are shorn of any sense of temporality and exist only in the present devoid of any certain meaning to which we can unequivocally pin them down:

The language of action is everywhere the language of non-symbolic signs in the present. Yet, in the present it has no meaning or, if it has meaning, it has it in a subjective way that is incomplete, uncertain and mysterious.

il linguaggio dell'azione è dovunque il linguaggio dei segni non simbolici del tempo presente, e, nel presente, tuttavia, non ha senso, o, se lo ha, lo ha soggettivamente, in modo cioè incompleto, incerto e misterioso. (243)

It is this mystery, this 'poeticità,' the sense of a presence perceived as an absence that gets lost when narrative form, turning the present into the past, turning 'cinema' into 'film,' is imposed on the language of action. From a valorization of 'film' as a corrective to the limits of 'cinema,' we come back to 'cinema' as a corrective to the violent constrictions of 'film.' We can trace the theoretical instability characterizing these texts through observing the shifts in the connotations that accompany their major metaphor, the figure of death. At times, it carries a positive connotation as a principle of order; at other times it is negative as order brings premature death to the ongoing process of signification.

The death metaphor takes on its negative connotations when Pasolini wants to emphasize the potential for semiosis inherent in signs. This is particularly characteristic of later essays collected in *Heretical Empiricism* like 'Res sunt nomina' (1971) and 'The Nonverbal as Another Verbality' ('Il non-verbale come altra verbalità,' [1971]), but can also be illustrated by the earlier short film *What Are Clouds?* (*Che cosa sono le nuvole?*, [1968]). When, for example, Pasolini writes in 'Res' of the 'greater propensity toward polysemia' ('maggiore disponibilità alla polisemia,' 264) that the sign acquires when it is taken out of a communicative context ('film') and put into an expressive one ('cinema'), he is restating in more scientific language the same idea contained in the earlier, far more dramatic statement we find in 'Is Being Natural?' ('Essere è naturale?' [1967]): 'Making cinema is like writing on burning paper' ('Fare del cinema è scrivere su della carta che brucia,' 249).

In the short film *What Are Clouds?*, the negative connotations of the death metaphor take the form of a critique of the tyranny of naming. Here Totò explains to Ninetto Davoli, as bemused as he almost always is in Pasolini's films, that the externalization of the truth we hold unexpressed within us is tantamount to the destruction of that truth. Ninetto, who in the film, like Totò, is a puppet controlled by a puppet master, a figure for the oppressive nature of narrative structure, begins the exchange by asking:

NINETTO: But what is the truth? Is it what I think of myself, or what other people think or what that person up there thinks?
TOTÒ: What do you feel inside? Concentrate. What do you feel?
NINETTO: Yes, I feel something there.
TOTÒ: What you feel is the truth, but ssshhh don't give it a name, because as soon as you name it disappears.

NINETTO: Ma qual è la verità? È quello che penso io di me, o quello che pensa la gente o quello che pensa quello là lì dentro?'
TOTÒ: Cosa senti dentro di te? Concentrati bene. Cosa senti?
NINETTO: Sì, sì si sente qualcosa che c'è.
TOTÒ: Quella è la verità ma ssshhhh non bisogna nominarla perché appena la nomini non c'è più.[11]

On other occasions, when Pasolini puts the emphasis on narrative order and not semiosis, when he seeks to correct the naturalism of the uninterrupted long take through montage,[12] the death metaphor takes on positive connotations. In fact, the first metaphors of death we find in *Heretical Empiricism* are used in such a context as a corrective to the boredom of Warhol's films: 'In my opinion, the authors of new cinema do not die enough inside their films' ('Secondo me, gli autori del nuovo cinema non muoiono abbastanza dentro le loro opere,' 250). Through its interruption of 'cinema's' infinite long takes, the metaphoric death that montage brings enables us to know the world and ourselves as other than it and we are. This is what Pasolini means when he writes: 'death carries out an immediate montage of our life' ('la morte compie un fulmineo montaggio della nostra vita,' 245); 'as long as we are alive we are without meaning' ('finché siamo vivi manchiamo di senso,' 245); 'it is only thanks to death that our lives help us to express ourselves' ('solo grazie alla morte, la nostra vita ci serve ad esprimerci,' 245); 'as long as a man has a future he is unexpressed' ('finché ha futuro un uomo è inespresso,' 244–45). Elsewhere Pasolini is at pains to point out that his idea of death was aimed not at the afterlife but at better understanding the world around us:

But my idea of death had to with the way we behave and with morality. It was concerned with what happens before death, not after it. Not with the afterlife, but with life itself.

Ma la mia idea della morte, dunque, era una idea comportamentistica e morale: non guardava al dopo la morte, ma al prima: non all'al di là, ma alla vita. (256)

More dramatically, Pasolini also expresses political and moral reservations about 'cinema' and the disengagement from the world it implies. At the heart of 'cinema,' in fact, Pasolini glimpses a deep immorality.[13] The link between the immortality of 'cinema' and its immorality is hinted at when he says the passage from 'cinema' to 'film' is founded 'on the abolition of time as continuity, and therefore on the abolition of its transformation into significant and *moral* reality' ('sull'abolizione del tempo come continuità, e quindi sulla sua trasformazione in realtà significativa e morale,' 256). Although to live entirely in the suspended sense of the eternal present and so to escape from death may seem an attractive proposal, just as many of Pasolini's own innocent characters are attractive, such escape is ultimately unforgivable insofar as it leads to a retreat from the writer's commitment to the world. The ethical and political irresponsibility of 'cinema' can be illustrated by reference to a short film *The Paper Flower Sequence* (*La sequenza del fiore di carta* [1969]), also sometimes known as *The Barren Fig Tree* (*Il fico secco*). In this film Ninetto, his usual picture of perfect poetic innocence, a Cheshire cat grin spread wide across his face, walks blissfully down Rome's via Nazionale while, in superimposition, we see newsreel footage of the atrocious events of the late 1960s: African famine, atrocities in Vietnam, and so on. Oblivious to such things, Ninetto continues on his way until he is struck down by an angry vengeful God who condemns him for his sin of irresponsible innocence:

Tell me, who did Christ speak to, son of mine, if not to the innocent? And why did he do that? So that they could have knowledge ... Listen to me, Curly, listen to me. A single nod of your head, a glance upwards toward the sky is all I need. Listen to me, if you don't want to be one of the lost. Innocence is a sin, innocence is a sin, understand? The innocent have to be damned because they no longer have any right to be innocent. I cannot pardon those who walk around with the happy look of the innocent when there is injustice, war, horror and chaos in this world.

Like you, there are millions of innocents all over the world who want to disappear from history rather than lose their innocence. And I have to make them die, even if I know that they can do nothing else, I have to damn them like the fig tree. Die, die, die.

Dì, a chi ha parlato Cristo, mio figlio, se non agli innocenti? e perché? Perché sapessero ... Ascoltami, Riccetto, ascoltami. Un solo cenno del tuo capo, uno sguardo verso il cielo mi basterebbe. Ascoltami, se non vuoi perderti. L'innocenza è una colpa, l'innocenza è una colpa, lo capisci e gli innocenti saranno condannati, perché non hanno più il diritto di esserlo. Io non posso perdonare chi passa con lo sguardo felice dell'innocente tra l'ingiustizia, la guerra, tra gli orrori e il caos.

Come te, ci sono milioni di innocenti in tutto il mondo che vogliono scomparire dalla storia, piuttosto che perdere la loro innocenza. Ed io li devo far morire, anche se lo so che non possono fare altro, io debbo maledirli come il fico. Morire, morire, morire.[14]

Ninetto, one might say, is guilty of having committed poetry. He is guilty, that is, of being innocent, in a world where innocence is no longer an option. To be detached from the world, especially this world, even in the sphere of attractive poetic disengagement that is Pasolini's 'cinema,' is now a criminal act deserving divine punishment, even if it means that an attractive innocent like Ninetto gets punished.

In perhaps its most dramatic formulation, we find in this film fable Pasolini's apprehension of the deep immorality that runs through 'cinema.' If our lives are to mean anything as examples to others, he writes in 'Living Signs and Dead Poets' ('I segni viventi e i poeti morti' [1967]), they must be brought out of the presentness of 'cinema' into the pastness of 'film.' The role he assigns to death, to interrupt life in order that it be understood as other is both political and moral: we are under a political and moral imperative to know the world in order to be able to change it. As *The Paper Flower Sequence* suggests, to ignore the real world of war, injustice, famine, and poverty is to be derelict in the duty that comes with our being in the world (see Nowell-Smith 1977, 15). At some stage, then, sense must be drawn from the suspended sense of 'cinema':

Each one of us ... in living carries out a moral action whose sense is suspended. Hence the logic of death. If we were immortal we would be immoral, because our example would never come to an end and would, therefore, be indecipherable, eternally suspended and ambiguous.

Ognuno di noi ... fa vivendo un'azione morale il cui senso è sospeso. Da ciò la ragione della morte. Se noi fossimo immortali saremmo immorali, perché il nostro esempio non avrebbe mai fine, quindi sarebbe indecifrabile, eternamente sospeso e ambiguo. (255)

The link Pasolini here establishes between immortality and immorality is a variation of an earlier formulation that appears on two occasions in the essays 'Is Being Natural?' and 'Living Signs and Dead Poets': 'either immortal and unexpressed or express ourselves and die' ('o essere

immortali e inespressi o esprimersi e morire,' 251) and 'express ourselves and die or be unexpressed and immortal' (o esprimersi e morire
o essere inespressi e immortali, 255). On both occasions the emphasis
falls not so much on the priority of one term over the other, but on the
tensional relationship that obtains between them.[15] The same can be
said of the relation between 'film' and 'cinema': when Pasolini speaks
of unexpressed immortality, he is referring to 'cinema'; when he speaks
of expressing oneself and dying, he is referring to 'film.' The bias toward
'cinema' we heard in Totò's remark in *What Are Clouds?* is deceiving;
and so is the emphasis given to the value of death by God's words
in *The Paper Flower Sequence*. The question Pasolini attempts to answer
in *Heretical Empiricism* never comes down to an unequivocal choice between 'cinema''s presentness and potential for on-going semiosis over
'film''s pastness, order and metaphorical death. Rather, the question
hangs on realizing that 'film' looks good from the standpoint of the
limits of 'cinema,' and vice versa. 'Film' appears a viable alternative
when it seems to correct the shortcomings of 'cinema,' while 'cinema'
looks equally good when it promises to preserve the potential for semiosis that 'film' threatens. The real issue Pasolini addresses is that 'film'
and 'cinema' are both, at different times, answers to questions that are
equally vital. At some stage 'film' must be the privileged term if our political selves are to function; at other times 'cinema' must be privileged
if our equally important poetic selves are to have a role to play.

The vacillation resulting from the ongoing renegotiation of these two
key terms is part of a broader instability brought on by the shifting subject positions occupied by the narrative voices we find in Pasolini's film
writings. At times, attracted by the potential for semiosis inherent in
signs, the voice we hear is that of the poet; at other times, aware of
the necessity to know and describe the world, the voice belongs to the
narrator figure or genial analytic mind. In Pasolini's theory both subject
positions are equally respectable and equally pressing and each establishes a temporary supremacy over the other as circumstances dictate.
But the moment of supremacy for each passes as the limits inherent in
their respective positions become apparent. The temporary hierarchy
reverts back to the tensions I have attempted to map out here.

Pasolini's theoretical writings, then, remain an elusive 'illegible' text,
peopled by voices staking competing claims. Pasolini's writings have
been the object of numerous critical attempts, by now spanning more
than a generation of commentators, to stabilize and make sense of
them. But they continue to elude stable unity and so remain ultimately

unknowable in any unequivocal sense. However, if we choose to read the essays contained in *Heretical Empiricism* as a grouping of unstable texts, where distinct voices vie to make their separate reasons heard, we succeed in recovering at least one problematic moment in Pasolini's writing that has resisted all attempts to control his film theory: namely, his gesture toward the commutability of the signified in 'The Nonverbal as Another Verbality': 'In reality, there is no signified. Because the signified is also a sign' ('In realtà non c'è significato: perché anche il significato è segno,' 268).

We are alerted to the problematic nature of this remark by the contrasting ways two critics have recently treated it. For Christopher Wagstaff (1985) such a statement stands outside the main thrust of Pasolini's film writings as 'a theoretical oversight in his system' (124). For Giuliana Bruno (1991), the same moment takes pride of place and serves as Pasolini's passport into the realm of postmodernist and feminist thinking.[16] Read from the perspective I have been here suggesting, that of a text which continually puts into question its own unity, the same statement need no longer be considered either an exception or a pinnacle in Pasolini's theorizing. Rather, it would become a stage in *Heretical Empiricism* in which the voice of the poet, whose project is to push the semiotic potential of language to the limit, takes precedence over the equally powerful voice of the narrator figure. Neither culmination nor oversight, Pasolini's valorization of the semiotic potential of the sign is one more stage in an on-going, multi-faceted project that after poetry, prose, dialect, cinema, and theory will lead him into a new area, theatre.[17]

Notes

1 Although the draft versions of Pasolini's six verse tragedies were written in April 1966, during his convalescence after an ulcer, they were, with the exception of *Calderón* (1973), only published in book form posthumously. All six texts and the *Manifesto per un nuovo teatro* have now been collected in *Teatro*. My page reference refers to this edition.

2 Published in 1972, *Empirismo eretico* is a collection of essays that were written and first appeared from 1964 to 1971. For each of the essays from which I quote I have supplied the date of first publication. An English translation of the text *Heretical Empiricism* is now available. The translations that appear here are, however, my own.

3 In the Lawton/Barnett translation, 'Osservazioni sul piano-sequenza' is translated as 'Observations on the Sequence Shot.' I prefer 'Observations on the Long Take.'

4 See Pasolini's interview with Jean Duflot for his comments on verbal language as a wall between reality and our access to it, in *Il sogno del centauro*, originally published as *Les dernières paroles d'un impie*, 28: 'These poetic or novelistic mediations placed a kind of symbolic screen, a wall of words between life and me' ('Ma queste mediazioni poetiche o romanzesche frapponevano tra la vita e me una sorta di parete simbolica, uno schermo di parole'). In addition, see Roberto Turigliatto (1976) for an extended exposition of Pasolini's love for reality, 'La tecnica e il mito,' 113–55, especially 117–20.

5 In this section, my argument draws heavily on recent critical work that has been concerned with the epistemological function of narrative. According to these theories, narrative enables us to get to know the world by highlighting significant aspects of reality and inviting us to reflect on them more deeply than we would do in the course of our everyday engagements with reality. W. Wolfgang Holdheim has called this a process of 'enhanced repetition.' See Holdheim 1984, 226–70; Hans-Georg Gadamer 1985, 122–3; and Hillis Miller 1991, 66–79.

6 In fact, the tourist Abraham Zapruder was using an 8 mm home movie camera. Pasolini mistakenly refers to this footage as 16 mm.

7 The entire quotation from which these extracts have been taken is as follows:

Now let's suppose that among the investigators [into the Kennedy assassination] who have seen the various, and unfortunately hypothetical films, the one tacked on to the other, there is a genial analytic mind. His genius could only consist in coordination. Through his intuitive powers, combined with an attentive analysis of the various pieces of naturalistic footage made up of the 16 mm films, he would be able to reconstruct the truth. But how? Choosing the really significant moments of the various subjective long takes and finding, as a result, their actual order. Put bluntly, this would be a montage. As a result of his work of choice and coordination the various visual angles would dissolve and the existential subjectivity would be replaced by objectivity ... we would have a narrator. This narrator changes the present into the past.

Ora facciamo ancora una supposizione: cioè che tra gli investigatori che hanno visto i vari, e purtroppo ipotetici filmini, attaccati uno all'altro, ci sia una geniale mente analizzatrice. La sua genialità non potrebbe dunque consistere che nella coordinazione. Essa, intuendo, la verità – da un'attenta analisi dei vari pezzi ... naturalistici, costituiti dai vari filmini – sarebbe in grado di riscostituirla, e come? Scegliendo i momenti veramente significativi dei vari piani sequenza soggettivi, e trovando, di conseguenza, la loro reale successività. Si tratterebbe, in parole povere, di un montaggio. In seguito a tal lavoro di scelta e coordinazione, i vari angoli visuali si dissolverebbero, e la soggettività, esistenziale, cederebbe il posto all'oggettività ... ci sarebbe un narratore. Questo narratore trasforma il presente in passato (243–4).

8 The closest Pasolini comes to elaborating this point is in another essay, collected in *Heretical Empiricism*, 'The Fear of Naturalism' ('La paura del naturalismo,' [1967]), where the significant moments of a recently deceased person's life make their own presence felt spontaneously:

The moment we die, in fact, a rapid synthesis of our life takes place. Billions of actions, expressions, sounds, voices, words fall to the wayside, while only ten or a hundred survive. An enormous number of sentences that we said every morning, mid-day, evening and night of our life fall into an infinite and silent void. But some of these sentences resist, almost miraculously, and make their way into our memories as epigraphs. They remain suspended in the morning light, in the sweet darkness of an evening. Our wife and friends weep when they remember them. These are the sentences that remain in a film.

Non appena uno è morto, infatti, si attua, della sua vita appena conclusa, una rapida sintesi. Cadono nel nulla miliardi di atti, espressioni, suoni, voci, parole, e ne sopravvivono alcune decine e centinaia. Un numero enorme di frasi che egli ha detto in tutte le mattine, i mezzodì, le sere e le notti della sua vita, cadono in un baratro infinito e silente. Ma alcune di queste frasi resistono, come miracolosamente, si iscrivono nella memoria come epigrafi, restano sospese nella luce di un mattino, nella tenebre dolce di una sera: la moglie o gli amici, nel ricordarle, piangono. In un film sono queste frasi che restano (253).

9 If it were not for his later interest in mythical and medieval texts, whose vitality and essence reside in the retelling of their narratives, on this score one could accuse Pasolini of a singularly ingenuous hermeneutics. He suggests on several occasions that once all the material pertinent to a finished event has been collected then that event may be completely knowable. He is unwilling, it would seem, to accept a hermeneutics that would allow for

further elucidations of the truth achieved as a result of the ongoing fusion of the horizons of the past (the 'finished' event) and the present. In this way, myths, although 'finished' as stories, relive and grow as they meet the horizon of the present in which they are told.

On the other hand, the primitive hermeneutics that seems to emerge from these essays may once again only be a by-product of Pasolini's hyperbolic mode of argumentation, which causes him to shuttle to and fro between extreme positions. Against the radical life of the incomprehensible present that can never be completely knowable, he posits, overstating the case for effect, the radical death of the clear cut and finalized past.

10 See Christopher Prendergast's (1986) chapter 'Narrative: A Matter for the Police,' in *The Order of Mimesis: Balzac, Stendhal, Nerval and Flaubert* for a discussion of the pros and cons of treating narrative as a manifestation of a fascist culture. For narrative order as a 'matter for the police' see Jacques Derrida (1979), 'Living On: Border Lines,' 104–5: 'The narratorial voice is the voice of a subject recounting something, remembering an event or a historical sequence, knowing who he is, where he is, and what he is talking about. It responds to some 'police,' a force or order of law ... In this sense, all organized narration is 'a matter for the police,' even before its genre (mystery, novel, cop story) has been determined.'

11 To the best of my knowledge there is no published screenplay of *What Are Clouds?* The quoted lines have been taken down during my viewings of the film.

12 Pasolini's actual films do little to illustrate his notion of 'cinema.' Concerned that 'cinema' renders reality 'natural' or everyday, the intervention of montage interrupts the linear temporality of the long shot to accentuate the mystery of reality:

This is why I avoid the long take: because it's naturalistic, and therefore ... natural. My fetishistic love for the things of the world does not allow me consider them natural ... That is why I substitute montage for the long take in my films. The linear continuity and infinity of the ideal long take that characterizes cinema as the written language of action becomes a 'synthetic' linear continuity and infinity through montage.

Ecco perché evito il piano-sequenza: perché esso è naturalistico, e quindi ... naturale. Il mio amore feticistico per le 'cose' del mondo mi impedisce di considerarle naturali ... Nel mio cinema perciò il piano-sequenza è completamente sostituito dal montaggio. La continuità e l'infinità lineare di quel piano-sequenza ideale che è il cinema come lingua scritta dell'azione, si fa continuità e infinità lineare 'sintetica,' per l'intervento del montaggio (235).

13 I have drawn on Richard Rorty's (1982) 'Idealism and Textualism,' 139–59 for this section of my argument.

14 As with *What Are Clouds?*, there is no published screenplay of *The Paper Flower Sequence*. The quoted lines have been taken down with the assistance of the Associazione Fondo Pier Paolo Pasolini.

15 Some attempt at a synthesis of the two positions is attempted when Pasolini speaks of the *Man of Aran*, a film that exemplifies 'an idea of montage which goes in the direction of a narrative technique of cinema of poetry' ('un'idea del montaggio piegato a una tecnica narrativa di cinema di poesia,' 254). But his strongest statements underline not the synthetic but the antithetical relationship that obtains between 'cinema' and 'film.'

16 Like Stefano Agosti's (1982) 'La parola fuori di sé,' and Teresa de Lauretis' 'Language, Representation, Practice: Re-reading Pasolini's Essays on Cinema,' Giuliana Bruno's 'The Body of Pasolini's Semiotics: A Sequel Twenty Years Later' (reprinted in the present volume) performs the valuable and welcome task of treating Pasolini as a forerunner of developments in recent theoretical work, thus rescuing him from the backwaters of reactionary thinking to which he had been relegated by earlier commentators (Costa, Eco, Garroni, Heath). While wholeheartedly supporting and appreciating the 'political' necessity of redressing an inaccurate bias that has haunted Pasolini studies, I would like to suggest that Pasolini's achievement lies in having anticipated not only the strengths but also the limits of postmodernist thinking. Strengths and limits are also apparent in Christopher Wagstaff's (1985) 'Reality into Poetry: Pasolini's Film Theory.' Its strengths, particularly the useful translation of Pasolini's semiotics into Peircean terms, is its 'empirical' approach to *Heretical Empiricism*; this strength, however, is also its limit as it underestimates how the 'heretical' elements in Pasolini's text problematize the entire notion of 'system.' See also Naomi Greene (1990), 'Theory: Towards a Poetics of Cinema,' in her *Pier Paolo Pasolini: Cinema as Heresy*, 92–126.

17 For Pasolini's theorization of theatre as a space of on-going, open-ended dialogue as an attempt at elaborating a narrative form that is neither, on the one hand, a 'matter for the police' nor, on the other, a place of epistemological irresponsibility, see my 'Pier Paolo Pasolini and the Events of May 1968: 'Il manifesto per un nuovo teatro',' forthcoming in *The Italianist*.

References

Agosti, Stefano. 'La parola fuori di sé,' *Cinque analisi*. Rome: Feltrinelli, 1982
– 'The Word Beside Itself.' Translated by John Meddemmen. In Beverly Allen,
    ed., *Pier Paolo Pasolini: The Poetics of Heresy*. Saratoga, CA: Anma Libri, 1982
Asor Rosa, Alberto. *Scrittori e popolo*. Rome: Savonà e Savelli, 1965
Bruno, Giuliana. 'Heresies: The Body of Pasolini's Semiotics.' *Cinema Journal*
    30, no. 3 (Spring 1991)
Calvino, Italo. 'Les romans de Pasolini.' *Pasolini: Séminaire dirigé par Maria
    Antonietta Macchiocchi*. Paris: Bernard Grasset, 1980
de Lauretis, Teresa. 'Language, Representation, Practice: Re-reading Pasolini's
    Essays on Cinema.' *Italian Quarterly* 82–3 (Fall/Winter 1981)
Derrida, Jacques. 'Living On: Border Lines.' In Harold Bloom et al., eds.,
    Deconstruction and Criticism. New York: 1979
Duflot, Jean. *Les dernières paroles d'un impie*. Paris: Pierre Beffond, 1981
– *Il sogno del centauro*. Edited by Gian Carlo Ferretti. Rome: Editori Riuniti,
    1983
Ferretti, Gian Carlo. *Letteratura e ideologia*. Rome: Editori Riuniti, 1964
Gadamer, Hans-Georg. *Truth and Method*. Translated by Sheed and Ward.
    Edited by G. Barden and J. Cumming. New York: Crossroad, 1985
Greene, Naomi. *Pier Paolo Pasolini: Cinema as Heresy*. Princeton: Princeton
    University Press, 1990
Holdheim, W. Wolfgang. *The Hermeneutic Mode*. Ithaca: Cornell University
    Press, 1984
Miller, J. Hillis. 'Narrative.' In Frank Lentricchia and Thomas McLaughlin,
    eds., *Critical Terms for Literary Study*. Eds. Frank Lentricchia and Thomas
    McLaughlin. Chicago and London: University of Chicago Press, 1991
Nowell-Smith, Geoffrey. 'Pasolini's Originality.' In Paul Willemen, ed., *Pasolini*.
    London: British Film Institute, 1977
Pasolini, Pier Paolo. *Ragazzi di vita*. Milan: Garzanti, 1955
– *Una vita violenta*. Milan: Garzanti, 1959
– 'La poesia dialettale del novecento.' *Passione e ideologia*. Milan: Garzanti, 1959
– 'Il manifesto per un nuovo teatro.' *Nuovi Argomenti* 9 (1968)
– *A Violent Life*. Translated by William Weaver. Manchester: Carcanet, 1968
– *Empirismo eretico*. Milan: Garzanti, 1972
– *The Ragazzi*. Translated by Emile Capouya. Manchester: Carcanet, 1986
– *Teatro*. Milan: Garzanti, 1988
– *Heretical Empiricism*. Edited by L.K. Barnett. Translated by L.K. Barnett and
    B. Lawton. Bloomington: Indiana University Press, 1988

Prendergast, Christopher. *The Order of Mimesis: Balzac, Stendhal, Nerval and Flaubert*. Cambridge: Cambridge University Press, 1986

Rorty, Richard. 'Idealism and Textualism.' *Consequences of Pragmatism*. Brighton, Sussex: Harvester Press, 1982

Turigliatto, Roberto. 'La tecnica e il mito.' *Bianco e nero* 1, no. 4 (1976)

Wagstaff, Christopher. 'Reality into Poetry: Pasolini's Film Theory.' *The Italianist* 5 (1985)

Manifesto for a New Theatre

PIER PAOLO PASOLINI

Translator's Introduction

Pier Paolo Pasolini's response to the events of May 1968 was highly controversial. He sympathized not with the student revolutionaries but with the police. The real victims of society, said Pasolini, were not the students, the spoilt products of corrupt bourgeois culture, but the police, the sons of the proletariat, forced by lack of educational opportunity and chronic unemployment to take the jobs nobody else wanted.[1] Pasolini interpreted the confrontations between students and police differently from most left-wing intellectuals, not as the first steps in a liberation but as confirmation of the extent to which bourgeois ideology had taken control of every aspect of existence.

It was also in 1968 that Pasolini published his 'Manifesto for a New Theatre' ('Il manifesto per un nuovo teatro') and its appearance coincides with a turn in Pasolini's work toward a head-on involvement with the political issues of the day. His six verse tragedies represent his attempt to address the question of bourgeois hegemony. Written originally in the mid-sixties, but revised in the next few years, the verse tragedies illustrate the diminishing space for difference and change that the ideology of advanced capitalist society leaves. Protest itself has been co-opted as both students and police act out the roles that this ideology has assigned them. The overriding concern of the tragedies is to expose how sameness has seized control over any possibility of difference. Sons, like the one in *Affabulazione*, are supposed to do nothing but replicate their fathers; heirloom wedding rings, like the one in *Calderón*, are figures of identical links in a chain that ensures continuity of the past into the present and the future. Revolutionaries, like the son in *Porcile*, realize that their revolt is only a masked, but ultimately sanctioned, protest supervised by power. And the dialogue between Revolution and Capital that concludes

Bestia da stile confirms that all activity, whether conformist or revolutionary, takes place under the aegis of Capital. Difference and Revolution are left to dream while Capital, enveloping all, goes ahead.[2]

Pasolini's 'Manifesto' does not offer the interpretive keys to his verse tragedies. Although taking up the broad issues the plays address – poetry, dialogue, recuperation of the intellectual – the 'Manifesto' makes no direct mention of Pasolini's own dramas but is more profitably read as notes toward the elaboration of a new cultural politics. The opening paragraph bears, for example, on this issue of 'starting again,' and indicates the initial aim is to outline what a genuinely new theatre would look – and sound like. But how, Pasolini asks, can one describe a new theatre when our expectations are all drawn from the world of old theatre?

Pasolini divides modern theatre into two types: the bourgeois 'theatre of chatter' (instanced by Anton Chekov and Edward Albee) and the anti-bourgeois theatre of 'protest,' which he terms the 'theatre of the gesture and the scream' (exemplified by the Living Theatre). For Pasolini 'anti-bourgeois theatre' is the product of the same culture that has produced the 'revolutionary' students of May 1968. Neither type offers anything in support of Pasolini's attempts to develop a new theatre, for both of them are bound up together in the same kind of culture. Although they each approach theatre from different sides of an ideological divide, each represents a ritual confirmation of the already known. If the bourgeois theatre has no interest in revolution in theatre, the ideological shortsightedness of the 'anti-bourgeois bourgeois theatre' means that its allegedly oppositional force is merely reinscribed within the network of bourgeois power structures.

The new theatre Pasolini proposes in his 'Manifesto' is an attempt to create a space of debate to which intellectuals are called to take part in a 'cultural ritual'; it is to be a forum that gives voice to intellectuals ('the progressive group of the bourgeois') who otherwise would have no role in society. For Pasolini these are the survivors, the idiosyncratic figures whose marginality has meant that while they have not been taken over by the dominant ideology, they have been forced to the edges and no longer have a voice. Perhaps the major aim of the 'Manifesto' is to recover these marginal intellectuals and bring them into purposeful debate on the issues of the day. Indeed, Pasolini's verse tragedies are full of such figures, poets of the margins, who have lost any political function.

Pasolini's new theatre is first and foremost a place of dialogue and not a theatre of scenic action. Here the protagonists are ideas expressed and elaborated through the interaction between texts and public. It follows that this new theatre is to be the place where language comes into its own as a means of sustaining dialogue. The language of the new theatre is grounded in the physical presence of its referents. Against the written word, the spoken word of the theatrical texts generates a space where signifier and referent are bound together. Further, the dialogue which the new theatre organizes deals with the 'dramatic' question of closure by deferring it into an undisclosed future. Pasolini's dialogical model of theatre projects its debate (its very textual form) into a 'virgin' future on which narrative design exerts as little pre-interpretive pressure as possible.

The difficult questions are to be debated in this new intellectual forum. Open-ended in nature, the dialogue recognizes the problematic social and ideological questions by discussing them but without claiming to close or even enfold them. Focusing on beginnings rather than endings, new theatre seeks to organize a continuing debate on and into the ideological sedimentations present in society, not as closed matters but to re-open their problematicity.

David Ward
Wellesley College

Notes

1 See Macciocchi, 'Le crime est politique,' Le monde, December 1975.
2 There are two critical studies in English that treat his verse tragedies: Pia Freidrich, Pier Paolo Pasolini (Boston: Twayne, 1982) and William Van Watson, Pier Paolo Pasolini and the Theatre of the Word (Ann Arbor, MI: UMI Research Press, 1989). These works contain quite full synopses of the plays.

(To the Readers)

1) The theatre you expect, even at its most innovative, will never be the theatre you expect. When you expect a new theatre, you necessarily expect it within the limits of the ideas you already have. Besides, something you expect is in a sense already there. Of a text or a performance none of you can resist the temptation to say: 'This IS THEATRE,' or 'This IS NOT THEATRE.' This means that already deeply rooted in your head you have an idea of what THEATRE is. But innovations, even the

greatest, as you well know, are never ideal but always concrete. Their truth and their necessity are therefore miserable, annoying, and disappointing: they are either not recognized as innovations or are discussed in such a way as to become once again part of old habits.

Today, then, you all expect a new theatre, but you all have in your heads an idea which comes from the old theatre. These notes are written in the form of a manifesto so that whatever innovations they contain are presented explicitly and perhaps even autocratically as such.

(In the entirety of this manifesto, Brecht will never be named. He was the last man of the theatre to bring about a revolution within theatre itself because in his time the hypothesis was that the traditional theatre existed [which it in fact did]. Now, as we shall see through the various sections of this manifesto, our hypothesis is that the traditional theatre no longer exists [or is ceasing to exist]. In Brecht's days, reform, even hard-hitting reform, could be carried out without opening up the whole question of theatre. In fact, the aim of his reforms was to make theatre more authentically theatre. Today, however, what is put into question is theatre itself. The aim of the present manifesto is paradoxically this: theatre should be what it is not.

One thing is certain: the days of Brecht are gone forever).

(The Audience of the New Theatre)

2) The audience of the new theatre will not be composed of the bourgeois who generally make up the theatre public, but rather the *progressive groups of the bourgeoisie.*

These three lines, typical of the minutes of a meeting, are the first revolutionary aim of this manifesto.

They mean that the author of a theatre text will no longer write for a public which by definition has always been the theatre public, a public which goes to the theatre to have a good time and which sometimes is scandalized.

The public of the new theatre will be neither *amused* nor *scandalized* by the new theatre because, as part of the progressive groups of the bourgeoisie, they are the *equals* of the texts' author.

3) A *signora* who goes to city theatres and never misses the opening nights of Strehler, Visconti, or Zeffirelli is strongly advised not to come to performances of the new theatre. Or, if dressed in her symbolic, pathetic fur coat, she does come she will find in the entrance hall a

sign which says that *signore* dressed in fur coats are required to pay thirty times the price of the ticket (which will normally be very low). On the other hand, the sign will also say that fascists (as long as they are under twenty-five) can come in free. There will be one other request: people will be asked not to applaud. Whistling and heckling will be welcome, but in place of applause spectators will be asked to show faith in the democracy which allows a disinterested and idealistic dialogue to focus on the problems raised and debated (open-endedly!) by the text.

4) By *progressive groups of the bourgeoisie* we mean those few thousand intellectuals found in every city whose cultural interest may perhaps be ingenuous and provincial but is nonetheless *real*.

5) Objectively, these groups are made up of most of those who call themselves 'left-wing' progressives (including those Catholics who tend to make up a New Left in Italy). A smaller part of those groups is formed by those élites who have survived Crocean liberal lay culture. Another group is formed by radicals. It goes without saying that this list is and goes out of its way to be schematic and terrorist.

6) The new theatre is neither an academic theatre[1] nor an avant-garde theatre.[2]
   It is not part of tradition but neither does it oppose it. It simply ignores it and out-manoeuvres it once and for all.

(The Theatre of the Word)

7) Even at the risk of seeming banal and sounding once again like the minutes of a meeting the new theatre defines itself as 'theatre of the word.'
   Its incompatibility both with traditional theatre and with all types of protest against traditional theatre is contained in this self-definition.
   Completely ignoring the whole recent tradition of bourgeois theatre, not to mention the modern tradition of Renaissance theatre and Shake-

---

1 Old and modern theatres with velvet seats. Theatre companies, repertories like the *Piccolo Teatro*, etc.

2 Cellars, old disused theatres, the repertory companies' second strings, etc.

speare, the 'theatre of the word' is not ashamed[3] to hark back to the theatre of Athenian democracy.

8) Come and listen to the performances of the 'theatre of the word' with the idea of listening more than seeing (this is a necessary constraint in order to understand better the words you will hear, *and therefore the ideas, which are the real characters of this theatre*).

(What the Theatre of the Word Is Against)

9) All existing theatre can be divided into two types, which can be defined – according to conventional terminology – in a number of ways. For example: traditional theatre and avant-garde theatre; bourgeois theatre and anti-bourgeois theatre; official theatre and protest theatre; academic theatre and underground theatre, etc. Instead of these conventional definitions we prefer two sharper ones: a) the theatre of Chatter (following Moravia's brilliant definition); and b) the theatre of the Gesture or the Scream.

To make things clear right away: in the theatre of Chatter, the Word is replaced by chatter (for example, instead of saying, without humour, without any sense for the ridiculous and without manners, 'I would like to die,' one says bitterly, 'Good evening'); in the theatre of the Gesture or the Scream, the word is completely desecrated, destroyed in favour of pure physical presence (see below).

10) The new theatre calls itself of the 'Word' against:

I) the theatre of Chatter, with its naturalistic settings and spectacular structures without which:

a) the events (murders, robberies, dances, kisses, embraces, and subplots) would be unrepresentable;

b) saying 'Good night' and not 'I would like to die' would have no sense in the absence of the atmospheres of everyday reality.

The new theatre also stands against:

II) the theatre of the Gesture or the Scream, which protests against the theatre of Chatter by razing to the ground its naturalistic settings and deconsecrating its texts, but whose *scenic action* – its basic fact (which it takes to extreme limits) – it cannot abolish.

---

3 With all the candour of the novice.

From this double opposition comes one of the basic characteristics of the 'theatre of the word': in other words, as in Athenian theatre, *its almost total lack of scenic action.*

The lack of scenic action implies, of course, the almost total *disappearance of the mise-en-scène* – lights, scenery, costumes, etc. All this will be reduced to a minimum (because, as we shall see, our new theatre will by necessity continue to be a form, even if an as yet untried form, of RITUAL: therefore, the switching on and dimming of lights to indicate the beginning and the end of the performance will always be necessary).

11) Both the theatre of Chatter[4] and the theatre of the Gesture or the Scream[5] are two products of the same bourgeois culture. They both share a hatred for the Word.

The former is a ritual in which the bourgeoisie mirrors itself, more or less idealizing itself, at the very least always recognizing itself.

The latter is a ritual in which the bourgeoisie on the one hand recognizes itself for cultural reasons as the producer of that theatre (thus reacquiring through its own anti-bourgeois culture the purity of a religious theatre), while at the same time experiencing the pleasure of provocation, of condemnation and scandal (through which, finally, it receives nothing other than the confirmation of its own convictions).

12) The theatre of the Gesture or the Scream is the product of bourgeois anti-culture,[6] set up in opposition to the bourgeoisie, and uses against it the same destructive, cruel, and separate process that was used by Hitler (adding practice to madness) in the concentration and death camps.

13) If not only the theatre of the Gesture or the Scream but also our theatre of the Word are both produced by anti-bourgeois cultural groups of the bourgeoisie, what is the difference between them?

Here it is: while the theatre of the Gesture or the Scream has as its perhaps even absent addressees the bourgeoisie whom they shock (and without whom such a theatre would be inconceivable, like Hitler without the Jews, the Poles, the gypsies, and the homosexuals), the theatre of the Word, on the other hand, *has as its addressees the same culturally progressive groups who produce it.*

---

4 From Chekov to Ionesco up to the horrible Albee.

5 The amazing Living Theatre.

6 From Artaud to the Living Theatre, above all and on to Grotowsky, such a theatre has often been of a very high standard.

14) The theatre of the Gesture or the Scream – in the clandestine world of the underground – seeks in its addressees a complicity in struggle or a common form of asceticism. In other words, it represents for the progressive groups that produce it and enjoy it as addressees nothing more than a *ritual confirmation* of their own anti-bourgeois convictions, the same ritualized confirmation of bourgeois convictions that traditional theatre represents for the average, normal public.

In direct contrast, during the performances of the theatre of the Word, even if there will be many confirmations and checks (it is no accident that authors and addressees belong to the same cultural and ideological circle), there will be above all an exchange of opinions and ideas, in a relationship that will be far more critical than ritualized.[7]

(Addressees and Spectators)

15) In practice will a merging of addressees and spectators be possible?

We believe that in Italy the progressive cultural groups of the bourgeoisie can numerically form a public and so produce their own theatre. In this relationship between author and spectator the theatre of the Word represents something completely new in the history of theatre.

For the following reasons:

a) the theatre of the Word is – as we have seen – a theatre made possible, demanded, and enjoyed in the specifically cultural circles of the progressive groups of a bourgeoisie.

b) as a result, it represents the only way toward the rebirth of theatre in a nation in which the bourgeoisie has been unable to produce a theatre that is neither provincial nor academic, and whose working class has been completely deaf to the problem (and where its chances of producing its own theatre are only theoretical. Or better: theoretical and *rhetorical*, as all attempts at a 'popular theatre' *directly* addressed to the working classes have shown).

c) the theatre of the Word – which as we have seen avoids any possible relationship with the bourgeoisie, and is addressed only to progressive cultural groups – is unique in being able to reach the working class, not by *partie prise* or rhetorically, but realistically. *In fact, the working class is directly linked to progressive intellectuals.* This is a traditional

---

7 It may even happen that those same progressive cultural groups will from time to time be shocked and above all feel let down. Especially when the texts are open-ended when, that is, they raise problems without ever claiming to offer answers.

and inalienable notion of Marxist ideology on which both heretics and the orthodox agree, as if it were a natural fact.

16) Do not misunderstand. No workerist, Stalinist, Togliattian, or conformist dogma is here being invoked.
    Rather, what is being reinvoked is the great illusion of Majakowsky, of Essenin and of the other touching and great young people who worked with them at that time. It is to them that ideally our new theatre is dedicated. No official workerism, then, even if the theatre of the Word will go with its texts (*but with no scenery, costumes, musical motifs, tape-recorders, or mime*) into factories and communist cultural circles, into big rooms with the red flags from 1945.

17) Read the preceding two articles 15 and 16 as the foundation of the present manifesto.

18) The theatre of the Word, here being defined through this manifesto, is also a practical task.

19) We do not rule out that the theatre of the Word may experiment with texts dedicated explicitly to working-class audiences. But only in an experimental mode, because the only correct way to guarantee a working-class presence in such a theatre is to carry out what is stated in point (c) of article 15.

20) The calendar of the theatre of the Word – which will take the form of tasks or activities – will not follow a normal rhythm. There will be no previews, first nights, or matinées. Two or three plays will be prepared at a time to be staged in the company's theatre and in the places (factories, schools, cultural circles) where progressive cultural groups, to whom the theatre of the Word is addressed, have their headquarters.

(Linguistic Parenthesis: Language)

21) What language do these 'progressive cultural groups' of the bourgeoisie speak? Like almost the whole bourgeoisie they speak Italian. In other words a conventional language, whose conventionality, however, has not come about 'on its own' as a result of a natural accumulation of phonological commonplaces. Or better: as a result of a political,

historical, bureaucratic, military, scholastic, and scientific as well as literary tradition. The conventionality of Italian was established at a given abstract date (let's say 1870), and from above (firstly by the courts at an exclusively literary level and to a lesser extent at a diplomatic level, then by Piedmont and the first state bourgeoisie of the *Risorgimento*).

From the point of view of the written language, such an authoritarian imposition may appear inevitable, even if artificial and purely practical. In fact, we have seen a clear-cut acceptance of *written Italian* all over the nation (geographically and socially). But as to spoken *Italian*, to accept nationalistic demands and practical necessity has been simply impossible. No one, in fact, can be insensible to the farcical claim that a *uniquely literary* language be forced on an illiterate people through artificial and scholarly phonetic norms (in 1870 more than 90 per cent of the population was illiterate). It is however a fact that if an Italian today *writes* a sentence he writes it in the same way no matter what his geographical or social position may be, but if that same person says it he says it in a way different from that of any other Italian.

(Linguistic Parenthesis: The Convention of Spoken Language and the Convention of Theatrical Diction)

22) Traditional theatre has accepted the convention of spoken Italian, which has been emanated, so to speak, by edict. It has accepted, that is, an Italian that does not exist. It is on such a convention, or better, on nothing, on the non-existent, on death, that it has founded the conventionality of its diction. The result is repugnant. Above all when purely academic theatre is presented under its most 'modern' banner, that of the theatre of Chatter. For example, the 'Good evening,' which in our example replaces the 'I would like to die' that goes unsaid, has in the real life of spoken Italian as many phonetic aspects as there are real groups of Italians who utter it. But in the theatre it has only one pronunciation (used only in actors' diction). In the theatre, then, one is required to 'chatter' in an Italian in which no one actually chatters (not even in Florence).[8]

---

8 The text, in other words, dresses down while the unaware actor dresses up (it is because of this that in Italy the theatre is even unpopular among the bourgeoisie, who do not recognize in the text their own dialectal idiom).

23) As to the theatre of protest (what we are here calling theatre of the Gesture or the Scream), the problem of spoken language is either not raised or if at all only as a secondary concern. In such a theatre, in fact, the word integrates and backs up physical presence. And it usually carries this out through a simple desecrating act of counterfeiting. It tends, that is, when it does not limit itself to caricaturing theatrical convention (which is itself founded on the impossible convention of spoken Italian), to imitate the gesture, and to be therefore pregrammatical to the point that it becomes interjection: groan, grimace, or simply scream.

24) The theatre of Chatter would have a perfect form in Italy: dialect or dialectal idioms [koinè dialettizzata].[9] But it does not make use of this form partly for practical reasons, partly out of provincialism, partly out of uncouth aestheticism, partly out of a servile attitude toward the nationalistic tendency of its public.

(Linguistic Parenthesis: The Theatre of the Word and Spoken Italian)

25) Nonetheless, the theatre of the Word excludes both dialect and dialectal idioms from its self-definition. Or, if it does include them, it includes them exceptionally and tragically in a way that places them at the same level as cultivated language.

26) The theatre of the Word, then, produced and enjoyed by the progressive groups of the nation, cannot help having to *write* its texts in that conventional language which is spoken and read Italian (and only rarely raises *purely spoken* dialects to the same level as written and read languages).

27) Of course, the theatre of the Word must also accept the convention of spoken Italian, since its texts are also written to be represented, or, as in the present case, and by definition, *said*.

---

9 In fact, the only occasions in Italy on which theatre is tolerable are when the actors speak either dialect (regional theatre, especially in the Veneto or in the Naples area, with the great De Filippo) or dialectal idioms (cabaret). Unfortunately, however, on the whole, where there is dialect or dialectal idioms there is also almost always vulgarity and a 'what do I care?' attitude (*qualunquismo*).

28) There is, of course, a contradiction: a) because in this specific (and essential) case, insofar as it accepts a convention that does not exist, the theatre of the Word behaves like the most abject of bourgeois theatres. Or better: it accepts the unity of a spoken Italian that no real Italian speaks); b) because, while the theatre of the Word aims to outflank the bourgeoisie by appealing to other addressees (intellectuals and workers), at the same time it envelops itself in the bourgeoisie. This is because only through the development of present bourgeois society will it be possible to fill the 'missing links' in the formation of a phonetic and historical convention of Italian, and so reach that unity of spoken language that for now remains abstract and authoritarian.

29) How can we resolve this contradiction? Above all, by avoiding any purism in pronunciation. The spoken Italian of the texts of the theatre of the Word must be checked so that it stays real. That is to say, up to the border between dialect and the pseudo-Florentine canon, without ever going beyond it.

30) In order that this theatrical and linguistic convention, founded on an actual phonetic convention (the Italian spoken by 60 million phonetic exceptions) does not become a new academy, it will be enough:
a) to be aware at all times of the problem;[10]
b) to stay faithful to the principles of the theatre of the Word. *Or better: to a theatre that is first of all debate, exchange of ideas, literary and political struggle*, at the most democratic and rational level possible. It is, then, a theatre that pays attention to meaning and sense and excludes any formalism, which, at the spoken level, leads to complacency and phonetic aestheticism.

31) All this requires the foundation of a true and proper school of linguistic re-education to lay the bases of acting technique in the theatre

---

10 Apart from one or two exceptions, Dario Fo, for example, no Italian working in the theatre has ever raised this question, and has always accepted the identification between the conventional orality of Italian and the convention of theatrical diction which is taught by even the most shabby, ignorant, and exalted maestros of the academy. Take the extraordinary case of Carmelo Bene, whose theatre of the Gesture and the Scream is completed by the theatrical word he desecrates and which, not to mince words, shits on itself.

of the Word, whose main object is not language but the meaning of words and the sense of the work.

A total effort which, combined with critical acumen and sincerity, necessitates a complete rethinking of the actor's self-image.

(The Two Existing Types of Actor)

32) What is Theatre? 'THEATRE IS THEATRE.' This is the answer everyone gives today: theatre is understood as 'something.' Or better: it is 'something else' that can only be explained by itself and can only be understood charismatically.

Actors[11] are the first victims of this kind of theatrical mysticism and so often become presumptuous, ridiculous, and ignorant figures.

33) But as we have seen, just as today's theatre is of two types: bourgeois and bourgeois anti-bourgeois, so actors are of two types.

First, let us observe the actors of bourgeois theatre.

Bourgeois theatre finds its reason for existence (not as text but as performance) in the life of society: it is a display of rich, prosperous people who also have the privilege of culture.[12]

Now, this kind of theatre is going through a period of crisis: it is now forced to reflect on its own condition and to recognize the reasons that push it from the centre of society to the margins, as if it had become a relic or a leftover.

The theatre itself has had little difficulty in reaching this conclusion: traditional theatre soon understood that a new type of society, massively flattened out and widened, formed by the petit bourgeois masses, has replaced it with two kinds of social event that are both more modern and appropriate: cinema and television. It has not been difficult to understand that something irreversible has happened in the history of theatre: the Athenian 'demos' and the 'élites' of old capitalism are but distant memories. The days of Brecht are indeed gone for ever!

Traditional theatre has gone into a state of historical decay that has created around it, on the one hand, an atmosphere of conservation as

---

11 But also critics.

12 At least official culture, which comes from the privilege of being able to go to school.

tenacious as it is short-sighted, and on the other, an air of regret and unfounded hope.

This too is a conclusion to which traditional theatre has more or less confusedly been able to come.

What traditional theatre has never been able even remotely to understand is what it is. It defines itself as Theatre and nothing else. When placed before the oldest and shabbiest of bourgeois audiences even the most wretched and jobsworth of actors vaguely knows that they are no longer participating in a triumphant and justified social event and are forced to explain their presence and performance (which now has no following) in mystic terms: a 'theatrical mass' in which Theatre appears in such a shining light as to induce blindness. In fact, like all false sentiments, it produces an intransigent, demagogic, and almost terrorist awareness of its own truth.

34) Let us now look at the second type of actor, the one from the bourgeois anti-bourgeois theatre of the Gesture or the Scream.

This kind of theatre has, as we have seen, the following characteristics: a) it appeals to a cultivated bourgeois audience and involves them in its own unrestrained and ambiguous anti-bourgeois protest; b) it looks for spaces where it can put on its performances outside official circles; c) it scorns the word, and also the languages of the national ruling classes, in favour of either a diabolic and disguised word or nothing other than a provocatory, scandalous, incomprehensible, obscene, and ritualistic gesture.

How can we explain all this? The reason lies in an inexact (but equally efficient) diagnosis of what theatre has become, or simply, what theatre is. And what is that? The THEATRE IS THE THEATRE, once again. But while for bourgeois theatre this is nothing more than a tautology that implies a ridiculous and triumphant mysticism, for the anti-bourgeois theatre this is a true and proper – and conscious – definition of the sacrality of theatre.

This sacrality is founded on the ideology of the rebirth of a primitive, originary theatre that takes the form of a propitiary, or better orgiastic ritual.[13] This is an operation typical of modern culture, according to which a form of religion crystallizes the irrationality of formalism into something that is born inauthentically (that is from aestheticism) and

---

13 Dionysus . . .

becomes authentic (or a true and proper type of life like pragma outside and against practice[14]).

Now, in some cases, this archaic religiosity, given new vigour out of anger toward the idiotic lay culture of consumerism, ends up by becoming a form of authentic modern religion (which has nothing to do with ancient peasants and everything to do with the modern industrial organization of life). Look at the Living Theatre, for example, and their almost monk-like collegiality, and the idea of the 'group,' which does nothing other than take the place of traditional units like the family, etc. Look also at how drugs are used as a means of protest, how 'dropping out' is seen as a form of violence, at least in gesture and language, and how the performance is almost a moment of sedition, or – as one says today – guerilla warfare.

In most cases however such a conception of theatre *ends up as the same tautology as bourgeois theatre*, and obeys the same inevitable rules.[15] Religion, then, from that form of life that is realized in the theatre becomes simply 'the religion of theatre.' And from this cultural vagueness, from this second-rate aestheticism, the actor in mourning and under the influence of drugs is made to look just as ridiculous as the co-opted actor, the type who wears a double-breasted suit, and who also works for the television.

(The Actor in the Theatre of the Word)

35) It will therefore be necessary for actors in the 'theatre of the word,' as actors, to change nature: they will no longer have to feel physically as if they were the carrier of a word that transcends culture in a sacred idea of the theatre: *they will simply have to be men of culture.*

No longer will they base their ability on personal charisma (bourgeois theatre) or on a kind of hysterical or spiritual force (anti-bourgeois theatre), which exploits demagogically the public's desire for performance (bourgeois theatre), or abuses the public by forcing it to take part in a sacred ritual (anti-bourgeois theatre). Actors will now have

---

14 Here once again looms the figure of Hitler, who has already been mentioned in other articles of this manifesto.

15 Anti-bourgeois theatre could not exist: a) without the bourgeois theatre to protest against and to massacre (this is its main purpose); b) without a bourgeois public to shock, even indirectly.

to base their skills on their ability to understand the text fully.[16] As actors they must not be the interpreters of a message (the Theatre!) that transcends the text. Rather, they must be the living vehicle of the text.

Actors will have to become transparent mediators of thought, and will be judged good the more, listening to the actors say the text, the public understands they have understood.

(Theatrical 'Rite')

36) Theatre is however in all cases at all times and in every place a RITE.

37) Semiologically the theatre is a sign system in which non-symbolic, iconic living signs are the same signs as in reality. The theatre represents a body with a body, an object with an object, an action with an action.

It goes without saying that *at an aesthetic level* this sign system has its own specific codes. But *at a purely semiological level* it does not differ (like cinema) from the sign system of reality.

The semiological archetype of the theatre is the performance that takes place every day before our eyes and within range of our ears, in the street, at home, in public places, etc. In this sense social reality is a representation that is not completely unaware of its status as representation, and therefore has its own codes (manners, behaviour, body language, etc.): put otherwise, it is not completely unaware of its own status as rite.

The archetypical rite of the theatre is therefore a NATURAL RITE.

38) Ideally, the first theatre that can be separated from the theatre of life is religious in character: chronologically, the birth of such a theatre as 'mystery' cannot be dated. But it occurs in every analogous historical (or rather prehistoric) situation. In all the 'ages of origins' and in all the 'dark' or middle ages.

The primary rite of theatre, as propitiatory rite, exorcism, mystery, orgy, magic dance, etc., is a RELIGIOUS RITE.

---

16 This is what all serious actors do, with genuine commitment: the critical results, however have been disappointing. In fact, they have been obscured by the tautological idea of theatre that implies materials and styles historically different from those of the text in question (if we are dealing with texts that pre-date Chekov or post-date Ionesco).

39) Athenian democracy invented and instituted the greatest theatre ever – in verse form – as POLITICAL RITE.

40) The bourgeoisie – with its first revolution, the protestant revolution – created, on the other hand, a new type of theatre (whose history begins perhaps with the *teatro dell'arte*, certainly with Elizabethan theatre and the theatre of the Spanish Golden Age, and now reaches us). In the theatre it invented (which was immediately realistic, ironic, adventurous, escapist and as we would say today politically complacent [*qualunquista*] – even if we are talking about Shakespeare or Calderón), the bourgeoisie celebrates the height of its worldly pomp and circumstance, which is also poetically sublime, at least up to Chekov, that is up to the second bourgeois revolution (the 'liberal' one). The theatre of the bourgeoisie is then a SOCIAL RITE.

41) Accompanying the decline of the bourgeoisie's 'revolutionary greatness' (unless, perhaps correctly, we want to consider 'great' its third revolution, this time technological) we have also witnessed the decline of the greatness of that SOCIAL RITE that was *its* theatre. So, if on the one hand a part of that social rite has survived, thanks to the bourgeoisie's conservative spirit, on the other it is gathering a new awareness of its own status as rite: an awareness that has been completely taken on board – as we have seen – by bourgeois anti-bourgeois theatre, which, in launching itself at the bourgeoisie's official theatre and the bourgeoisie itself attacks above all its official status as *establishment*, its lack of religion. The theatre of the underground – as we have said – attempts to revive the religious origins of theatre, as orgiastic mystery and necromantic violence. However, in this kind of operation, the aestheticism that goes unfiltered by culture works in such a way that *the real content of this religion is the theatre itself*, just as the myth of form is the content of every formalism. We cannot say that the violent, sacrilegious, obscene, desecrating-consecrating religion of the theatre of the Scream or the Gesture is without content or is inauthentic, because it is often filled by an authentic religion of the theatre.

The rite of such a theatre is then a THEATRICAL RITE.

(The Theatre of the Word and Rite)

42) *The theatre of the word does not recognize as its own any of the rites here listed.*

It refuses with anger, indignation, and nausea to be a THEATRICAL RITE; that is, it refuses to obey the rules of the tautology produced by an archaeological, decadent, and culturally generic religious spirit that has been easily co-opted by the bourgeoisie through the very scandal that it wants to arouse.

It refuses to be a bourgeois SOCIAL RITE: in fact, it does not even address itself to the bourgeoisie and excludes it, slamming the door in its face.

It cannot be the POLITICAL RITE of Aristotelian Athens, with its 'many' who were just a few thousand people: and where *the whole city* was contained in its stupendous open-air social theatre.

Finally, it cannot be a RELIGIOUS RITE, because the new technological middle age seems to exclude it on the grounds that it is anthropologically different from all previous middle ages . . .

Addressing itself to a public of 'progressive cultural groups of the bourgeoisie,' and, *therefore*, to the more enlightened working classes, through texts that are based on the word (hopefully poetic) and on topics that could be typical of a lecture, a possible political speech, or scientific debate, the theatre of the Word is born and operates completely in the sphere of culture.

Its rite, then, can only be defined as CULTURAL RITE.

(Summary)

43) To sum up:

The theatre of the Word is a completely new phenomenon because it addresses itself to a new type of public, outflanking once and for all the traditional bourgeois public.

Its originality consists in being of the Word: it stands against the two typical theatres of the bourgeoisie, the theatre of Chatter and the theatre of the Scream or the Gesture, whose basic unity is confirmed by their both having: a) the same public (which the former entertains, the latter shocks), and b) a common hatred for the word (hypocritical the former, irrational the latter).

The theatre of the Word does not seek out its theatrical space in any setting other than the head.

Technically, this 'theatrical space' is frontal: text and actors facing the public, with absolute cultural parity between these two interlocutors who, looking each other in the eyes, provide the guarantee of its adherence to true, even scenic democratic principles.

The theatre of the Word is popular not because it addresses itself directly or rhetorically to the working class but because it addresses it indirectly and realistically through those progressive intellectuals of the bourgeoisie who make up its audience.

The theatre of the Word has no interest in spectacle or worldliness, etc.: its only interest is cultural, shared by the author, actors, and public who, therefore, when they gather, take part in a 'cultural rite.'

Translated by David Ward

Accattone and *Mamma Roma*

P. ADAMS SITNEY

After a short apprenticeship in filmmaking as scenarist and dialogue adviser in the 1950s, the decade in which he also published his two 'Roman novels,' Pasolini abruptly abandoned writing fiction for film directing, beginning with *Accattone* and *Mamma Roma*. Taking Pasolini's quotations of Dante as a leitmotif, P. Adams Sitney situates his 'strange fascination with filming versions of the *via crucis*' ('way of the cross') within, and also against, the predominant genre of 'spiritual biography' of art cinema in the period. Sitney precisely locates Pasolini's precedents in Dreyer, Bresson, Fellini, Bergman, and De Sica, but measures the distances Pasolini sets between their works and *Accattone*, noting as well that while the film offers 'the illusion of immediacy and simplicity' suggestive of a return to neorealism, Pasolini's strategies differ in crucial ways. Indeed, Sitney shows the intricacy of Pasolini's style and allusions in both his early films was such that Pasolini transported the 'spiritual biography,' by 1960 firmly set in the middle class, into the ethos of the criminal subproletariat.

In considering the opening epigraph of *Accattone* (1961) I hope to cast some light on Pasolini's use of Dante, and then speculate on his strange fascination with filming versions of the *via crucis*. In this way I shall be prepared to make some claims about the genre of *Accattone* and about its uniqueness in that genre, and finally its relationship to *Mamma Roma* (1962).

Pasolini was known as an authority on prostitutes and pimps, above all as a student of their language. Fellini had hired him as a script adviser in that capacity for *Le notti di Cabiria* (1957). Fellini too had offered to finance *Accattone*, but he welshed on the deal when he saw the test footage he had ordered Pasolini to direct. In a sense *Accattone* is a critique and a revision of *Cabiria* and even an homage to Fellini's master and precursor, Rossellini, whose benign prostitute in the Roman episode of *Paisà* (1946) shares with Adriana, the heroine of Moravia's 1949 novel, *La Romana*, the exemplary role of a long line of generous whores in Italian cinema and literature.

Fellini's Cabiria is, characteristically, the sweetest of them all and the least sexual. The pathos of her exploitation and deception ironically crosses over into the narrative of Christian redemption that the film unfolds. Even after the man she unexpectedly met after praying at the shrine of the Madonna di Divino Amore for liberation from her profession, turns out to be a thief who takes all the money she made from the sale of her beloved shack, she cannot resist the redemptive lure of music and festive people. Instead of finding the petit-bourgeois paradise for which she prayed, she attains unanticipated Grace in the spirit of the simple-minded lay monk who earlier had offered her spiritual encouragement.

Accattone, the pimp, has neither Cabiria's charm nor innocence. He will betray his own friends for a meal (somewhat like Augusto, the protagonist of Fellini's *Il Bidone* [1955]); rob his baby son, whom he does not support, of a gold necklace; force his first woman (Maddalena) onto the street with a broken leg the very day he accuses her of turning in her former pimp (Ciccio), which leads to her beating and consequent arrest; and then seduce, abuse, and exploit a second (Stella) when the first goes to prison. His virtues are limited: he feeds the jailed Ciccio's wife and children after moving into her house with Maddalena, and he is sufficiently moved by the horror Stella feels, after her first night on the street, to try to support her by manual labour or by theft.

The titles end with the quotation of Satan to the Angel of God that took Buonconte Montefeltro's soul (*Purgatorio*, V, 106–7):

You carry off with you the eternal part of him for one little tear which takes him from me. (trans. Singleton)

> Tu te ne porti di costui l'etterno
> per una lagrimetta che 'l mi toglie.

Where Vittorio Spinazzola takes the *lagrimetta* to be Accattone's saving kindness toward Stella, I find the idea of salvation by good works runs counter to both Pasolini and Dante.[1] The point of *Purgatorio* V is that Grace may come instantaneously at the final moment even of a life that had been immersed in sin. Pasolini generally puts more emphasis on the moment of death than on the concept of sin. As the guarantee of meaning, death marks the conclusion of his 1967 essay, 'Observations on the Sequence Shot':

It is therefore necessary to die, *because so long as we live, we have no meaning,* and the language of our lives (with which we express ourselves, and to which we therefore attribute the greatest importance) is untranslatable; a chaos of possibilities, a search for relations and meanings without resolution ... *It is only thanks to death that our life serves us to express ourselves.*[2]

The point at which the Dantean model intersects with this Heideggerean, or more precisely existential-ontological, idea of being-towards-death would be hagiography, the lives of the saints. And this may be a part of what Pasolini had in mind when he acknowledged early Renaissance painting and Dreyer's films as the primary sources of his cinematic style. Doubtless, the Dreyer film closest to his project was *La Passion de Jeanne d'Arc* (1928). His memory of the film seems to have sheared away the intricate camera movements which articulate over and over again the figure of a circle with Joan at its centre (a Boethian-Augustinian theological geometry); instead, he seized upon the monumental closeups of carefully chosen 'types' and the problematic cohesion of the space they inhabit to guide what he called the *sacralità tecnica* ('sacred technique') of his own first cinematic style.

Often Pasolini pans from one speaker to another, especially when the *ragazzi* are grouped together. Sometimes the pans describe the movement of a glance. The very frontality of the shot-countershot elements and the autonomy of the panning movements suggest a distillation and an abstraction of the stylistic features of La *Passion de Jeanne d'Arc* without any obvious indication of their linkage to the original. Superficially the film bears a closer resemblance to Robert Bresson's films of the fifties because of the elliptical progress of its narrative – stressing significant accidents and relentlessly driving toward its culminating moment – and its use of a single, culturally prestigious, musical source: here excerpts from Bach's *St. Matthew Passion* function as Mozart's *C Minor Mass* did in *Un Condamné à mort s'est échappé* (1956) and Lully in *Pickpocket* (1959). The obsessive use of questions and answers, which Rinaldi explores in his discussion of *Accattone*,[3] may be yet another outgrowth of the influence of the interrogatory form of Dreyer's film.

In 1959 Pasolini had used a similarly skewered hagiographic model to shape his novel, *Una vita violenta*, the fictive life of Tommasso Puzzili, a *ragazzo di vita* who had been a Missino thug[4] and a daydreamer of Christian Democrat respectability before dying a Communist hero. So a year later, making his first film during the most troubling political crisis of postwar Italy, the summer of Tambroni's alliance of the Christian Democrats with the extreme right, amid urban riots and widespread fear of a *coup d'état*, he narrates the last days of Accattone without a single overt reference to the political issues of the moment, as if despairing of any parliamentary solution to the situation of the Roman subproletariat. Instead, the idea of political action occurs only when Accattone attempts to start a conversation with Stella, the first time he meets her; calling her work as a bottle cleaner slavery, he says: 'Lincoln freed the slaves. But in Italy they put it in place. If I had a machine gun in my hands, anyone would be lucky to be left standing!' Here this is only idle chatter. In the same passage there is a virtual repetition of the final speech of *Pickpocket*: 'O Jeanne, what a strange path we took to find each other.' Accattone says, 'Eh, Stella, Stella ... Indicame er cammino!' ('A, Stella, Stella ... Show me the way!'), adding ironically, 'Insegna a 'st'Accattone qual è la strada giusta pe' arrivà a un piatto de pasta e facioli' (Teach this Beggar the right way ... to get to a plate of pasta and beans').[5]

Fifteen years later, Pasolini recognized two ways in which the film pointed to the 'perfect ... continuity between the Fascist regime and the Christian Democrat regime': the ghettoization of the subproletariat and the criminal violence of the police.[6] Actually, Pasolini's most 'political' gesture was to relocate the genre of the spiritual biography of the late 1950s (*Il Bidone, Wild Strawberries, Pickpocket*) outside of the middle class. *Le notti di Cabiria* may have anticipated this, but Fellini gave his heroine middle-class values and virtues; in short, he transposed her and her world into the framework and the ideology of the spiritual biography. Pasolini's more startling achievement was to deploy the genre without altering the world and values of the criminal subproletariat.

On the most elementary level, this transposition began with the casting of the film. In fact, one of the impetuses driving Pasolini toward filmmaking was his frustration with the use of actors to play the *ragazzi* in the two of the films he wrote for Mauro Bolognini, *La notte brava* (1959) and *La giornata balorda* (1960), according to his collaborator and informant on Roman dialect and slum life, Sergio Citti.[7] Citti's brother, Franco, played Accattone, and his friends from the *borgate* played the other *ragazzi*. As a first step toward his *sacralità tecnica*, this form of typecasting repeated a principle of neorealism, and to some extent a strategy of both Dreyer and Bresson.

The predominance of outdoor cinematography in urban locations, coupled with a distinctively stylized repertoire of compositional and montage strategies that give the illusion of immediacy and simplicity, also distances *Accattone* from the norms of the ambitious Italian films of the late 1950s in ways that suggest a refashioning of neorealism without actually repeating the strategies of films from the 1940s. Pasolini claimed he used only the middle-range 50mm and 70mm lenses to 'add weight to matter, highlight the depth and the light and shadow'[8] but there are clearly some minimal zoom movements in the finished film. Perhaps he meant that he never took advantage of the wide-angle and telephoto options of the zoom. When he told his cameraman, Tonino Delli Colli, that he wanted the image '*sgranata*,' which could mean 'open-eyed' or 'peeled,'[9] Delli Colli used a 'hard' stock from Ferrania and emphasized contrast and grain by printing a dupe negative from the original master. Such rawness plays up the difference between the texture of *Accattone* and the studio polish of Fellini's *La dolce vita* (1960) and the nuanced luminosity of Scavarda's images for Antonioni's *L'avventura* (1960).

But just as striking were the unfamiliar cityscapes of the Roman *borgate* in the brutal summer sun. Pasolini described the shooting conditions:

Those were stupendous days when summer was still burning in its purest form, and indoors there was hardly a lessening of its fury. Via Fanfulla da Lodi, in the middle of Pigneto, with low shacks, cracked walls, there was a granular magnitude in its extreme meanness; a poor, humble, unknown alley, lost under the sun in a Rome that wasn't Rome.[10]

Pasolini punctuated this vision of an unknown Rome with a series of remarkable images: Accattone's dive from the bridge with statues of angels; his drunken, wet face covered with sand, as if in premonition of his burial; his wearing a woman's hat and placing a basket on Fulvio's head; naked babies outside the cemetery; the thieves laughing themselves sick on the curb over Cartagine's smelly feet. The film proceeds through a series of gestural moments, consciously modelled on the fresco panels of the great Florentine masters of the early Renaissance.

The intense summer light takes on *thematic* importance in Accattone's dream: after following a funeral procession which turns out to be his own, he is barred from entering the cemetery. When he scales the wall, he finds only an old gravedigger preparing a plot for him in the shade of a tree. He talks him into digging a little farther away so that he will lie in the light. If we take this oneiric desire for light as the *lagrimetta* that saves Accattone's soul, then the *sacralità tecnica* of the film's style coincides with the typology of light in the Dantean allegory.

The musical quotations of Bach suggest that the film describes the 'passion' – the suffering endurance – of Accattone, his hagiographic suffering unto death. Of course, Dreyer had already emphasized this *imitatio Christi* in giving his film of Joan's trial such a title. Pasolini may also have been aware of the Anselmic dimension of Bach's theological polemic in *The St. Matthew Passion*: that salvation comes from Christ's willing gift of His death and cannot be earned by the action of men. So Pasolini's protagonist accepts salvation in his dying words ('Mo sto bene'; 'Now I'm fine') but he does not earn it.

Broadly speaking there are three movements in the film: Accattone's loss of Maddalena as his source of income, his destitution and attempt to convert Stella into a substitute for Maddalena, and the finale of his passion and death attempting to support himself and her. In all three sections accidents seem to guide the logic of events: at the opening Maddalena is hit by a motorbike, and at the very end a parked motorbike gives Accattone the illusion he can escape; but in a scene structured so much like the ending of *Ladri di biciclette* (1948) it must be deliberate, the motorbike he steals becomes the agent of his death. He meets Stella for the first time, accidentally, while conniving to exploit his estranged wife. More significantly, he meets her again at the very moment he is about to reap the reward of a plot against his friends to get their share of food from a church charity.

The spoken language of the *ragazzi di vita* is so embedded with fossilized Christian oaths (themselves layered on a linguistic palimpsest of invocations to Latin gods) that the theological markers in the text are easily disguised as signs of colloquial realism. So Fulvio opens the film with a note of doom: 'Ecco la fine del mondo' ('Behold, the end of the world'). He carries funereally a bouquet of flowers. The *ragazzi* call his work at a flower stand, 'martyrdom,' and the very word 'work' a 'blasphemy.' Later, after Accattone brutally presses Stella into prostitution, he remarks in exasperation: 'Madonna, fateme santo! Chè la penitenza mia già l'ho fatta! E quanta!' ('Madonna, make me a saint! What a penance I've already done! And how much!').

Accattone is no allegory of Christ's mission, but it is riddled with Gospel allusions ranging from the farfetched – Accattone's meal and his dive into the Tiber wearing gold ornaments as a parody of the Temptations in the desert – to the blatant – his death in the company of two thieves. In fact, the Christological focus seems to become sharper as the film moves toward its conclusion after the repeated *'falla finita'* with which the protagonist announces his firm decision to keep Stella off the streets. Fulvio covers the hand cart with wilted flowers as if parodying the entry into Jerusalem as Accattone banters that he is on the way to the Madonna of Divine Love. The night before, when Accattone had dreamed of his own death, the images literalized the Parable of the Shepherd: 'I tell you the truth, the man who does not enter the sheep pen by the gate, but climbs in some other way is a thief and a robber' (John 10:1). Barred from entering the cemetery as part of his own funeral procession, he scaled the wall to confront the gravedigger. So even in his dream Accattone subverts the symbolism of salvation, rendering any orthodox interpretation of his final justification uncomfortable.

Therefore the redemptive narratives of Manfredi-Episcopo, Cabiria, and Augusto are less problematic than that of Pasolini's hero. Pasolini's obsession with the *via crucis* dominates all his early black and white films: there is the Christlike death of Ettore in *Mamma Roma*, the film of the Crucifixion in *La ricotta*, the full-scale biblical narrative of *Il Vangelo secondo Matteo*, and even the parodic trinity of Father, Son, and Bird in *Uccellacci e uccellini*. But his obsession is not a measure of his piety, but almost the reverse, that is, the ground from which he argues with the Church and with the Italian tradition, from the perspective of a self-proclaimed 'heretic' or 'Lutheran,' not in the sense of a Protestant sectarian, but a prophetic rebel.

In the middle of *Accattone* one of the prostitutes seated with the *ragazzi* when Accattone first offers Stella to a man at another table quotes Dante: 'Lasciate ogne speranza, voi ch'entrate' ('Abandon all hope you who enter here') as if Hell and prostitution were identical. When *Mamma Roma* picks up the Dantean undersong of *Accattone* it remains in this Infernal register.

The ending of *Mamma Roma* went through at least two major changes before the film was shot. The treatment published in *Ali dagli occhi azzurri*[11] lacks the recitation of Dante in Ettore's prison infirmary cell, but it has an elaborate fantasy, brought on by his fevered delirium in which Mamma Roma magically crosses a sea and encounters an incarnation of Joy, who enacts with her a parable about a partisan and a soldier, while Ettore is being humiliated by a gang of boys.

In the published script this complex dream, inspired probably by Bergman's *Wild Strawberries* (1957), shrinks to a superimposed fantasy of elephants attacking and killing Mamma Roma in Guidonia where Ettore was raised, while a Sardinian prisoner recites the end of *Inferno*, Canto XVIII. In the final film there are no dreams or delirious fantasies, but the Dantean recitation remains. Only now the beginning of Canto IV is quoted.

What do these changes mean? I would surmise that the contextual aptness of Canto XVIII – at the moment of the Pilgrim's vision of panderers, seducers, and flatterers buried in faeces – carried too absolute a condemnation of prostitution for a film which bestows so much sympathy on Mamma Roma. Nevertheless Pasolini wanted to invoke the *Inferno* within that film, rather than announce his Dantean theme with a quotation in the beginning as he had done in *Accattone*. Therefore, he substituted the more generic opening of Canto IV, the first sight of Hell in the *Divina Commedia* for the problematic specificity of XVIII.

For technical or aesthetic reasons Pasolini dropped the dream sequence from the same scene, depriving us of participation in Ettore's subjectivity and rendering his agony in prison the parallel of that earlier moment in the film when his restlessness in his mother's apartment signals his decision to steal and sell her records.

The changes in the ending of *Mamma Roma* point to three lines of convergence with *Accattone*: a moral ambivalence about their shared theme of prostitution, a pseudo-biographical form that would have included an oneiric premonition of death, and a carefully chosen allusion to the *Divina Commedia*. The dark irony of Pasolini's second, and less successful, film is that the meliorated world of the INA Casa tenement building and the petit-bourgeois ethos of the reformed prostitute make up an even crueller hell than the slums. Mamma Roma's desperate attempts to keep Ettore from becoming a manual labourer, that is, her efforts to frustrate his natural class allegiances, ultimately lead to his death and her despair.

Brunetta identified the motorbike Mamma Roma gave Ettore as both a symbol for the yearning to escape from the confines of the subproletarian ghetto and as a displacement of her own desperation to escape prostitution.[12] She makes her one political statement while riding on it behind her son: in response to his statement of dislike for the middle-class waiters with whom he works – 'they think they are somebodies when they have a little of their fathers' money in their pockets' – she worries that he is becoming a communist.

In Pasolini's first films upward mobility is a descent into Hell. If *Accattone* is a parodic saint, he owes his salvation to the very horror of his situation; for Pasolini suggests that only the most humble and despised know salvation. Yet the cinematic genre through which he operates, the spiritual biography, had emerged in the European art cinema of the 1950s as the privileged locus of bourgeois sensitivity within alienation. But by inscribing allusions to the *Divina Commedia* in both films Pasolini claims a pedigree for his vision outside of the immediate cinematic context.

Notes

From *Vital Crises in Italian Cinema (1945–1950 and 1958–1963)* by P. Adams Sitney. Copyright 1994 by the University of Texas Press. Reprinted by permission of the publisher.

1 Vittorio Spinazzola, *Cinema e pubblico: Lo spettacolo filmico in Italia 1945–1965* (Milan: Bompiani, 1974), 279. Quotations from Dante's *Divina Commedia* are from the Petrocchi edition, translated by Charles Singleton.

2 Pier Paolo Pasolini, *Heretical Empiricism*, ed. Louise K. Barnett, trans. Ben Lawton and Louise K. Barnett (Bloomington: Indiana University Press, 1988), 236–7

3 Rinaldo Rinaldi, *Pier Paolo Pasolini* (Milan: Mursia, 1982), 228–32

4 'Missino' denotes a member of the neo-fascist Movimento Sociale Italiano (MSI) political party.

5 Gian Piero Brunetta, *Forma e parola nel cinema* (Padova: Liviana, 1970). Brunetta writes convincingly of the alternative goals of women and food in this film. At one point he identifies 'Stella-Beatrice.'

6 Pier Paolo Pasolini, *Lutheran Letters*, trans. Stuart Hood (Manchester: Carcanet, 1983), 100

7 Franca Faldini and Goffredo Fofi, eds., *L'avventurosa storia del cinema italiano: raccontata dai suoi protagonisti 1960–1969* (Milan: Feltrinelli, 1981), 39

8 Laura Betti et al. eds., *Pier Paolo Pasolini: A Future Life* (Rome: Fondo Pier Paolo Pasolini, 1989), 19. Translator unspecified.

9 *L'avventurosa storia*, 46

10 Ibid., 40

11 See 'Accattone,' in *Alì dagli occhi azzurri* (Milan: Garzanti, 1989 [1965]), 249–362

12 Brunetta, op. cit., 108

To Film a Gospel ... and Advent of the Theoretical Stranger

BART TESTA

The 'sacred' and 'epic' qualities of Pasolini's film style are the focus of Bart Testa's analysis of Pasolini's adaptation *Il Vangelo secondo Matteo* (*The Gospel According to St. Matthew* [1964]) and the later allegorical film *Teorema* (1968). Testa sidesteps the dominant auteurist approach to *Il Vangelo*, and focuses upon a detailed analysis of Pasolini's adaptation, his stylistic solutions in filming a pre-modern, 'laconic' text, and he demonstrates the significance of Pasolini's film through a comparison with other examples in the 'Jesus film' genre. Pasolini's film avoided many of the pitfalls of traditional approaches to this genre (from Griffith to Scorsese), which produced 'novelistic' adaptations of the gospel. This tendency in gospel films, which is explained as the result of the 'laconism' of the original text, is not reproduced by Pasolini, and Testa describes how Pasolini abandoned certain editing conventions (such as the 'interval': dissolves or fade-outs) but, on the other hand, creatively used other editing figures (such as shot/counter-shots or close-ups) and camera motion (dynamic panning, for example) as the filmic equivalents of narrative accelerations, and elliptical jumps in the original story. Testa describes how Pasolini's style leads to a de-psychologization or de-individualization of point of view. This process of de-individualization is repeated in the later film *Teorema*, in which the characters in the film undergo a traumatic loss of self-identity after their encounter with an allegorically divine 'visitor.'

... To Film a Gospel

Il Vangelo secondo Matteo (*The Gospel According to St. Matthew* [1964]) was the most famous and popularly successful of all Pasolini's films and clearly marked his arrival as director of international reputation. *Il*

Vangelo came after *Accattone* (1961), his directorial debut, and *Mamma Roma* (1962), two feature films that recapitulate the two 'Roman novels' of the fifties. In this period there were also three shorts, including *La ricotta* (1963), a satirical fiction set during the production of a conventional 'Jesus film,' and the documentary *Sopralluoghi in Palestina* (*Locations in Palestine* [1964]) in which Pasolini scouts locations in the Holy Land, although he eventually decided not to shoot the gospel there.

Il Vangelo restated Pasolini's complicated ambivalence as an experimental-realist and a modernist-traditionalist, adding to these 'Marxist-Catholic.' Discussion of these, and further conflicted facets of the artist's sensibility, have continued ever since. However, it should be recalled that the question of 'Marxist-Catholic' dialogue, opened in the pontificate of John XXIII, was hardly limited to Pasolini himself. In its success, partly propelled by the new openness of the Catholic Church after the Second Vatican Council, *Il Vangelo* appeared fortuitously as an emblematic work arising from such religious-political exchange. As that contemporaneous setting has faded from view, however, more recent critics have tended to downgrade *Il Vangelo* somewhat.[1] Emphasis in writing about Pasolini has shifted to his later films, polemics, and theorizing, and *Il Vangelo* is not conveniently fitted into this project. The film falls uneasily between two major moments in Pasolini's cinema: to one side, *Accattone* and *Mamma Roma* are restatements of neorealist cinema, however qualified;[2] to the other side, is *Uccellacci e uccellini* (*Hawks and Sparrows* [1966]), the open break with the neorealist 'generation of the Resistance.'[3] This division prefaces the start of the myth-based quartet of films, which finds Pasolini alternating adaptations of classic texts – *Edipo Re* (*Oedipus Rex* [1967]), *Medea* (1969) – and his own stylized inventions – *Teorema* (1968) and *Porcile* (*Pigsty* [1969]) – through the later sixties.

Although Pasolini's own commentary sometimes suggests an anticipation of his later mythic cinema, *Il Vangelo* was received as a much-needed alternative to the blue-eyed, holy-picture Jesus of the Hollywood religious epics satirized by *La ricotta*. On closer inspection, *Il Vangelo* is even more strikingly anomalous both for what we might call its 'genre' and for Pasolini. Starting from the generic context, we can raise some analytical concerns with the film. Most contemporary approaches to Pasolini's films are auteurist, and understandably so given Pasolini's self-explanatory energy. However, the present discussion will shift emphasis a bit away from the artist's project, and from his film theory, the start of which suggestively coincide with *Il Vangelo*.[4] This shift in emphasis can be significant. It is only a slightly extreme instance of auteurism, for example, that one critic's discussion of *Teorema* (my concern in the last part of this essay) makes the film into an illustration of his theory.[5] Here the focus will fall on issues of structure and narration. Nevertheless, we begin, as one must with Pasolini, with the artist, by lingering on his extraordinary decision – to film a gospel.

Il Vangelo is the first time Pasolini films a *given* text. His first two features, and his early shorts, were idiosyncratic inventions. But now, Pasolini decided to conform to a text, the Gospel of St. Matthew, promising to film it precisely as written because his own 'words and images could never reach the poetic heights of the text.'[6] We should remember how extremely rare it is to film a gospel. Although film history offers many 'Jesus films,' none go directly to scripture for the text. Instead, filmmakers adapt an historical novel, like *Ben Hur*, *The Robe*, or *Barabbas*, in which Jesus figures crucially as an agent of the narrative but only peripherally as a character. Or, they make a 'Life of Christ,' as with *King of Kings* and *The Greatest Story Ever Told*, in which biblical material is freely synthesized and adapted – again, in effect, novelized.[7] These novelizing solutions reach back to D.W. Griffith's *Intolerance* (1916), perhaps the genre's *locus classicus*, and even further, to the first filmed versions of European Passion-plays.[8]

Martin Scorsese's notorious *The Last Temptation of Christ* (1987) provides a recent and vivid example. The film is an adaptation of a modern and very fictional 'Life of Christ' by Nikos Kazantzakis.[9] Scorsese claims that his film is intended to be at once historically authentic and contemporary. The strategy he devises to satisfy this double intention is to create an expressionist film-novel with Jesus as a protagonist, which is to say a hero equipped with a fully drawn modern psychology, and then to throw him into an historical reconstruction of the confused stew of ancient Palestinian religions. The strategy leads Scorsese to restage the main events of Christ's biography and, with Kazantzakis' novel as his source, to invent a few as well. As many commentators have correctly observed, the film's failure lies precisely in the collision of modern psychologizing and historical reconstruction, which creates both a religiously confused and psychologically overwrought Jesus. Scorsese's modern Jesus never congeals as either an ancient or a modern personality but, as a novel-protagonist, he consists of a set of neurotic mannerisms.

If filmmakers from Griffith to Scorsese have pursued a novelistic solution, usually to unsuccessful ends, what is the problem? It is the laconism of the Bible. The scriptures do not depict Jesus by elaborating the psychology of a novelistic protagonist. The novel is a modern genre with a bourgeois provenance, while the gospels, as ancient texts, offer little that can be translated into the modes of conventional narrative films that invariably derive their modes of characterization from those of the novel. The scriptures refuse to speak the novel's elaborated psychological terms; they are unyieldingly laconic. Directors and scriptwriters have sought a solution to this problem – really the historical crevasse that lies between ancient texts and modern narrative techniques – by doing what André Bazin suggests filmmakers do when faced with any daunting task of adaptation: 'film-makers ... feel justified in treating [texts] simply as very detailed film synopses ... [they] go to novelists for character, a plot, even – and this is a further stage – for atmosphere.'[10] Scorsese's *Last Temptation* is only the most recent, and controversial, example of 'Jesus films' taking the gospels to be pretexts – offering characters, plot, and atmosphere – for novelized biographies.

Pasolini did not resort to this solution. When he decided to film a gospel he meant directly, using the actual text of Matthew. In a famous remark, he also declared that his decision to film a gospel was driven by a 'furious wave of irrationalism.'[11] Despite appearances, Pasolini does not use the word 'irrational' to describe a state of mind. In his account of modern Italian literary culture, for example, he suggests three moments: the irrationalism of hermeticism (the poetic manner his first writings adopted); the sentimentalism of neorealism; and the rationalism of the fifties, which he associates with *Officina*, the journal he co-founded in the late 1950s. He explains that this rationalist moment sought to correct the sentimentalism of neorealism and its political appropriation by the Italian Communist Party.[12] In the sixties, however, Pasolini felt the rationalist-Marxist vein had run dry and this shook his politics, which caused him to turn to religion. 'In me,' he said, '[ideological uncertainty] took the form of this regression to certain religious themes which nonetheless had been constant in all my work.'[13] Naomi Greene suggests that Pasolini felt Marxism could be revitalized through contact with Christianity and that this possibility opened up for him in the personality of Pope John XXIII (to whom *Il Vangelo* is in fact dedicated). Pasolini claimed, 'The great enemy of Christianity is not Communist materialism, but bourgeois materialism.' And, on the other side of the 'dialogue,' he added, 'So too Marxism must face the religious moment of humanity. There will always be an irrational, religious moment.'[14]

The 'wave of irrational impulses' was not, despite Pasolini's subjective rhetoric, just personal. Making a film of Matthew's gospel, he added, transformed his earlier 'precious' religious themes into 'faith, myth and collective mythology.'[15] What Pasolini says he saw in Matthew – and it was the text itself that so struck him[16] – and what he sought to duplicate in his film was the quality of what he termed 'national-popular epic.' That is, he read Matthew through a Gramscian theory of literature developed in the rationalist *Officina* period. In a discussion with Jean-Paul Sartre after the film was released, he insisted

I have been faithful to myself and I have created a national-popular work in the Gramscian sense. Because the believer through whom I see Christ as the son of God is a humble Italian ... seeing the world through his eyes I came close to Gramsci's national-popular conception of art.[17]

In these quotations, Pasolini suggests a paradox – that through 'a furious wave of irrational impulses' he came to film the gospel, a work of 'collective mythology,' that became a 'national-popular work in a Gramscian sense,' a sense associated with 'rationalism.' This paradox is echoed in another, Pasolini's frequently repeated claim that the film was made by a non-believer but through the eyes of a humble believer.

While these splits cannot be resolved, they can be understood as a consequence of Pasolini's decision to conform to Matthew's text. In his introduction to the script, Pasolini mentions two features he discerns in the gospel that should give us pause:

By literally following Matthew's 'stylistic accelerations' – the barbaric-practical workings of his narration, the abolition of chronological time, the elliptical jumps within the story which inscribe the 'disproportions' of the didactic, static moments such as the stupendous, interminable, discourse on the mountain – the figure of Christ should finally assume the violence inhering in any rebellion which radically contradicts the appearance and shape that life assumes for modern man: a grey orgy or cynicism, irony, brutality, compromise and conformism.[18]

This sentence begins by insisting that he has literally followed Matthew's 'barbaric-practical' style of narration, which he begins to characterize quite specifically in terms of elliptical jumps, sharp disproportions of temporal modes, from accelerated to 'static.' It ends by contrasting Christ's 'interminable' Sermon on the Mount and the corrupt ethos of modern man, suggesting that the text's Christ will 'assume the violence' of rebellion against the present age. For Pasolini, then, a 'regressive' surrender to religious impulses will restore ideological certainty – or at least a radical contradiction with modernity.

Given these strong claims Pasolini made for the very text of Matthew, and for his film of it, it should be mentioned that the four gospels – Matthew, Mark, Luke, and John – are not the same. This is not just a matter of a few differences in episodes (i.e., whether or not a particular miracle is depicted), but a complex and profound textual difference. Theological themes, and particularly their Christology, are embedded in each gospel, and narrational, even linguistic, specifics carry a particular charge of significance. So, to adapt the text literally, as Pasolini claims, means conforming to these textual specifics. We should point to another remark of Pasolini's, namely that in Italy (this is doubtless also true of most Catholic countries) no one reads the scriptures even once in a lifetime. Although he reported being filled with great 'energy' upon reading Matthew for the first time in Assisi, Pasolini expressed some surprise no one he knew had read the gospels. He did not add that in Catholicism scripture is heard rather than read through the liturgy where it is excerpted. Reading scripture is, in fact, a Protestant – and modern – idea descending from the Lutheran doctrine of *sola scriptura* ('by scripture alone').

Why did Pasolini choose Matthew? Negatively, he claimed that John was too mystical, Mark too vulgar, and Luke too sentimental. His evaluative tone aside, these are clichés of biblical criticism: John is the most mystical of the four evangelists, and Luke is regarded as a humanizer. Pasolini's dismissal of Mark is more problematic. Although Matthew is traditionally considered the first evangelist, the grounds for this are spurious. Mark is the earliest of the gospels to be composed and, in fact, Matthew incorporates considerable portions of the Marcan text. Given Pasolini's fascination with the primal in language, and his decision to film on the stark landscapes of southern Italy, by a process of 'analogy' (where the Italian locales stand in for ancient Palestine), the primitivism of Mark should have offered some advantages. Positively, however, Pasolini explains he chose Matthew because of the harshness of the Saviour's words, the abruptness of the evangelist's narration, and the 'absolute' fashion with which Matthew stages Christ's confrontations: in short, because of the 'violence' of Matthew's Jesus.

Pasolini's fidelity to these qualities of the gospel have drawn durable criticism: that Pasolini's Jesus is cold and distant, that his followers are silent and passive, which critics claim contradict the Gramscian intent of the film. Moreover, it is said that Pasolini ignores the historical realities of Jesus' time and so the confrontations between Christ and the Pharisees are 'abstract' confrontations of oppressor and oppressed. Summarily, the solitude of Jesus, and not his solidarity, is the hallmark of the film's hero. In drawing on these criticisms to make her own synoptic critique, Greene suggests *Il Vangelo* 'betrays a deep political pessimism' that Pasolini would only come to recognize later – and express to Oswald Stack in 1968 when he speaks of the film as 'an unpleasant and terrible work, at certain points outright ambiguous and disconcerting, particularly the figure of Christ.'[19]

What critics have discerned within the film leads back, I believe, to Pasolini's basic decision: to film a gospel. Critics insistent that he should have invented – for example, more dialogue between Jesus and his followers, or a whole ancient politics – are calling for another 'Life of Christ,' another novel. By composition, the gospel is organized around the *ipsissima verba* ('the very words of Jesus'), with the result that the gospel is largely a monologue while Matthew's narration, and with it his political scene-setting, is boldly diagrammatic: between the things of men and the things of God there can be no compromise; the violence of worldly power and the violence of divine eschatological power are incommensurable. The modern temptation to elaborate 'characters' around Jesus, to make them more loquacious, and to draw out a politics of ancient Palestine require the filmmaker to rewrite Matthew as a modern historicized fiction, precisely the strategy the 'Jesus film' genre has always pursued and Pasolini resisted when he decided to film a gospel.[20]

There is also the older temptation, as well, to elaborate by iconic illustration. The classic strategy of Western religious drama (i.e., the Passion-play) and visual art is to freeze the action of the gospel narrative as tableaux and to elaborate the anecdote pictorially in ways that treat the *verba* as emblematic captions.[21] Pasolini claimed, 'I wanted to do the story of Christ plus two thousand years of Christianity. At least for an Italian like me it has had an enormous importance in these two thousand years, indeed it is the major element in the Christological tradition.'[22] Although he does draw on painting, the instances are isolated and far less important in shaping the film than this remark suggests. Pasolini abandoned what he calls his *sacralità tecnica*, or 'sacred technique,' used for *Accattone* early in the production.[23] This is usually, and rightly, accounted as a stylistic reversal for Pasolini – sacred style for the gritty world of *Accattone*, a 'mixed' or 'magmatic' style, with *cinéma-verité* flourishes, for *Il Vangelo*.[24] More telling, Pasolini denied himself the elaboration of the gospel by iconic illustration. He stripped himself of the pictorial defence against the textual difficulties of filming a gospel: finding cinematic narrational equivalents to the laconic text. This means visualizing episodes as narrative and setting them in an order and to a rhythm. The problem of filming a gospel, Pasolini recognized with a sure discernment, is pre-eminently a problem of narrating Matthew's text, not of forging a pictorialist style. Critics overly impressed with details, like the Pharisees hats derived from Piero della Francesca, fall under an impression symmetrical with those who, prescribing the film to be a sort of religious social realist novel, criticize Jesus' lack of solidarity with the masses.

Segmenting Matthew

There are several overlapping analytical topics touched on in the previous observations that arise from Pasolini's decision to film a gospel. These topics – narrative design, adapting laconic text to a film narration, and Pasolini's thematic preoccupation with the violence of Jesus – concern how Pasolini engaged in segmenting Matthew.

Matthew's gospel and Pasolini's film seem at first straightforward narratives composed of episodes arranged in a linear fashion. However, on closer reading, like Jack Dean Kingsbury's,[25] Matthew is textually divided

into three main sections that are demarcated by 'superscriptions' (4:17, 16:21; cf. also 1:1) that he himself (i.e., Matthew) wrote in order to inform the reader that the major purpose of his Gospel is to set forth (a) the genesis and significance of the person of Jesus (1:1–4:16), (b) the nature and effect of his proclamation (4:17–16:20) and (c) the reason and finality of his suffering, death and resurrection (16:21–28:20).[26]

To abbreviate in what follows: the Infancy (though it includes Jesus' fasting in the desert, temptation, and baptism); the Ministry and the Passion.[27]

We saw that Pasolini remarks on Matthew's use of sharp ellipses, and strong accelerations and decelerations, and that he admiringly applies the epithet 'barbaric-practical' to these features of the text. Matthew does use varying narrational rhythms in each section, and these suggest a preliminary segmentation. Elliptical acceleration is most emphatic in the Infancy and Passion sections, where ellipsis moves the story from episode to episode. The Ministry, however, is largely characterized by what Pasolini calls 'interminable' and 'static' discourses interspersed with summary narrative passages; acceleration and deceleration are both very much at play here. The Passion proves an even more complicated case. A film director would understandably be attentive to problems Matthew's stylistic diversity presents: problems of transitions, of negotiating ellipses between short episodes; and staging those long discourses as part of the narrative flow.

Matthew handles transitions between both large and small segments by means of verbal formulas. These are markers of thematic importance to which we will have to return. But, for now, it should be noted that they do not diminish but actually accent Matthew's abruptness. For example, transitions in the Infancy and Passion episodes, where the formulas are most numerous, serve as fast transits between scenes. Nor are they used to forge a cause-and-effect relation between incidents; modern narrational hooks between segments that build suspense are alien to Matthew's style.

Pasolini does not seek close narrational equivalents to these textual formulas, and he seldom punctuates ellipses with conventional devices like voice-overs or fades and dissolves.[28] Instead, he uses the straight cut, usually enters an action already under way, and represses establishing shots. Although once inside an event, he can be rather leisurely, often using long takes of matched duration, Pasolini emphasizes Matthew's abrupt style in being himself even more elliptical at almost every transitional point. The effect is that *Il Vangelo* conforms to Matthew's ellipticality and episodic structure, with the further structural consequence that the film is as emphatically segmented as the gospel.

Perhaps the most remarked, if not wholly typical, example of this abruptness is the sequence opening the Ministry. In a strong transitional passage between the last Infancy episode – the Temptation in the Wilderness – and the start of the Ministry, Pasolini inserts a short, invented scene[29] of John the Baptist in prison. John hears a voice-over that quotes Isaiah describing the people who live in darkness but have seen a great light. Pasolini then cuts to a hand-held shot of Jesus alone moving quickly down a road and, with a series of rapidly cut moving-camera shots, shows him declaring to baffled peasants 'Repent, the Kingdom of God is at hand.' The evangelist is similarly abrupt in initiating the Ministry and, following Matthew exactly again, Pasolini then cuts to the call of the Apostles, which is rendered in a series of contrasting mobile shots: Jesus in close-up and the Apostles, at first in series of close-ups, and then running in panning long shots. This roughened mixture of shot types, and the speed of these two sequences taken as a whole, are made more emphatic through the rhythmic contrast between the transitional scene with John, which is slow and static, and the moving-camera intercutting that follows. The break between the Infancy and the start of the new segment, the Ministry, is very pronounced.

But to see Pasolini's more typical accomplishment in sustaining narrational equivalents to Matthew's segmentation, a fuller example is needed: the Infancy. Pasolini starts the film very slowly, with Joseph and Mary in a series of nine lengthy takes, arranged in frontal reverse-angle close-ups as the troubled Joseph withdraws from his pregnant fiancé. After the tenth shot, a point-of-view from Joseph, he collapses. Then, Pasolini expends four more shots before the angel appears and explains that Mary is 'with child' through divine intervention. The sequence then reverses almost exactly over another six lengthy takes, as Joseph returns to Mary until we are back where we began: Joseph and Mary each in close-up seen in frontal reverse angles, now smiling. What Pasolini has done here is to distend a rather densely narrated – but sketchily dramatized – passage of the gospel into a lucid and dramatic, but very laconic, narrative series whose symmetry has the same effect as Matthew's text, namely to seal the episode as a whole into itself.

Pasolini then moves, without transition, to the Magi from the East. Like Matthew, he divides their tale into three succinct scenes: the interview with Herod, the visit with the Child, and the angel leading them away in a different direction. The exchange with Herod announces the birth of Jesus (which Pasolini, like Matthew, does not show) and the Magi name him 'King of the Jews,' which in Matthew perturbs Herod and 'the whole of Jerusalem': textually, the significance here is the opposition between the politically powerful (centred in Jerusalem) and Jesus, which Matthew insists upon here at the outset. Narratively, the Magi's encounter with Herod sets up the Slaughter of the Innocents and Pasolini reproduces this narrative coherence by simple straight succession, without suturing the episodes into a unit or offering additional narrative material. Instead, he slightly ceremonializes the visit of the Magi to the child – in a wordless series that, after establishing long shots (a rarity in the film), settles into a relaxed series of long-take close-ups – as if the encounter was of no narrative consequence but possessed of solemn internal significance. (Both are true in Matthew: although the Magi's visit does lead to the Slaughter, in contrast to 'perturbed' Jerusalem, the men from the East also represent a first, and serene, recognition of the Messiah on the part of the Gentiles.) Pasolini then cuts to shots of the sleeping Holy Family (using close-ups again) and the angel speaks to Joseph, ordering him to flee into Egypt. This event is reduced to three shots of departure (two of them close-ups of Mary) with a brief voice-over quoting Matthew quoting Hosea (11:1): 'I called my son out of Egypt.' In contrast, the Slaughter of the Innocents, which follows immediately, is extended into multiple shots, many of them long shots taken in newsreel fashion (most using telephoto lens) and arranged as a series of rapid pans tied loosely with disjunctive cuts, concluded with a voice-over, also from Matthew, quoting Jeremiah (31:15).

The effect of these contrasting sequences is that of events linked only very loosely into a narrative line but well defined internally as episodes. The rhythm of each sequence is set internally, and disjoined stylistically across the segment as a whole. So, the sweetness of the Adoration of the Magi, and the slow lyricism of the Holy Family in flight forcefully collide with the kinetic violence of the Slaughter. Particularly notable is Pasolini's refusal to reconstruct the narrative here as a parallel sequence, remaining faithful to Matthew's strict and elliptical episodic succession. Pasolini continues like this, too, after the Slaughter, devoting a longish, but starkly simplified, sequence to the anguished death of Herod, and, reverting to the style of the opening sequence, offering a portrait of the Holy Family, with Jesus now a boy, after the angel returns to Joseph telling him to return to Israel. The overall effect is to match, even at times to exaggerate, Matthew's accelerated-decelerated rhythms and his abrupt transitions.

If Pasolini matches Matthew's quickened episodic narrative in the Infancy, he also stays close to the structure of the Ministry. However, these segments are something of a different story in the gospel, for they are, in the main, a series of monologues spoken by Jesus punctuated with miracles and summary narrative passages.[30] Unlike the Infancy, the Ministry is not a linear concatenation of marked episodes, but a cycle of apparent narrative repetitions. Although they form a dramatic arc at least suggesting a segmentation, it is subtle and 'textual' rather than dramatic. The abrupt start of the Ministry has already been described. After this comes the 'interminable' discourse of the Sermon on the Mount, then episodes showing the gathering of followers in crowds and the miracles. Then, the inquiry of John's disciples, John's death, and Jesus' three prophecies of his own death and the commission of Peter form the series that ends the Ministry.[31]

In a reading of Matthew, however, this segmentation of events is not readily apparent and one of the most acute discernments of *Il Vangelo* lies in Pasolini's use, in several variations, of a cinematic figure to demarcate Matthew's narrative progression. It is shot/counter-shot. This figure is conventionally used in film to depict conversations, usually showing the interlocutors in matching spatial configurations, using close-ups and sight-lines and angles to match speakers. Pasolini's interest in improvising on this figure is already apparent in *Accattone*.[32] In *Il Vangelo* shot/counter-shot provides a key motif from the very start, since, as we saw above, Pasolini chooses a long, wordless shot/counter-shot exchange to depict Joseph and Mary at the beginning of the Infancy. In the Ministry, Pasolini generally represses the counter-shot and also medium shots and long shots when Jesus preaches. This is rather surprising for it constitutes a refusal of the classic iconography of the preaching Jesus amid the crowds. Visually, in Pasolini's film Jesus and his message do not resonate through the crowds, either through reaction shots or pans over and through the crowds. Instead, Jesus' preaching is seen in close-up, which makes it paradoxically intimate and distant – the camera is close to him but does not mediate Jesus to his listeners. Indeed, the Sermon on the Mount, the first and longest discourse, has virtually no visible listeners at all. Pasolini renders it with an intercut series of close-ups, verse-by-verse, completely suppressing the counter-shot. When Pasolini depicts intimate exchanges, as with the leper, the rich young man and his apostles, shot/counter-shot is used, but configured as matched straight angles to Jesus, who appears frontally in either close-up or medium shot. In the case of confrontations with the Pharisees, the reverse angle to them is usually a low-angle grouping (most often a trio). For the cures, the same editing figure simply articulates Jesus' power: he speaks and, cut, the leper is clean. With the Apostles, brief exchanges prompt Jesus to withdraw a bit, turn, and then deliver a discourse, as with the three prophecies of his death and the testimony of Simon-Peter. Finally, there are also passages in which Jesus reacts silently, again in close-up, to reverse-angles, as with passages involving children; here Pasolini introduces two or three point-of-view shots, then cuts to Jesus, who speaks.

Although these variations are formally simple, even this partial enumeration suggests two points. First, Pasolini has systematized the shot/counter-shot figure in *Il Vangelo* in order to sustain episodes in the Ministry through a carefully ordered repetition/variation; second, breaks within the system are potentially significant as segmental markers. The strong examples confirming this include the episodes of Jesus' 'dismissal of his relations' and the 'commission of Peter.' The 'dismissal' episode starts with shots of the crowds and Jesus heard, then seen on high preaching against those who were first chosen and have not believed. In angle (low) and camera position (long shot), then, Pasolini noticeably breaks with his stylistic system here. When Jesus is interrupted by a disciple who says his mother and brethren are waiting, he turns – with a cut to a side-angle close-up – to ask 'Who is my mother? Who are my brethren?' Pasolini introduces a short series of close-up shots of Mary (now aged since the Infancy)) looking up and, in reverse angle, Jesus looking over his shoulder – a proper shot/counter-shot construction. Pasolini's invention (Mary does not appear by name in Mt 12), the exchange of glances points visually toward Mary's role in the Passion, as we will see below. Segmentally, in other words, the exchange is a prolepsis pointing toward the Passion.[33]

The 'commission of Peter' is more elaborate and itself punctuates a major segmental shift in the film. It is preceded by the death of John, itself a significant event that, in Matthew, concludes the major phase of the Ministry. *Il Vangelo* devotes three successive sequences to John's demise: Salome's dance, John's execution, and Jesus' mourning of John. In the last, Pasolini cuts directly to a silent Jesus' weeping in close-up and then, leading the Apostles away, he says the 'Son of Man has no place to put his head.' Jesus and the Apostles withdraw – in effect, from the Ministry – in fact, into a hilly wilderness, pursued by a hand-held camera. At this point, Pasolini adjusts the shot/counter-shot system so that Jesus now speaks *with* his Apostles and the reverse angles include dialogue. But this occurs in a curious fashion because the sequence is broken by camera movements as the group moves along, and Jesus also at times speaks with his back turned away. He delivers the three prophecies of his death, which Pasolini compacts into a single elliptically cut and highly mobile discourse that roughly alternates moving camera shots and static close-ups. In other words, the whole sequence recalls the rough mix of shot types that start the Ministry. Indeed, the slight excision and rearrangement of the later portions of Matthew's Ministry chapters permit Pasolini to arrive more directly at this symmetrical and dramatic conclusion of the Ministry.[34] Stylistically, this ending is marked with a reconfiguring of the system of shot/counter-shot built up through the preaching and miracles sequences. Like his use of ellipsis and acceleration, here the film's visualization serves as a structural-narrational equivalent to Matthew's segmentation. Thematically, too, the evangelist counterposes individuation of the apostles with both the crowds and the Pharisees.[35]

Structurally Pasolini also rearranges Matthew slightly so that the murder of John by the king and Jesus' rejection by the home-town crowd of Nazareth form a narrative sequence of events that articulate the failure of Christ's Ministry to be believed by the leaders (complicit in John's murder) and the people (the Nazareth crowd) alike. Both episodes are marked by close-ups of Jesus that show him silent, a significant variation of close-ups of him preaching, and these are counterposed at the end of the Ministry by the commission of Peter. It is prompted by the apostle's declaration of faith and, therefore, it accents the dramatic arc of the Ministry – from the first declarations, through the calling of the Apostles, through the preaching and miracles to the failure – the visit to Nazareth and murder of John – and the prophecies of Jesus' death, finally to arrive at Peter's commission. Visually, at the end, through shot/counter-shot reconfigurations, Peter and the other Apostles belatedly enter into dialogic space with Jesus. While in the Ministry Pasolini alters Matthew's text (by rearrangement and excision), he does so in order to bring the evangelist's narrative segmentation to the fore and the director lends a strong and flexible cinematic-figural support to its articulation.

Perhaps most striking, however, is Pasolini's handling of the Passion, which is in Matthew composed, like the Infancy, of a set of short episodes, though more complexly linked as a drama. Actually in Matthew, what we have abbreviated as 'the Passion' is really two large segments, as Kingsbury indicates above: the first segment falls between the prophecies of the Passion (which, in the film directly precedes the entry into Jerusalem [Mt 21:1–9]) – through the Last Supper/Garden of Gethsemane (Mt 26:1). The second segment, which is the commonly recognized 'Passion narrative,' starts at the end of Jesus' arrest in the Garden and concludes with his death.

In the gospel the first large segment superficially seems to be a continuation of the Ministry: Jesus is still preaching, giving parables, and talking with the Apostles as before. In Matthew's second Passion segment, however, Jesus is alone and speaks very little, and never in discourses. The pace of the later episodes (the two trials, Judas' despair and death, etc.) accelerates until the Crucifixion and Resurrection. However, textually, the character of the preaching and of the parables changes in Matthew once Jesus enters Jerusalem. Jesus now confronts the Pharisees much more often; he prophesies the fall of Jerusalem and the

apocalypse, and speaks of his own death in parables. Matthew emphasizes the failure of the people and the leaders to believe for, although
the crowds see Jesus as a great prophet, they do not grasp he is the
Messiah (as the Apostles do) and their leaders now ask him only trick
questions and plot against him. These are textual rather than narrational shifts, and Matthew does not alter his method of presentation.
But the filmmaker must.

Pasolini marks these changes – and so segments Matthew – in several
ways. After the entry into Jerusalem, he accelerates his montage, using
high-angle panning long shots intercut with close-ups of Jesus. This
does not so much speed up the narration, however, but dynamizes it:
once Jesus arrives in Jerusalem, the film becomes tense with potential
violence, starting immediately with Jesus driving the money-changers
from the temple. (Indeed, Pasolini shoots the episode in a manner that
answers, in miniature, the violent and disjunctive pans he used for the
Slaughter of the Innocents.) Quite unlike the Ministry sequences, now
there are many shots of crowds in motion, and the confrontations with
the Pharisees are staged in crammed courtyards.

Gradually Pasolini, like Matthew, isolates Jesus as we approach the
Passion itself: markedly with the Fig Tree parable, which begins with
shots of the sleeping Apostles and then wordless close-ups of Jesus
alone, and then his violent prophecy. The Last Supper, which is all
close-ups, emphasizes Judas' betrayal and Jesus' desertion more than
the Eucharist itself. Finally, the Gethsemane episode, where Pasolini at
last resorts to dissolves, distends Jesus' lonely and anguished prayer to
his Father. Pasolini cinematically forms these episodes into an arc toward
a final isolation, deftly conforming his filmic segmentation to successive
emphases of Matthew's text: confrontations followed by isolation.

In contrast, after the capture in Gethsemane – during the trials, the
march to Calvary, and the Crucifixion – which Matthew narrates swiftly
and laconically, Pasolini's camera withdraws into long-shot distance
from Jesus, redolent of television-news shooting. Moreover, he further
distances Jesus during the trials by introducing point-of-view mediators
of the wide-angle spectacle through reverse angles to Judas and Peter
seen in close-up (counterpointing the betrayer of Jesus and the Apostle
who denies him). Finally, he cuts regularly to Mary, who mediates the
Crucifixion and Resurrection scenes, so resuming and developing her
role begun earlier in the 'dismissal of the relations' sequence.

Rarely does Pasolini return to close-ups of Jesus; even when the
opportunity of dialogue offers itself, as in the first trial, Jesus' voice is

heard in long-shot. This narrational visualization conforms to Matthew, who, during the first sections of the Passion, draws closer to Jesus – as eschatological preacher, then as Son addressing his Father – and then later withdraws from him for the final steps of the Passion. Pasolini also shapes the narrational structure of his film to the dynamic of narrational distance and pace. There is one important exception. Where Matthew accelerates the last parts of the Passion, Pasolini slows his cutting – his frequent long shots are also long takes – and, by narrative elaboration, distends the drama of Judas' suicidal despair, the anecdote of Peter's betrayal, and Mary's anguish at the Crucifixion.

Pasolini characterizes Matthew as an 'epic' and claims his film is as well. The point of my discussion of segmenting Matthew is that the question is: How to narrate in film what Matthew can narrate in language. Kingsbury notes that Matthew's narration is 'third-person,' omniscient and omnipresent,[36] but it must also be noted, from a cinematic perspective, that Matthew cues focalization minimally. Matthew's narration has a 'point-of-view' in the usual sense, but it does not clearly position the narrator visually in relation to the scenes, which is what cinematic point-of-view must do. Like his elipticality and rhythmic variety, this is another effect of the evangelist's laconism, and his difference from a modern novelist. It presents the gravest problems for a filmmaker in that he or she must choose how to narrate visually while also being burdened with cinematic codes (that of the close-up, for example) that are at once conventional connotators of a novelistic psychology as well as indispensable tools of narrative denotation.

Pasolini's response is to develop a 'mixed style' for *Il Vangelo*, a style he also termed 'epic.' It is an 'epic style' in that compression, ellipsis, and distension alternate in accord with a principle that Pasolini sometimes terms 'absolute' representation, distinguishing it from naturalistic verisimilitude. Sergei Eisenstein is the great master of this epic style in cinema and he associates it with a process of eliminating the intervals between, and distensions of, significant moments.[37] In *Il Vangelo*, which alludes to Eisenstein more than once,[38] Pasolini's elimination of the interval – specifically, fades, dissolves, establishing and medium shots, reverse-angle counter-shots, etc. – is everywhere visible as the key strategy of his editing patterns, as is the emphatic use of ellipsis and systematic suppression of classical cinematic continuities. On one hand, eliminating the interval allows Pasolini to cut to the essential image – in *Il Vangelo* characteristically the frontal close-up – crucial to his 'absolute' style and so escape psychological connotation. On the other hand, ellipsis and distension allow him to segment Matthew and conform to the evangelist's 'epic' narrational system.

However, the epic nature of the gospel is not just narrational and stylistic; textually, Matthew writes under a determining assumption about what is to be understood as 'epic.' Matthew's epic of time, or history, is recorded in the Hebrew scriptures and that is why virtually every episode in the Infancy and in the Passion is sealed with a formula (which also serves as a narrational coda/transition) that pronounces the episode to be a 'fulfilment of scriptures' through direct citation of scriptural precedent. It is this intertextual formulation of the gospel that provides episodes with epic significance. In the main, Pasolini eliminates these formulas, though in instances they are spoken – by the angel, by John, by Jesus himself, and by a voice-over – and, at the end of the Crucifixion, over black leader. Nonetheless, they no longer possess the quality of a refrain, and the epic significance of the gospel is textually attenuated.

This has a pointed relevance to the 'violence' of Jesus in *Il Vangelo* that Pasolini is so taken with. As mentioned above, critics have complained about the solitude of Jesus, implying Pasolini failed to show his solidarity with the people. Pasolini in turn has repeatedly remarked on the violence of Jesus and suggested that this violence is revolutionary.[39] The criticism and the director's testimony belong together. In Matthew, once Jesus is born, and Jesus has spoken, something ends and something new is being born; the violent imagery that runs through so much of the preaching and the parables derives from the epic structure of Jesus' mission, which is eschatological. Pasolini misses much of the textual, and intertexual, sense in his treatment of the Infancy especially. However, the narrative pattern of what should be understood as epic-violence that marks this process in Matthew is retained as a structural pattern: the birth and recognition by the Magi are followed directly by the Slaughter of the Innocents; Pasolini cuts sharply from John's prophecy of the fire that will consume the chaff to the first close-up of the adult Jesus; John's recognition that Jesus is the One, which occurs again later, is followed by his murder; and Jesus' fullest self-proclamation concludes his Ministry and is woven with prophecies of his death; in the Passion, finally, his prophecies of the destruction of Jerusalem conclude at his death with an earthquake that rends Jerusalem (and Pasolini introjects a montage of same), proleptic of the apocalypse.

Pasolini's segmentation of Matthew pulls these epic-violent patterns into high relief by building both on contrasts – in the Infancy, the Holy Family/the Innocents – and counterpoints – John/Jesus, even inventing a scene for John to keep him present in the film. John in particular, as the last prophet, in Matthew is the image of a double, or eschatological, temporality, and Pasolini goes to great trouble to represent this pattern. But that sense is everywhere carried in the gospel by expressions like 'these days' and 'this generation,' uttered by Jesus and Matthew's narrator alike. In some contrast to Luke and John, Matthew uses formulas of condemnation and threat, which lend Jesus' preaching its violently confrontational tone. Pasolini's staging of the preaching carries that tone not only through Enrique Irazoqui's severe performance as Jesus but through framing and cutting: one result of the 'absolute' style is it never allows Jesus to seem conversational. His preaching is visualized as the incommensurable confrontation between the Messiah and his listeners. This is not a dialogue, but an absolute speaking, something Pasolini's use of frontal close-ups makes emphatic.[40] During the Passion segment, that confrontation becomes violent in both tone and text: the people are now a mob seen around Jesus, and the leaders framed in massed trios, face-to-face with him; the cutting is tense and sharp.

The solitude of Jesus in *Il Vangelo* is not the solitude of the 'alienated intellectual' as some critics have suggested, imagining the film to be an attempted modernization of the gospel, but a consequence of Pasolini's narrational and stylistic tactics seeking cinematic equivalents to the gospel. Matthew's text is not modern, but both ancient and eschatological in its violence and absolute character – and for Pasolini that very likely was its appeal, compelling his 'irrational' decision to film a gospel.

Advent of the Theoretical Stranger – A Note on *Teorema*

In one interview, when asked, Pasolini expressly denies that *Teorema*'s mysterious visitor relates to the Christ of *Il Vangelo*. 'The character cannot be identified with Christ; rather with God, God the Father (or a messenger who represents the Father). It is an Old Testament, not a New Testament visitor.'[41] Elsewhere he says of the stranger,

Originally, I intended the visitor to be a fertility god, the typical god of pre-industrial religion, the sun-god, the Biblical god, God the Father. Naturally, when confronted with things as they were, I had to abandon my original idea and so I made Terence Stamp [who plays the stranger] into a generically ultra-terrestrial and metaphysical apparition: he could be the Devil, or a mixture of God and the Devil. The point is that he is something authentic and unstoppable.[42]

Although the director was planning a life of St. Paul, and drafted a script in 1968,[43] his films in this period were generally more involved with non-Christian mythological materials, as this quotation indicates and his two adaptations of classical plays attest. Yet there is another contrast: his Oedipus and Medea are passionate, even overwrought works while *Teorema* has most often been seen as cold, harsh, theoretical, and even mathematical.[44] Set in the contemporary world, constructed in a symmetrical, even telegraphic programmatic manner, and bearing a title meaning 'theorem,' the film is the converse of its companions in this period.

The claims of precisionism, mathematical or otherwise, however, are somewhat exaggerated. Although Pasolini does obsessively unfurl a programmatic structure, it is limited formally to narrative organization. There are three prologues: the first is a pre-credit sequence that proves to be proleptic (workers have been given ownership of their factory, shot in verité style); following the credits is the second, enigmatic prologue (a long-take pan over a barren wilderness, with a supertitle from Exodus 13:18; bits of this footage are inserted at intervals throughout the film). The third prologue is expository, a silent montage of members of the Milanese family seen in black and white going about their daily business. Then a messenger arrives and delivers a telegram read during the affluent family's dinner which says the visitor will arrive tomorrow. He does, at a party in progress, where he is identified just as 'a boy.'

The first long segment follows immediately and moves through the sexual encounters the visitor has with each of the family members: the maid Emilia, the son Pietro, the mother Lucia, the daughter Odetta, and the father Paolo. Then, at another matching dinner scene, a new telegram arrives and the visitor announces his imminent departure. In a series of briefer scenes, each member of the family comes to him in private and confesses he has transformed them and that they do not know what they will do after he is gone. After the visitor leaves, a second long segment begins in which each of them undergoes a cataclysmic change: the maid returns to her village and becomes a folk-mystic; the daughter falls into a rigid trance and is hospitalized; the son becomes a painter; the mother goes about town picking up adolescent boys; the father strips in the train station and wanders naked across the bleak waste seen in the second prologue.

Expressed in a brief narrative synopsis, the program of the film seems emphatic and precise. But on slightly closer inspection, *Teorema* is not as strictly organized as it first seems. Once we get past the tripartite, regimented succession of seductions, confessions, and after-effects – and the fact that virtually nothing else happens – and we begin to move inside the film's narrative segments, they reveal themselves to be unevenly distributed. The seduction of the daughter is folded into the seduction of the father and both are dispersed over several sequences, while the encounters with the maid and the mother are short, self-contained, and undeveloped. The son and the stranger become friends as well as lovers, and, at one point, they join a group of boys for some sort of outing. Emilia's mysticism is developed over the whole third segment through parallel montage, and the son's decay is elaborated over three sequences. But the father's, mother's, and daughter's transformations are shown in blocked sections.

There are many suggestive episode-rhymes: Odetta's trance sends her to the hospital, while, in the next scene, Emilia's trance leads to the miraculous cure of a child. As the mother and father disintegrate psychically, they desert the family home but the children burrow deeper inside it. These contrastive rhymes and correlates do not, however, reinforce the initial programmatic impression of *Teorema*, nor do they form a consistent second or subordinate system. Finally, while the film's tripartite narrative segmentation is programmatic, and some passages are deliberately stylized, Pasolini's stylistic strategy is actually less systematic than it is in *Il Vangelo*, *Edipo Re*, or *Medea*. Some episodes are strongly iconic (Lucia's seduction, Odetta's trance, Emilia's ascension); others are loosely constructed anecdotes (Pietro's seduction, Lucia's pick-up spree, Paolo's sessions by the river). Indeed, it is really only on the anecdotal level – who, what, and in what order – and not in the way the narrative is articulated cinematically that *Teorema* seems a precisionist work.

The point is that we should not seek the textual mystery of *Teorema* in its formalism. In fact, the form of the film only makes signification in *Teorema* blunter and more obvious. Its narrative structure reduces one kind of narrativity into demonstrating a significance that rests upon a theoretical system. As a preliminary, this system may be described as a reductive de-individuation of characters. Although *Teorema* has a contemporary setting, it effaces naturalism and psychology; or more exactly, it effaces the novelistic psychological interpretation of the modern middle class. The novelistic mode is virtually irresistible to conventional cinema, and especially to the European art film. However, Noel Purdon rightly refers to the process of reduction as Pasolini's condensation of characters to 'psychiatric case history.'[45] On slightly adjusted reading, we might add that *Teorema* cruelly parodies novelistic psychological narration by allegorizing it as psychiatric case history.

As much as he deploys parody, Pasolini also deploys a classic allegory,[46] which by its nature is reductive: allegory creates a program of characters and images/episodes in accord with a doctrinal system. In traditional Christian allegory, like *Pilgrim's Progress*, the characters even bear doctrinal names and their character 'traits' are highly reduced, even singular. In *Teorema*, character psychology is reductive in a similar way. In the erotic presence of the stranger, the family members' transformations are all reductions to a simple state of desire. When he leaves, desire transmutes into a collapse of the self, a regression to a pre-ego state. The daughter falls into a rigid psychosis; the son's painting decays into fecal play (he pisses on his paintings); the mother's promiscuity is coded as an obsessive repetition; the naked father traverses a black, voidlike landscape. As for the exception, Emilia, we will have to come back to her, though she regresses as well, to selfless mysticism.

In comparison with the mode of the psychology of modern novelistic cinema, in *Teorema*, character, then, is diminished to a single and, as Purdon says, psychiatric condition. This process of diminishment – to desire, then collapse – is what drives the film's narrative structural program. This is also how the film functions as an allegory, working out a parody of novelistic character psychology by reducing it to doctrine, or better, to theory. Also, nothing else happens in the film. Its social texture is a bland and indifferent nullity. The political significance of *Teorema*'s diegesis is evacuated in advance, into the first (the newsreel-factory) prologue. When someone asks during the bustle of that sequence if the bourgeois are not absorbing everyone into their class, the remark keys the parody politically as Pasolini's ideological nightmare – that the bourgeois world is becoming the whole world.[47] After the prologue, the film's airless diegesis is emblematic of that whole world.

The rigid tripartite structure – of the seductions, confessions, and catastrophic transformations – and the coming and going by the stranger that motivate it bear more striking homologies with the 'violence of Jesus' and the structural eschatology of *Il Vangelo* than they do with the other films of what Greene calls 'the mythic quartet.'[48] In Matthew's 'epic,' there is the time of the Law (the Infancy), the time of the Ministry, and the time of Passion, with its prophecies of the apocalypse. As we have seen above, Pasolini discerned and registered this eschatology in the narrational segmentations of his adaptation of Matthew. In *Teorema*, he again registers it, as a homology of programmatic tripartition of the film's narrative movements. There are also several blunt cues: the telegrams are delivered by an 'Angelino' who flaps his arms as he dances across the courtyard. Pasolini's includes a verse from Exodus 13 over the second prologue: 'God led the people about, through the way of the wilderness.' And fragments of that passage, images of a black wasteland, appear as a refrain through the film. As discussed above, Matthew uses angels to announce the advent of Christ, and Matthew also places citations from the Hebrew scriptures as formulas at the end of many episodes of the gospel, to fix their eschatological significance. Pasolini imitates the evangelist here, not necessarily suggesting that the film is an gospel allegory, but that *Teorema*'s structural template is the triplex segmentation of the gospel.

If taken as a reductionist allegory mapped on the gospel, the rigid structure of *Teorema* could be described as: the bourgeois dispensation or law; the stranger's erotic ministry/the confessions of the family; the bourgeois apocalypse. The first dispensation is characterized by the laws of repression – laws against incest, homosexuality, and promiscuity – that sustain the order of a class and the order of 'personality' as well. Paradoxically, selfhood under this law is at once denied and sustained by these laws of repression. The stranger smashes these laws, ending the daughter's attachment to her father, the son's and father's heterosexuality, the mother's chastity, and they then confess to their new, 'authentic,' but unsustainable identities or selves.

Repressive modern laws of the self in *Teorema* are not identifiable with the Law of Moses that Jesus fulfilled/abolished in the new Christian dispensation. The film is not 'historical' in that sense but 'theoretical.' The laws of the bourgeoisie that govern this film are produced by Pasolini's reductive, faux-psychiatric discourse. The stranger is not Christ but a 'theoretical redeemer.' Yet, these laws function in a homology with Law in Matthew: they define and structure social ego identities; when they are destroyed, so is the self. Jesus prophesies the destruction of Jerusalem as a sign of the Kingdom, and promises that he who will lose his life will gain it. In *Teorema* the confessions the characters offer to the stranger are at once parodies of professions of faith – faith in the stranger who has revealed their inner selves. But the dilemma of desire will finally spell madness, the loss of the self. The confessions, which are also the only protracted dialogue passages in *Teorema*, are elaborate parodies of novelistic-spiritual confessions of the sort that European, and especially Ingmar Bergman's, films made the serious 'spiritual' argot of sixties cinema.

After their erotic-parodic 'conversions' to the visitor, the new dispensation becomes a vicious type of desublimation. Pasolini's cruellest parody occurs in the long bourgeois apocalypse of part three, after the visitor's departure. With the removal of the repressive laws, and the withdrawal of the stranger – 'the authentic' figure of 'divine love' says Pasolini – each member of the family loses him/herself but, by doing so, does not gain an authentic self. The visitor's desertion leaves them alone with his and her defining 'spiritual' problem, but figured as a psychiatric reduction: each of them is reduced to a 'case.' Several critics have read the third part of the film as attempts to regain something of the visitor. The son paints, starting with portraits of the stranger; the mother picks up boys who vaguely resemble him. Taken as a psychiatric parody of the Catholic sacramental real-presencing of Christ, these attempts, and Odetta's psychotic trance and the father's wandering in the desert, could likewise be seen as parodies of the mystical loss of self into the One who has gone.

The One who comes and goes, but who changes everything is not necessarily a Christological figure, as Pasolini says. He has only the violence of Jesus, and the visitor's mission is counter-redemptive, his preaching is a 'theory,' and, unlike Christ's, his ministry produces merely miracles and damnation. Here figured as a gentle, actually somewhat distracted sexuality, the stranger's violence is ironized because it is really violence only against the bourgeois self constructed by repression. It is, then, an allegorical violence, not a Christological-epic violence. Its force lies in its constructed theoretical meaning, the faux-psychiatry on which Pasolini constructs his cruelly reductive cases. Indeed, it is a theoretical stranger whose advent into the family and whose vague and abstract sexual acts, hypothetical chimera of the text, *Teorema* narrates so rigidly as to their effects.

There is, nonetheless, the surplus of *Teorema*, Emilia, the maid who is transformed into a folk-mystic. The usual and appropriately schematic (if also sentimental) reading of her transformation is that Pasolini regards the peasantry positively but despises the bourgeois. But what to make of her sexual encounter with the stranger? Pasolini treats it like a weird Chaplin film, in which Emilia runs around the garden several times while the stranger sits reading Rimbaud. She then goes into the kitchen and, after staring in the mirror, attempts suicide by sticking a gas hose in her mouth. (The grim earnestness of Laura Betti as Emilia makes this a decidedly joyless frolic.) The stranger intervenes and ends this absurd comedy to make love to her. Emilia never speaks to him – there is no confession – and leaves immediately after he does. She then traces out an *imitatio Christi* of fasting, mission (the cure of the child), transfiguration (her ascension), and the tomb (which is not a final death). Clearly, Emilia lives within a different law, a different selfhood, and without benefit of Pasolini's theory, before and after the encounter. When she loses herself, she alone finds herself, to be recognized by the villagers both as Emilia and as a saint. Pasolini leaves her enigma open, but it is also classical as an *imitatio*, while he systematically nails down the 'meaning' of the other characters, whose case histories form a predicatable theoretical arc. He makes a point of this by cutting from key moments in Emilia's transformation to each of theirs – Emilia's tale hovers over almost all of the third segment – and suggests that, for her, the 'violence' of Jesus actually has come in the form of the theoretical stranger. For Emilia, he is not the theoretical stranger, but God, although a sexual, and so a heretical (more precisely, a Gnostic) God.

Notes

1 For example, see Geoffrey Nowell-Smith, 'Pasolini's Originality,' in *Pier Paolo Pasolini*, ed. Paul Willemen (London: The British Film Institute, 1977), 11. Referring to *Il Vangelo* and *Uccellacci e uccellini*, Nowell-Smith remarks, 'Since these were the films that earned him the dubious title of Catholic Marxist, it is worth saying something briefly about them – although, in light of his subsequent development, they are undoubtedly less important than they seemed at the time.' In some contrast to Nowell-Smith, however, also see Zygmunt G. Barański's 'The Texts of *Il Vangelo secondo Matteo*,' *The Italianist*, No. 5 (1985), 77–106. Barański's main point in this meticulously researched article is that *Il Vangelo* is a very much a 'Pasolinian' text.

2 See Peter Bondanella's discussion of *Accattone* in his *Italian Cinema: From Neorealism to the Present* (New York: Frederick Ungar, 1985), 180–2. See also P. Adams Sitney's essay in the present volume.

3 For a discussion of the film that takes this fully into account, see Naomi Greene, *Pier Paolo Pasolini: Cinema as Heresy* (Princeton: Princeton University Press, 1990), 80–9 .

4 Pasolini's essay 'Cinema of Poetry,' which initiated his activity as a film theorist, was published in 1965, the year following release of *Il Vangelo*.

5 See Millicent Marcus, *Italian Cinema in Light of Neorealism* (Princeton: Princeton University Press, 1986), 245–62.

6 Cited in ibid., 73.

7 I should explain the distinction. A 'Life of Christ' is always a novelization, a story in which Jesus is the protagonist and his life story told as if it were a fiction. Even when the author, like a Jim Bishop, who wrote *The Day Christ Died*, strives for complete historical veracity – rather than, say, piety, or to reshape the story for children – the resulting text is not the same in its form or narrational means as any of the four gospels. The distinction is basic to modern scripture scholarship.

8 It also happens to be the case that Jesus movies were the first feature-length films made, arising in the so-called primitive period before 1907. For detailed accounts of representations of Jesus in early cinema, see Roland Cosandey et al., eds., *Un invention du diable? Cinéma des premiers temps et religion* (Sainte-Foy, Québec: Les Presses de l'Université Laval, 1992).

9 See Theodore Ziolkowski, *Fictional Transfigurations of Jesus* (Princeton: Princeton University Press, 1972), 124–33 for a discussion of Kazantzakis.

10 André Bazin, *What Is Cinema?* vol. 1 (Berkeley: University of California Press, 1971), 53–4

11 Cited in Naomi Greene, *Pier Paolo Pasolini: Cinema as Heresy*, 70.

12 Pasolini quickly lays out this 'history' quickly in the course of his interview with Oswald Stack concerning *Il Vangelo* in *Pasolini on Pasolini: Interviews with Oswald Stack* (London: Thames and Hudson/British Film Institute, 1969), 79–81. The pertinent passage is: '*Officina* provided the first critical revision of a rationalist kind of neo-realism and of the whole of Italian literature, naturally in a fairly sporadic and fragmentary way. This rationalism had marxist origins, but with heterodox tendencies, and although it had marxist origins it was very much in polemic with the Communist Party.'

13 Cited in Greene, *Cinema as Heresy*, 70.

14 Cited in ibid., 71.

15 Cited in ibid., 72.

16 The anecdote Pasolini tells is that he came upon St. Matthew's gospel quite by accident when stranded in a traffic jam in Assisi during a visit

by Pope John XXIII. His reading so enthused him that he felt compelled to 'do something.' Pasolini tells this anecdote in *Pier Paolo Pasolini – A Future Life*, edited by Laura Betti and Lodovico Gambara Thovazzi (Rome: Associazione Fondo Pier Paolo Pasolini, 1989), 63. Also see 'Interview with Gunnar D. Kumlien' in *Commonweal* 82 (July 1965), 471–2.

17 Cited in Greene, *Cinema as Heresy*, 74.

18 Cited in ibid., 73.

19 See ibid., 77–80 for Greene's careful summary of what she takes to be the enduring criticisms of the film. But see Pasolini's remarks to Stack, *Pasolini on Pasolini*, 77. Greene's excerption of the director's remarks cited here suggest a repudiation of the film. However, Pasolini makes them to contrast *Il Vangelo* as a 'terrible work' with a 'Catholic work' it only superficially resembles. A few sentences later, Pasolini renews his Gramscian claim, 'so making The Gospel was to reach the maximum of the mythic and the epic' while also embracing the film as his own: 'But internally nothing I've ever done has been more fitted to me myself than The Gospel.'

20 It is beyond the scope of this paper to dispute critics who question the 'Gramscian sense' of *Il Vangelo*. However, it should be obvious that Pasolini takes this sense to refer to the text itself, its 'epic' composition and historical role as 'popular mythology.' Pasolini is not interested in the politics of the Roman Empire or a modern historical reading of Jesus as an ancient revolutionary.

21 See Meyer Shapiro, *Words and Pictures: On the Literal and the Symbolic in the Illustration of a Text* (The Hague: Mouton, 1973) for an art-historical semiotic study of this process that takes a text from Exodus as an example. Also see Leo Steinberg's *The Sexuality of Christ in Renaissance Art and Modern Oblivion*, *October* 25 (Summer 1983) for a close study of the process with respect to selected motifs of the depiction of Christ in a particular period. In the silent Italian cinema, there is an exemplary instance of such an iconographic 'Jesus film,' Giulio Antamoro's *Christus* (1915).

22 Stack, *Pasolini on Pasolini*, 91

23 *Pier Paolo Pasolini: A Future Life*, 64. Pasolini says, 'When I began to shoot *Il Vangelo*, I believed I had a ready formula for it, i.e., my way of filming, my idea of sacred technique ... I began to shoot and I did some horrendous, awful, intolerable things ... And the reason is clear. To perform *Il Vangelo* according to sacred, stately, religious technique was carrying coals to Newcastle ... And therefore in a few days, and after a few sleepless nights, I was forced to revolutionize my technique, and I changed it to a completely different one, the so-called magma technique. That is to say,

instead of having symmetry in frames as my main objective, or using short precision tracking shots, or pans, etc. as I had done in *Accattone*, I really did change everything.

'I used the strangest lens, I put different close-ups together, one with a 25 mm and another with a 100 mm and I used a zoom opened up to its limit, like one does for bicycle races, and I used it to show the Apostles following behind Christ. Namely, an absolutely chaotic technique due to a moment of anger, to such an extent that I ended up filming the two trials of Christ, the one by Pilate, and the other by Caiaphas, in cinéma-verité.'

24 See Bondanella, *Italian Cinema*, 182, for a short discussion of the 'mixed style' of *Il Vangelo*.

25 In what follows I will be drawing on two of Kingsbury's studies of Matthew, *Matthew: Structure, Christology, Kingdom* (Philadelphia: Fortress Press, 1975) and *Matthew as Story* (Philadelphia: Fortress Press, 1986). The methodological context for Kingsbury's work, which is based in narrative analysis, has been extensively described in Stephen D. Moore, *Literary Criticism and the Gospels: The Theoretical Challenge* (New Haven: Yale University Press, 1989), esp. 3–55.

26 Kingsbury, *Matthew: Structure, Christology*, Kingdom, 36

27 In *Matthew as Story*, Kinsbury further develops this analysis, devoting a chapter to each of the three sections of the gospel. See 41–93.

28 There are exceptions. In the Infancy, when Joseph returns to Mary after the apparition of the angel, a voice-over accompanies him, replicating Matthew. Similarly, a voice-over and a fade out concludes the 'Slaughter of the Innocents' and Jesus's Baptism, both taken directly from Matthew. In the Passion section, at the end of the Crucifixion, a span of black leader is seen with a voice-over quotation from Isaiah, which Pasolini interpolated into the text. Further exceptions are noted below.

29 This invention is a close visualization of Mt 4:12: 'Hearing that John had been arrested he [Jesus] went back to Galilee.' And the passage John hears in prison is excerpted from Isaiah 8:23-9:1 and in Matthew it appears as 4:15-16.

30 Barański, 'The Texts,' 88, astutely notes in this respect, '[Pasolini] was faced with a major problem. The original text is primarily a collection of Jesus's speeches interspersed with brief moments of activity, for example, the movements from one place to the next and the miracles. Matthew uses action descriptions principally as devices with which to introduce a new set of Christ's sayings.'

31 See Kingsbury, *Matthew as Story*, 57–77, for a much closer segmentation of the Ministry.

32 See Marc Gervais, *Pier Paolo Pasolini* (Paris: Seghers, 1973), 15, for his astute analysis of 'the beginning of a style of confrontation' in the use of close-ups in *Accattone*. I am indebted in this discussion to P. Adams Sitney's discussion of the shot/counter-shot in his *Modernist Montage* (New York: Columbia University Press, 1990), passim.

33 See Barański, 'Texts,' 87–89 and passim. Barański argues that Pasolini creates characters through a 'lingering on details' in the cross-cutting and between Jesus and his followers, and that he amplifies the roles of Judas and Mary well beyond Matthew's gospel. This is doubtless true, but not nearly so to the generalized extent that he claims. Moreover, although his analysis, while touching upon the inevitable necessity of showing specifically whom Jesus is addressing – a detail on which a camera cannot but linger – further leads him to conclude Pasolini is thereby engaged in a radical, though subtle, revision of the gospel through dilated characterization. Barański hinges his argument on Pasolini's dilation of the role of Judas, while in fact more notable is the expansion in the film of the role of John the Baptist, whose imprisonment and death Matthew describes elliptically and to which Pasolini devotes more than one invented scene. This, as I argue, typically in *Il Vangelo*, serves a structural function in segmenting the Ministry. Barański does not discuss the Baptist. Nor does he discuss the role of Peter for whom Judas is a foil in the film's Passion segment. This is suggested by the scriptures, which (as Pasolini does) juxtapose the traitor who despairs and commits suicide with the apostle who loses his courage but retains his 'investiture' and remains the 'rock' of the church.

The most reasonable, if critically modest, explanation of these character expansions, which Barański very persuasively suggests but then rejects, is that Pasolini dilates John, Judas, Peter, and Mary in light of the 'two thousand years' of expansion these figures have enjoyed in Christianity and which the director sought, to some degree, to incorporate into the film. Barański rejects this explanation because he seeks to find in such expansions evidence that 'in structuring the film, Pasolini eliminates Matthew and substitutes himself as a new 'evangelist' and a source of information about Christ.' (87) I prefer a more modest critical explanation. My view is that 'in structuring the film,' these somewhat expanded, somewhat traditionally sanctioned, characterizations, serve primarily narrational functions in Pasolini's strategy of segmenting Matthew.

34 See Barańsky, passim, for a very precise account of these excisions and rearrangements.

35 See Kingsbury, *Matthew as Story*, 10–27, for textual analysis of 'characterization' in the gospel.

36 See Kingsbury, *Matthew as Story*, 30–1.

37 Annette Michelson offers an account of Eisenstein's epic style in 'Camera Lucida/Camera Obscura,' *Artforum* 11, 5 (January 1973), 30–3. Also see Annette Michelson, 'The Wings of Hypothesis, On Montage and the Theory of the Interval,' *Montage and Modern Life, 1919–1942*, ed. Matthew Teitelbaum (Cambridge: MIT Press, 1992), 61–9.

38 The often-cited example is Pasolini's use of Prokofiev's music from *Alexander Nevsky* to accompany the *Slaughter of the Innocents*. But also notable are the recurring triangular groupings of Jesus' followers and, habitually shot from a low angle, the Pharisees, shots which recall Eisenstein's usage from *Battleship Potemkin* through *Que Viva Mexico!* Finally, although Pasolini's use of non-actors seemingly recalls neorealism, his practice in *Il Vangelo*, where very few of the performers are called upon to develop anything but minimal roles or characterizations (in contrast with, say, Rossellini's *Paisan* or De Sica's *Ladri di Biciclette*), is far more redolent of typage, the use of non-actors for their appearance, perfected by Eisenstein in *Potemkin*.

39 Pasolini: '"I have not come to bring Peace but a sword." This is the key by which I conceived the film. This is what drove me to make it.' *Pier Paolo Pasolini – A Future Life*, 63. However, see Barańsky, 'Texts,' 95–8, for a discussion of Pasolini's wavering on how Christ was to be represented.

40 Although Pasolini was likely unaware of this – or does not mention it – these frontal compositions participate in an historic code in Western visual art. According to Meyer Shapiro, *Words and Pictures: On the Literal and the Symbolic in the Illustration of a Text* (The Hague: Mouton, 1973), the frontal code is precisely that of confrontation, as opposed to the profile and three-quarter view, the code of participation. It is this pictorial coding I believe that helps Pasolini to override the codes of psychology of the close-up generally true of narrative film.

41 Stack, *Pasolini on Pasolini*, 162

42 Ibid., 156–7. The first quotation comes from an interview with Lino Peroni in 1968; the second from an undated BBC interview. Both are reproduced as appendices in Stack.

43 See Pasolini's *San Paolo*. Also see Walter Siti's discussion of the project in this volume, and also Stack, *Pasolini on Pasolini*, 95. This project is in itself suggestive with respect to *Teorema*, since St. Paul was struck down from his horse and made blind by God while on the road to Damascus to persecute the early church. Paul's conversion is the classic Christian

symbol of irresistible grace, which comes to the unregenerate sinner with cataclysmic force.

44 See, for example, Marcus, *Italian Film in the Light of Neorealism*, 248–9; also see Noel Purdon, 'Pasolini: The Film of Alienation,' in *Pier Paolo Pasolini*, ed. Paul Willemen (London: The British Film Institute, 1977), 46–7: 'But the most coherently followed model is that of geometry, albeit geometry adapted and refined for purposes of psychological reasoning.'

45 Ibid., 46

46 See Greene, *Cinema as Heresy*, 139–42, for a suggestive discussion of allegory in Pasolini. However, my analysis does not follow hers here.

47 See Stack, *Pasolini on Pasolini*, 157: 'The sort of indignation and anger against the classical bourgeoisie ... no longer has a rationale because the bourgeoisie is undergoing revolutionary change: it is assimilating everybody to the petit bourgeoisie: the whole of mankind is becoming petit bourgeoisie.'

48 Greene, *Cinema as Heresy*, 127ff

Stylistic Contamination in the *Trilogia della vita*: The Case of *Il fiore delle mille e una notte*

PATRICK RUMBLE

> The *Arabian Nights* are a narrative model ... Unlimited narration. One thing after the other, and one inside the other, to infinity.[1]

Although colourful, erotic, lively, and a pleasure to watch, Pier Paolo Pasolini's adaptations of three classic medieval 'proto-novels,' *The Decameron*, *Canterbury Tales*, and *The Arabian Nights*, comprising the *Trilogia della vita*, were, Pasolini said, 'the most ideological films I have ever made.' In this analysis of the trilogy, Patrick Rumble argues that we should not look to their surfaces but into their depths, which Pasolini understood to be the level of narrative structures and visual strategies where we will find 'homologies' with social and economic structures. Rumble focuses on the third film of the *Trilogia* along two vectors: Pasolini's use of embedded tales that play between the container and the contained in such a way as to question our modes of conceiving history; and Pasolini's 'contamination' of the ideologically freighted visual style of classical cinema (descendent of Renaissance perspective) with the visual codes of Oriental miniatures, in effect creating an 'alien language' within the dominant one. Rumble routes his detailed analysis back into Pasolini's literary and film theories to indicate how the *Trilogia* continues and enriches Pasolini's long, enduring political theory of culture.

Pier Paolo Pasolini's *Il fiore delle mille e una notte* (*Arabian Nights*) was released in 1974, and forms the third 'chapter,' following after the *Decameron* (1971) and *I racconti di Canterbury* (*Canterbury Tales* [1972]), of the *Trilogy of Life*. Much like the first two films of the *Trilogia*, in which Pasolini draws material from the medieval works of Boccaccio and Chaucer, *Il fiore* presents an adaptation of an important episodic model of storytelling (all three of the films of the *Trilogia* share the episodic structure of the original texts). For Pasolini, the *Arabian Nights* in particular offers a model of 'unlimited narration' or *il narrare illimitato*. But while he insists, in an interview with Gideon Bachman, that he made the *Trilogia* 'for the sheer joy of telling and recounting' (in Lawton 1981, 204), he suggests at the same time that

> the films of the *Trilogia della vita* are the most ideological films I have ever made. Certainly *Il fiore delle mille e una notte* is not, quite obviously, a topical and directly ideological film like *Uccellacci e uccellini* or *Accattone*. Its ideology is hidden deep below the surface. It is brought out not by what is explicitly said, but by representation. (Pasolini, *A Future Life*, 171)

Therefore, what interests us here is to describe some of the ways this ideologically engaged film is brought out from below the enjoyable surface of the *Trilogia*, to account for what we might call the 'ideological pleasure' of Pasolini's films, while focusing on *Il fiore* in particular. What I will argue is that for Pasolini, narrative structures and visual strategies offer an image of social structures. In *Empirismo eretico* he develops a theory of a homology, or structural parallel, between models of storytelling and models of social and economic aggregation, and thus reveals an ethical dimension of style.

Pasolini gains his homological understanding of the novel – that is, his understanding of how the linguistic or stylistic structure of the novel offered insights into analogical structures of conviviality as well as epistemological paradigms – from his studies of Lucien Goldmann carried out in the early 1960s. While Pasolini criticizes Goldmann for being too *contenutistico* (or 'content-oriented'), and not being sensitive enough to questions of style, he does adopt Goldmann's general structural approach (see Pasolini, *Empirismo eretico*, 126–47; Goldmann 1964). This approach underpins his attitude toward the 'proto-novels' he will adapt in the *Trilogia*.

As I will conclude, the pleasure of the *Trilogia* is never divorced from an awareness of ideology, an awareness brought about through stylistic experimentation. Pasolini attempts to bring his spectators, collectively, to 'recognize the experiences from which the deduction of the norm is born' (Pasolini, *Empirismo eretico*, 85). For Pasolini, styles of narration are always experienced as allegories of society. Finally, I will argue that Pasolini's *Il fiore* is an example of his 'genealogical' cinema, designed to reveal the historical nature of visual regimes, and to gesture toward new ones. He accomplishes this through disjunctive narrative structuration and through an experimentation with diverse styles of figuration, often bringing mutually incompatible visual codes into contact. In the process, Pasolini's films subvert the models of subjectivity presumed by conventional cinematic codes, provoking a perceptual disorientation in a spectator forced to become an active participant in, indeed a 'co-author' of, the narration.

Structural Contagion: Embedded Tales

As Naomi Greene (1990) points out, nowhere in the *Trilogia* is Pasolini's attraction to *il narrare illimitato*, or 'unlimited narration,' given such free reign (189) as in the *Arabian Nights*. The film offers itself as the prototype of 'pure' narration: that is, of narratives that live off of one another, that are embedded in one another to such an extent that it is often impossible to determine the containing tale from the contained. *Il fiore* will reproduce the image of the self-generating tales of the original text, and yet its expulsion of the original frame-tale, the story of Scheherazade, is a function of Pasolini's refusal to trace a possible outer limit to narration within the film itself. A 'politics' of narrative framing is carried on in this film much as it was in the *Decameron*; however, here there is no unambiguous frame inscribed within the film, as there was in the *Decameron* (where the tales are framed by the stories of Ciappelletto and Giotto's pupil [see Pasolini, 'A quattr'occhi con Pasolini,' 159; and Lawton 1981]) and in *I racconti di Canterbury* (where the motif of Chaucer/Pasolini at his desk serves as the framing device). The only tale that seems to have such a unifying function is that of Zumurrud and Nur ed Din; indeed, the enamoured Nur ed Din's search for his lost Zumurrud takes the form of an extended trajectory gag. Carried along by the momentum of his desire for reunification with his beloved, this character seems to crash through the other tales. Thus, this tale is often embedded in the very stories it embeds, as it were, 'parendo inchiuso da quel ch'elli 'nchiude' ('appearing enclosed by that which he encloses'), to cite a decontextualized Dante (*Paradiso* 30.12).

Narrative Embedding in *Il fiore**
1. *Tale of Zumurrud and Nur ed Din*
    1a. Tale of Harun ar-Rashid
        1aa.Tale of Harun and Zeudi
1. *Zumurrud and Nur ed Din*
    2. Tale of Munis

   1. *Nur ed Din*
   2a. Tale of Tagi: meets Aziz
     2b. Tale of Dunya, her dream, her tela
   2a. Tale of Tagi and Aziz
 2. Munis and *Nur ed Din*
   1. *Nur ed Din*
   2a Tale of Tagi and Aziz
     3. Tale of Aziz, Aziza, Budur
     2b. Dunya's tela
     2. Tale of Munis: beggars
   2a. Tale of Tagi, his desire for Dunya
     2d. Tale of Shahzaman
     2e. Tale of Yunan
   2a. Tale of Tagi: encounter with Dunya
 2. Tale of Munis
   1. *Nur ed Din*
1. Zumurrud and Nur ed Din
(*Primary frame-tale [or elements found therein] are in italics.)

As shown in this chart, the oft-noted Chinese box structure of the film, which Pasolini reproduces in part from the original text – a structure that presents tales within tales (potentially, as Pasolini says, on to infinity) – runs into a possible moment of confusion when the embedding tale, or some objects or characters from that tale, are found to be circulating in one or more of the embedded tales. Examples of this are found, as seen in the chart, when elements of the primary frame-tale find their way into Munis' tale; and there is Dunya's *tela*, which seems to circulate freely; and note the presence of the beggars in both Munis' and Aziz's tales. This contagion between narrative levels poses a threat to the logic of containment, and it denies the possibility of any meta-textual or, one might say, meta-historical perspective, on the margins of all stories, that could survey and account for all those stories. In a sense, history (*storia*) is subverted by stories (*storie*). That is, in this film, elements derived from the narrative's 'origins' – its initial frame, the first story (Nur ed Din and Zumurrud) – erupt within the structures of the other tales that follow, introducing a potentially destabilizing temporal disjunction, and putting into doubt the continuing presence of a founding meta-structure underlying the progress of narration. Indeed, when read in this manner, again as an allegory of textual but also social structuration, *Il fiore* appears to present a parable of a 'self-framing' structure, or a structure framed from the inside, as opposed to a structure whose legitimacy is guaranteed by an externalized, 'ahistorical' (extra-narrative) agency.

Pasolini's allegorical interest in *Le mille e una notte* is also found in the works of the American novelist John Barth, who appears, in this instance, to be of a kindred spirit.[2] Barth, who, like Pasolini, was drawn to the image of unlimited narration found in the *Arabian Nights*, writes in *Chimera* the story of his imagined visits and conversations with Scheherazade and her sister Dunyazadiad. The topics of their talks swing from problems of theme to those of structure. And as Barth writes, the characters 'speculated endlessly on such questions as whether a story might imaginably be framed from inside, as it were, so that the usual relation between container and contained would be reversed and paradoxically reversible – and (for my [the narrator's] benefit, I suppose) *what human state of affairs such an odd construction might usefully figure*' (Barth, *Chimera*, 32, emphasis mine; for a theoretical discussion of embedded tales, see Barth, 'Muse Spare Me'; 'Tales within Tales within Tales,' 218–38; and *The Tidewater Tales*, 639–51). Elsewhere Barth himself will explain the apparent political 'usefulness' of insights gained through the study of embedded structuration. He suggests that the problem of 'tales within tales within tales,' as found in the *Arabian Nights*, puts our 'concept-structures,' and the 'cultural consensus' that frames them, into crisis; that is, he suggests, it problematizes the models of social organization and personal comportment that we attempt to emulate in structuring the stories of our lives ('Tales within Tales,' 221). Barth will also allude to Borges' idea that embedded stories 'appeal to us because they disturb us metaphysically. We are reminded by them, consciously or otherwise, of the next frame out: the fiction of our own lives, of which we are both the authors and the protagonists, and in which our reading of *The 1001 Nights*, say, is a story within a story' (235).

Pasolini's film attempts to bring his spectators to this metaphysical and political-cultural awareness, in ways quite similar to those discussed by Barth. But whereas for Barth the reminder of 'the next frame out' does come to an end, at what he calls God the storyteller (219), Pasolini's image of the *narrare infinito* allows no such delimitation – although it does call attention to how the invocation of God's presence functions. Indeed, the fact that in his film the embedded tales are often 'infected' by properties found in adjacent tales (Nur ed Din's trajectory especially between the frame and Munis' tale, Dunya's painting of the gazelles, the same beggars found in Munis' tale and then in Aziz's tale, as it is told by Tagi, who is a character in Munis' tale, etc. [see chart]) provides not so much an image of textual layers ('Chinese boxes') moving outwards toward God as the ultimately arbitrary frame, but one of a structure that turns in on itself in Moebius strip fashion, so that the enabling 'ground' of the stories (and allegorically, that of our histories) is conceived of as a construct of these very stories. Thus, rather than conform to an idea of Chinese boxes, which may merely function (within certain approaches to this text) as a ploy designed to delay, or worse to *conceal*, the invocation of an ultimately extra-textual or meta-historical limit (what Roland Barthes [1977] once called 'God and his hypostases' [147] or what Barth calls the narrating God), Pasolini's film presents an allegory of an 'eversive,' self-effacing structure where the framing agency (an author, a state, a divinity) that had been held to exist outside of that structure – since its legitimacy and authority were derived from the uncontaminated or 'disinterested' status of this agency – is found to be located firmly within that structure, and thus open to radical alteration. The text everts, like a glove pulled inside out, rendering an image of continual 'frame-replacement.' *Il fiore* thus is an allegory of a text without an author and a society without a state.

Stylistic Contagion: Embedded Pictures

This 'eversive' nature of *Il fiore* is found in the other films of the *Trilogia* as well, and it explains the ironic presence of Pasolini within both the *Decameron* and in *I racconti di Canterbury*. And the *Trilogia* may be read as an allegory of textual and social organization given Pasolini's belief in the homological relation of textual and social ordering, derived from his study of Lucien Goldmann (Pasolini, *Empirismo eretico*, 126–47). However, neither the *Decameron* nor *Canterbury* reproduces the complexity of narrative layering as it is found in *Il fiore*, and neither of them present such contagion between individual tales themselves.

The forces of contamination that can be detected throughout Pasolini's *opera* have produced, in *Il fiore*, an image of structural contagion. However, the forces of pastiche or citation found at the level of style in most of Pasolini's work have not been excluded from this film. Nevertheless, stylistically speaking, *Il fiore* resembles the other films in the *Trilogia* very little insofar as Pasolini's visual sources are no longer the icons and masterpieces of the European tradition (except in his framing of Gaiwan the Thief's crucifixion: it seems Pasolini couldn't resist an allusion to Western representations of the Passion).[3] Rather, in this film Pasolini abandons this tradition, along with the codes peculiar to it, and draws his imagery from the art and architecture of the Orient; and, as Dante Ferretti, Pasolini's scenographer remarks, Pasolini is especially intrigued by the art of Oriental, Indian and Persian miniatures (see Bertini 1979, 191). Not only does Pasolini use Persian and Rajput miniatures as sources for costumes, architecture, decor, and so on, all elements found within the mise en scène, but he will also reproduce, as much as his medium will allow, certain distortions in spatial composition as found in these miniatures.

As Gian Piero Brunetta has noted, such distortion (what he calls a 'figural disorientation' caused by 'the mutation of certain visual codes') is introduced into the film through Pasolini's adoption of Oriental figural models, and it is a sign of an altered address to the film spectator (see Brunetta 1979, 662). The 'mutation' Brunetta describes has its origin in the fact that the miniatures that Pasolini translates to the screen do not conform to the perceptual codes characteristic of Western art since the Renaissance. Persian art does not organize space according to a single, idealized observer whose gaze 'controls' the representation. As John White (1987) observes, generally speaking this art avoids the types of perspectival cues used in Western art since the fifteenth century: receding orthogonals are avoided, as is the Western tendency of foreshortening. The point of view is usually an approximation of a humanly untenable bird's-eye view (68). Thus, the images often appear to suffer from a lack of spatial coherence given the absence of a single coordinating gaze.

Indeed, perceptual distortion (see illustrations) arises with a denial of a Cartesian organization of space. This perceptual code produces a specific response in spectators; it produces real, material effects within the psyches and upon the bodies of those whose vision it defines (see Crary 1992). Any experimentation with the 'play' between perceptual codes at work in cinematic representation entails a denial of the various narrative and formal strategies found in dominant or classical cinema: a denial of cinema as a *reproductive* technology of subjectivation (de Lauretis 1987). Furthermore, the presence of these 'alien' figural models within film, whose lens-system was developed out of post-Renaissance experiments in perspective and optics (see Baudry 1986; Comolli 1990; Corrain 1985), is part of Pasolini's attack upon the hegemonic forms of representation of the West, and ultimately an attack upon the cultural hegemony of the West as it spreads throughout the 'periphery' (in this case, particularly the Third World). As Pasolini himself remarks, in *Il fiore* 'my polemic was against the culture of the dominant Eurocentric class.'[4] And just as Pasolini celebrates the bodies and pleasures available to a pre-capitalist, non-industrialized society in the *Decameron*, in *Il fiore* he celebrates an analogous 'peasant' society, that of the Third World, with which he came to identify more and more in his own life.[5] For Pasolini, it was a society still on the margins of consumer capitalism, where the bodies and imaginaries of the people had yet to be fully 'homologated' by the culture of neocapitalism.[6]

For Pasolini, non-Western societies and traditions exist as cultural hold-outs providing a potential point of resistance to the cultural hegemony of the economic centre. Thus, the Oriental miniatures that he brings to life in his film should be taken as emblematic of this form of cultural resistance. They are 'visual dialects,' as it were, and their presence in the film is analogous to his use of dialects in his other writing and films. As he insists: 'Today dialect provides a means to oppose acculturation. As always, it will be a lost battle.'[7] The use of dialect in his writing is not simply a moment of linguistic resistance. From the beginning, as we can see in his Friulian poems, the choice of dialect also manifests Pasolini's nostalgia for the peasant culture of his childhood Friuli, the primarily agrarian region whose rituals and rhythms of life accompanied his first sexual experiences and made such an indelible impression upon his poetic imagination. The contamination of standard Italian and regional dialects found in his later works, inspired in part by the style of 'plurilinguism' as found in the writing of Pascoli and Gadda, is, in Pasolini's own words, 'characteristic of a collective style' (Pasolini, *Il portico della morte*, 63; translation mine). Moreover, the presence of dialect reveals both a nostalgia for a non-industrial society and non-bourgeois models of sexuality.

Pasolini carries these poetic tendencies over into his films. In *Il fiore* we have an analogous mixture of a 'standard,' classical cinematic language (i.e., the editing procedures of the continuity system) and visual 'sub-languages' functioning within the conventional cinematic code. These 'sub-languages' form an internal contestation of the standardized code they inhabit: Pasolini might call them a 'poetic' contestation of the 'cinema of prose' (the term he used to denote the classical style). The film is an *ibrido linguistico* (or 'linguistic hybrid') which, as Pasolini remarks concerning poetry, 'is always a product of a moral hybrid – I almost said historical hybrid'[8] Just as his early poems in the Friulian dialect formed a linguistic resistance to the standardizing culture of fascism in the early 1940s,[9] the contamination of visual languages characteristic of *Il fiore*, in its mixture of Western and Oriental pictorial models, is a manifestation of an analogous resistance to what he called in his 'angolo visuale' (or 'visual angle') of the conformist or even neo-fascist majority (Pasolini, *Lettere luterane*, 24). Regional dialects and visual subcultures serve as functions of Pasolini's search for counter-traditions and counter-sexualities.

Cinematic Codes and Spectatorship

In *Il fiore*, Pasolini creates an alien language within a dominant language. The narrative presents tales within tales, tales that are at times embedded within what they embed. As we mentioned above, the film (as an allegory of a nearly impossible structuration) comments upon the 'disinterested' framing agencies that are presumed to provide the 'ground' for the stories that combine into histories (the stories of the protagonists within the film and the protagonists watching it). Embedded tales thus present a continual delaying of the invocation of that 'ground' that could provide structural guarantee, and that could provide a principle of unity or identity. That is, embedded tales are an eternal deferral of the exercise of power: Scheherazade's narratives as a technique of delay is prototypical for Pasolini's 'embedded pictures.' The motif of enframing is carried over into the visual material as well. As Pasolini remarked concerning the *il narrare illimitato*, outside the limits of one story there begins another *ad infinitum*. For Borges, this led to an existential or metaphysical dis-ease; for Barth it brought him to contemplate God.

Embedded pictures in *Il fiore* bring one to a similar dis-ease concerning the referential nature of images, and a contemplation of the coded nature of reality itself. The contamination of diverse forms of visual space in the film brings the spectator to contemplate the nature of the organization of real space, and to call into question the agency and interests that oversee the 'composition' of what we might call the lived space of the 'world picture.' According to Marco Vallora, it is Pasolini's 'mannerist' aesthetic that reveals the coded nature of reality: reality as the product of 'layers' of languages, 'embedded' languages, struggling over objects and people. As he writes:

Nature, that is, is already artifice, culture, spectacle; anything elementary or primary no longer exists; all things refer to a preexisting code, art descends into life ... Reality presents itself as art or, better, it is already art; cultivated references are 'natural,' not simply imposed by the poet's own culture.'[10]

Pasolini's theory of cognitive codes, as it is found in *Empirismo eretico*, presents precisely this idea of eternal deferral of any ultimate 'underlying code' or *codice sottostante* (Pasolini, *Empirismo eretico*, 282–3). This is made clearest during his response to Umberto Eco's critique of Pasolini's insistence that the 'Code of Reality' and the 'Code of Cinema' are identical. For Eco, Pasolini's formulations suffer from a methodological 'dilettantism' (a 'semiological naïveté') in its theory of codes that, suggests Eco, reduces cultural facts (the objects of representation) to natural phenomena (283). Eco insists that a semiological theory of codes performs the opposite: it studies the facts of nature in order to reveal them as cultural phenomena (283). This is a rather strange criticism given Pasolini's insistence upon the necessity to render all 'natural' relations to our physical surroundings as cultural relations. In his argument with Eco he insists that 'all of my chaotic pages concerning this problem *tend to bring Semiology towards the definitive culturalization of nature* (I have often repeated that a General Semiology of reality would be a philosophy that interprets reality as a language).'[11] The *Semiologia Generale*, which is Pasolini's form of filmmaking itself, thus refuses to acknowledge any existence of a *codice sottostante* (which he insists Eco presumes, and which is the source of his resistance to Pasolini's formulations), a 'grounding' code that would enable any discourse that refers itself to that underlying code for its authority to assert itself as dogma: 'Non vorrei cioè che avesse nessun valore nessun dogma.'[12] Pasolini's cinema presents itself as a *semiologia generale* (a 'general semiology') that reveals reality as a Language from which subjects and objects (what he calls the *paroles* of the Code) derive their meaning. And the narrative structure and stylistic contamination found in *Il fiore* provide one of the most effective examples of such a radical semiology (put into action in the moment of its reception) that, 'making all of living into a speaking'[13] renders the 'object' a social relation – and therefore open to renegotiation – and the subject available to an altered 'suture.' As Pasolini remarks:

Sometimes I ask myself (without the least anxiety) if by chance this *Trilogia* to which I am giving myself body and soul (like an exile who lives in a marvelous foreign country) is not a form of political disengagement and ... indifference. But I know intimately that my recent works are political precisely because they do not want to be so ... The interruption of meaning is not only more honest, it is more universal than the meaning itself. (Pasolini, *A Future Life*, 153)

Pasolini's theory of codes as developed in *Empirismo eretico* is intended to enable a radical cultural politics: it 'suspends' or 'interrupts' the meanings of things and individuals, and opens them to different articulations (see de Lauretis 1980, Costa 1977, and Wagstaff 1985). In *Il fiore* Pasolini brings two antithetical 'visual spaces' into contact in a hybridized film style that manifests an *ibrido morale* (or 'moral hybrid'). Jacqueline Rose's (1988) discussion of Black filmmaking and visual regimes helps us to understand this moral conundrum as both a necessity and refusal of identification within prescribed psychic and visual regimes. This ambivalence can only be presented by constructing an alien language within the dominant one, or as Rose suggests, through a 'collision' of two forms of visual space: 'It seems that the sexual and political identification, what is both a necessity and a refusal of identification within the available visual and psychic parameters, can only be represented in the two forms of visual space' (125). This collision translates the filmmaker's ambivalence into filmic techniques that 'deconstruct the positionality of the spectator as controller of the field of vision' (125). As we mentioned, Pasolini carries out this form of deconstruction in *Il fiore* through a contamination of two figural traditions, containing two diverse approaches to the viewer. The cinematic 'suture,' built into and presumed by the photographic technology itself, is short-circuited from within by the 'contagious' presence of another figural tradition, another 'visual space,' which tends to subvert that suture and call upon an altered response in the spectator. This 'alien space' in the film is embedded within what Stephen Heath (1981) identifies as the 'Quattrocento space' presumed by the humanist codification of perspective. This code, which provides the ideological conditions and subjective disposition for the technical development of the camera, is the perceptual rule that underpins what Pasolini calls the bourgeois *angolo visuale* or world-view that continues to establish its hegemony. As Francastel writes, during the development of this code of perspective by artists such as Alberti and Brunelleschi,

it was a question for a society in process of total transformation of a space in accordance with its actions and its dreams ... It is men who create the space in which they move and express themselves. Spaces are born and die like societies; they live, they have a history. In the fifteenth century, the human societies of Western Europe organized, in the material and intellectual senses of the term, a space completely different from that of the preceding generations; with their technical superiority, they progressively imposed that space over the planet. (in Heath 1981, 29)

Pasolini's radical interrogation of forms of spectating, or of what we might call his search for a new erotics of spectating, as it is found throughout the *Trilogia*, is clearly what motivates his choice of certain Rajput representations of specifically erotic themes for *Il fiore*: representations that provide an inherent resistance to the imposition of bourgeois space, as described by Francastel. As shown in the illustrations provided, the highly (or even violently) metaphorical representation of Aziz and Budur's love-making, and the rather undefined spatial organization of the frame, present an ideal example of the 'alien' presence of another figural tradition that itself beckons an altered sexual 'language' (as Pasolini would call it). It would appear that Pasolini's source for this representation of Aziz and Budur was the seventeenth-century Rajput miniature as reproduced in the illustrations (although he left no documentation to support this claim). Clearly, for the Western observer, who can merely read the image literally, it seems rather shocking in its violent representation of love-making. Or perhaps the only resonance it contains for us is with the classical theme of sex as a 'hunt' – and in the miniature tradition the comparison of sex to a tiger hunt was a topos. Nevertheless, even at the thematic level, the image calls upon a visual literacy, and a sexual imaginary, that we as Westerners do not share: it is opaque, and this opacity is not lacking in the film's *riscrittura* of this miniature.

The difficulty we encounter as spectators in interpreting this image is also entirely appropriate given its situation within this particular episode. For throughout the tale, Aziz is constantly being baffled by the strange object-language that Budur uses to communicate with Aziz (a language in which banal, recognizable objects are given mysterious significance by an unknown, and apparently female, code) and he is continually running to Aziza for her competence in such language. In the end it appears that the real drama of the story is taking place between Aziza and Budur, with Aziz as the naïve vehicle of their cryptic messages (and his very incompetence in their language will cost him dearly). The difficulties we have as spectators of the scene between Aziz and Budur seem to be Pasolini's way of having us share in Aziz's drama of misreading; and it is an invitation to suspend habitual patterns of reading or reception, just as Aziz does, and consider other possibilities of interpretation.

But besides these thematic difficulties, we can see that something of the original's spatial organization (or 'distortion') has found its way into the film. As can be seen in the original miniature, the artist's abilities in foreshortening seem to us to be rather limited. The image presents at least two conflicting viewpoints, as revealed most clearly by the mats upon which the lovers are resting. The one on the left appears to locate the point of view high above the figures, with the mat existing, logically, on the same plane as the underlying rug. The mat beneath the character on the right, however, is seen from a much lower point of view, apparently very near to the floor, and thus the plane of the mat and the plane of the rug intersect, presenting a geometrical contradiction or distortion. The rug itself is not foreshortened while the figures are, and the resulting lack of any sense of verticality in the wall or horizontality of the floor destroys any possible illusion of depth that could have been provided by the figures themselves. The distortion of the image arises from its lack of a single organizing point of view that would unify the pictorial space and lend it 'firmness.' Its spatial 'incoherence' derives from compositional procedures not ordered according to European codifications of perspective.

Some of this incoherence finds its way into Pasolini's film. Along with the metaphorical and transgressive contents of this image, Pasolini's filmic translation of it captures some of the original's formal inconsistency (although, as we mentioned, the camera-based technology of the film would largely disallow the kind of radical disjunctions in point of view found in the miniature). We can see that the lack of receding orthogonals in the architecture enclosing Aziz and Budur detracts from the image's sense of depth; and the only real indication of such depth is offered by the slight movements and the foreshortening of the figures themselves, who are surrounded in a relatively undefined space of the tent. Relatively speaking, this frame contains an unusually small number of spatial cues that would lend the image an illusion of depth. It is a frame, that is, in which two visual spaces collide: the first derived from another aesthetic tradition, that of the miniature; and the second, the spatial organization imposed by film that is the technical expression of Western codes of vision and spatial organization, the mechanical guarantee of their reproduction. Furthermore this technology shrouds its codic operations within a discourse of naturalistic or realistic reproduction.

The 'alien language' of the Oriental pictorial tradition found within the dominant language of the cinema is deployed by Pasolini precisely to resist this ideology of technical reproduction: it is the presence of a visual subculture that exists as a moment of rupture within the rationalizing hegemony of Western forms of spatial and cultural organization – and a hegemony of a mode of production, insists Pasolini, that is spreading into and colonizing other non-European or Third World traditions and cultures – a mode of production that 'not only produces commodities, but also social relations, humanity.'[14]

Furthermore, as found in Pasolini's use of regional dialects in his writing, these visual subcultures not only form a resistant front to that cultural and economic hegemony (what he calls the new power of 'consumerism'), but also to its moral attitudes toward bodies and sexuality. For Pasolini finds in the erotic miniatures a correlation between (a) an apparent structural incoherence or representational disorder and (b) images of less constrained sexuality. The manner in which these images fail to offer an individualized, privileged point of view is the formal expression of another, perhaps less restrictive, attitude toward sexuality. That is, a certain lack of 'firmness' or rigidity in form seems to translate into a sense of flexibility in matters of pleasure, almost as if the absolute logical fixity of the location of point of view in bourgeois art somehow was a correlate of a fettering bourgeois code of personal, sexual comportment.

Conclusion: *Trilogia* as Auto-Lesionistic Cinema

The rationalization of perspective in the Renaissance is accompanied by a parallel rationalization of human comportment or by what Pasolini calls an anthropological modification of human bodies. The entire *Trilogia della vita* is one massive reaction to this modification of the language of human bodies that has 'traumatized' Pasolini (see Naldini 1989, 392). In bourgeois society, sexuality and pleasure satisfy 'a social obligation' (392; translation mine) and are betrayed by guilt. The *Trilogia* is an attempt to represent an image of sexuality untouched by this guilt, and pleasure as something 'against social obligations' (392; translation mine). This is found in the 'innocent' bodies of the *Decameron* and the sense of sexual *play* in *Il fiore* (while *Canterbury* appears as an exception here, given its presentation of generally corrupted and instrumentalized expressions of desire [on *Canterbury* as an anticipation of *Salò*, see Miccichè 1978]). As Pasolini writes concerning these films:

I made them in order to oppose the consumerist present to a very recent past where the human body and human relations were still real, although archaic, although prehistoric, although crude; nevertheless they were real, and these films opposed this reality to the non-reality of consumer civilization.[15]

The comparative innocence he projects onto medieval society and the ideal of pleasures unladen by guilt or bourgeois morality he detects in Third World societies exist as a reaction to the pressures of rationalization that have imposed a certain visual order and uniformity of space. Cinema (and later television), as a mass medium, is the most developed technology subtending this visual order. Therefore, 'cinema of contestation' may seem to be a contradiction in terms, since it is the technical expression of the hegemony of this order. Franco Fortini (1987), for example, claims that Pasolini's 'turn' to film made him complicitous with that hegemony: he was compromised by the medium itself (213–14). In another context, Adorno and Eisler (1969), likewise, see the cinema as a technology responsible for a rationalization of the eye: 'The eye has adapted to bourgeois rationality and ultimately to a highly industrialized order by accustoming itself to interpreting reality, a priori, as a world of objects, basically as a world of commodities' (41; quoted in Koch 1989, 13).

Yet for Pasolini, in the first place, a *refusal* to engage in the 'audiovisual technique,' so powerful in contemporary cultural formation, would render one complicitous. Imperative, however, is an ironic or 'heretical' use of the technology, a self-reflexive and necessarily 'autolesionistic' form of filmmaking, as Pasolini insists (Pasolini, *Empirismo eretico*, 273–80). As he writes in the poem 'Progetto per opere future':

It is necessary to frustrate people. Throw oneself upon the coals like roasted and ridiculous martyrs: the avenues of Truth often pass through the most horrendous places of aestheticism, of hysteria, of crazy, erudite re-makes.

Bisogna deludere. Saltare sulle braci come martiri arrostiti e ridicoli: la via della Verità passa anche attraverso i più orrendi luoghi dell'estetismo, dell'isteria, del rifacimento folle erudito. (Pasolini *Poesie in forma di rosa*, 522)

The *Trilogia della vita* subverts the traditional language of cinema, which, in the words of American filmmaker Stan Brakhage (1982), proposes 'a form of sight which is aggressive and which seeks to make of any landscape a piece of real estate' (Brakhage 205).[16] And it carries out this subversion in spite of the medium itself, in a self-deconstructing manner. Pasolini's cinema offers a genealogy of the modern visual order, gives it a history, and he does so through adaptations of premodern and non-Western texts, and through what he describes in his essay 'Cinema of Poetry' as a 'poetic' style that reveals 'another film,' the stylistic-expressive film that manifests the 'pre-grammatical,' or 'oneiric' basis of a cinematic language, a language that is 'extremely crude, almost animal' (Pasolini, *Empirismo eretico*, 173). It is this other film, a 'hypnotic monster' lurking below the logical surface of 'the prosaic language of narrative' (and threatening to disrupt this communicative language) that Pasolini's *cinema di poesia* celebrates (see Pasolini, *Empirismo eretico*, 176–7). It pushes its spectators to a renewed involvement in 'subconscious life' in order to reveal how 'the truth is not to be found in a single dream, but in many dreams' ('La verità non sta in un solo sogno, ma in molti sogni'), as the prefacing title to *Il fiore* announces.

In the *Trilogia* Pasolini adopts a mannerist style designed to tear cinema away from its 'naturalist' or realist ideology as a technology of reproduction, and he calls attention to the relation between camera and physical reality as a cultural relation: 'we must fight to the end, therefore, to demystify the 'innocence of technique'.'[17] Furthermore, through a contamination of styles, genres, and visual traditions, found throughout the *Trilogia*, Pasolini attempts to remind his viewers of preceding ways of seeing and thus intervening in the world (the compositional strategy of pastiche is maintained in the *Decameron* where intertextual references are to Giotto, Masaccio, Bruegel, and in *I racconti di Canterbury*, where we find citations from the medieval iconographic tradition, and from Bruegel and Bosch). What he calls, in a very Bakhtinian fashion, his 'translinguistic research' provides the source for stylistic contamination in a work that injects what he refers to in 'Progetto per opere future' as an 'ancient figurativity in the flank of the new generation'[18] This abrasive stylistic offensive, or *delusione* ('bisogna deludere'), is carried out by way of an often parodic recuperation of the past. In the process, Pasolini attempts to evoke a cultural memory in the spectator, to force a conflict between memory and perception, and to thus raise him or her to a position from which to critically judge the present – a present, that is, located in a society of forgetfulness, since the commodity and memory are at war with one another, since the ideal consumer would have no memory at all. Indeed, in the poem 'La poesia della tradizione,' Pasolini accuses the 'unfortunate generation' of May 1968 of being fooled into making a virtue of forgetfulness in their refusal of bourgeois cultural canon:

> The books, the old books pass before your eyes
> like the objects of an old enemy
> you felt the need to resist . . .
>
> you came into the world, which is huge yet so simple
> and there you found those who laughed at tradition,
> and you took this falsely rebellious irony literally
> erecting youthful barriers against
> the dominant class of the past.

> I libri, i vecchi libri passarano sotto i tuoi occhi
> come oggetti di un vecchio nemico
> sentisti l'obbligo di non cedere . . .
>
> venisti al mondo, che è grande eppure così semplice
> e vi trovasti chi rideva della tradizione,
> e tu prendesti alla lettera
> tale ironia fintamente ribalda,
> erigendo barriere giovanili
> contro la classe dominante del passato. (Pasolini, *Le poesie*, 670)

This 'generazione sfortunata' failed to understand that their 'disobedience' was naïve obedience:

> in this way you will understand to have served the world
> against which you 'carried on the struggle' with such zeal:
> it was the world that wanted to toss out
> its own discredited history
> it was the world that wanted
> to sweep out its own past.

> e così capirai di aver servito il mondo
> contro cui con zelo 'portasti avanti la lotta':
> era esso che voleva gettar discredito sopra

la storia – la sua
era esso che voleva far piazza
del passato – il suo. (670–1)

For Pasolini, this forgetfulness was yet another requirement of governability: memory provides the potential basis for resistance to the continual anthropological, ideological, and geographical mutations of the present. The refusal of 'tradition' is an example of what Pasolini sees as the obedient disobedience of the new radicalism of the sixties and seventies, and led him in theory to reject its followers as reactionaries of the Left.

Pasolini's work explores literary and figural traditions in an attempt to construct a 'counter-memory,' to keep his spectator from fully 'adapting' to the 'atrocious' and 'repressive' present. As he remarks, the *Trilogia* was not a typical film of political denunciation; however he made it

with such a violent love for the 'lost time,' to be a denunciation not of some particular human condition but a denunciation of the entire present (necessarily permissive). Now we are inside the present, at this point to an irreversible degree: we have adapted ourselves to it. Our memory is getting ever worse. We are living, therefore, that which happens today, the repression of the tolerant power which, of all repressions, is the most atrocious.[19]

In the cinema, the production of a 'counter-memory,' capable of pushing us 'outside' of this present, entails what we have described as the transgressing of the conventions of filmic representation, recalling historically superseded representational models, mixing visual 'dialects,' so to speak, with the standard language of cinema: he sets loose a *vecchia figuratività* (an 'ancient figurativity') in the flank of this unfortunate generation. This is a style of contamination (or *plurilinguismo*) that is found throughout Pasolini's entire *opera*, lending it its coherence across the variety of media and genres he adopted throughout his life. And as Jonathan Crary (1989) writes, concerning Walter Benjamin and regimes of looking, filmmakers especially must counter what he calls the 'redundancies of representation' found in standard cinematic fare, or what Pasolini called the cinema of prose: 'That kind of redundancy of representation, with its accompanying inhibition and impoverishment of memory, was what Benjamin saw as the standardization of perception' (Crary 1989, 103; Benjamin 1969). What was necessary was to locate 'the moment when a conscious rift occurred between memory and perception, a moment in which memory had the capacity to rebuild the object of perception' (Crary 1989, 103). Pasolini's cinema is designed to do just this: to call attention to the process of perception in order to defamiliarize spectators with traditional habits of viewing. And indeed, he calls upon a new *spettatore da farsi* (an incomplete spectator, in the process of becoming), 'in such a way that every spectator would be called upon to choose and to criticize, that is *to be co-author*, instead of being a wretch that sees and hears, all the more repressed the more he is adulated' (Pasolini, *Lettere luterane*, 177). By presenting us his 'translinguistic research' in the *Trilogia*, Pasolini invites us to become such 'co-authors' of the infinite sequence shot of reality (reality that is nothing but 'cinema in nature'): the 'magma without amalgam' of the *Trilogia della vita*.[20]

Notes

1 *'Le mille e una notte* sono un modello narrativo ... Il narrare illimitato. Una cosa dopo l'altra, e una dentro l'altra, all'infinito' (Pasolini in Naldini 1989, 380; translation mine).

2 John Barth has been an important figure in Italian cultural debates concerning postmodern literature, in particular (see Carravetta and Spedicato). Recent approaches towards a 'postmodern' Pasolini might find a theoretical comparison of these two authors productive.

3 Pasolini's clearest visual sources in the *Decameron* and *I racconti di Canterbury* include Giotto, Masaccio, Bruegel, and Bosch.

4 'La mia polemica era contro la cultura della classe dominante eurocentrica' (in Faldini and Fofi 1987, 9; translation mine).

5 'I feel better there' (in Naldini 1989, 250).

6 See Chris Bongie's (1992) recent critique of Pasolini's 'exoticist' *tiersmondisme*.

7 'Oggi il dialetto è un mezzo per opporsi all'acculturazione. Sarà, come sempre, una battaglia perduta' (in Naldini 1989, 388; translation mine).

8 'È sempre prodotto di un ibrido morale – qui verrebbe voglia di dire storico' (Pasolini, *Il portico della morte* 105; translation mine).

9 Pasolini reports that he was ostracized at the University of Bologna for this (see Naldini 1989, 388, and also 99–109).

10 'La natura, insomma, è già artificio, cultura, spettacolo; non esiste più nulla di elementare, primario; ogni cosa rimanda ad un codice preesistente, l'arte scende nella vita ... La realtà si atteggia ad arte, meglio è già arte, i riferimenti colti sono 'naturali,' non già imposti dalla cultura del poeta' (Vallora, 1978, 120; translation mine).

11 'Tutte le mie caotiche pagine su questo argomento ... *tendono a portare la Semiologia alla definitiva culturizzazione della natura* (ho ripetuto sette otto volte che una Semiologia Generale della realtà sarebbe una filosofia che interpreta la realtà come linguaggio)' (Pasolini, *Empirismo eretico*, 283; emphasis his, translation mine).

12 Ibid.

13 'Facendo dell'intero vivere un parlare' (Pasolini, *Empirismo eretico*, 288).

14 'Non produce solo merce, produce insieme rapporti sociali, umanità' (Pasolini, *Lettere luterane*, 183; translation mine).

15 'Li ho fatti per oppore al presente consumistico un passato recentissimo dove il corpo umano e i rapporti umani erano ancora reali, benché arcaici, benché preistorici, benché rozzi, però tuttavia erano reali, e opponevano questa realtà all'irrealtà della civiltà consumistica' (Naldini 1989, 348; translation mine).

16 Brakhage is one of the only American filmmakers, along with Warhol, that Pasolini mentions in *Empirismo eretico* (258), though his name is mistyped as Burkage.

17 'Dobbiamo batterci, dunque, per demistificare l' 'innocenza della tecnica,' fino all'ultimo sangue' (Pasolini, *Empirismo eretico*, 230; translation mine).

18 'Una vecchia figuratività nel fianco della giovane leva' (Pasolini, *Le poesie*, 521). Although the actual work he is describing is his *Divina mimesis*, his descriptions found in this poem are entirely relevant to the *Trilogia* along with many of his other films.

19 'Con un amore così violento per il 'tempo perduto,' da essere una denuncia non di qualche particolare condizione umana ma di tutto il presente (permissivo per forza). Ora siamo dentro quel presente in modo ormai irreversibile: ci siamo adattati. La nostra memoria è sempre più cattiva. Viviamo dunque ciò che succede oggi, la repressione del potere tollerante, che, di tutte le repressioni, è la più atroce' (in Naldini 1989, 392; translation mine).

20 'Gioisco come si gioisce seminando, col fervore che opera mescolanze di materie inconciliabili, magmi senza amalgama, quando la vita è limone o rosa d'aprile' (Pasolini, 'Progetto per opere future,' *Le poesie*, 520).

References

Adorno, T., and H. Eisler. *Komposition für den film*. Munich: Roger and Bernhard, 1969.

Barth, John. 'Muse Spare Me.' In *The Sense of the Sixties*. New York: Free Press, 1968

230   Patrick Rumble

– *Chimera*. Greenwich, CT: Fawcett, 1972
– 'Tales within Tales within Tales.' *The Friday Book*. New York: Putnam, 1984
– *The Tidewater Tales: A Novel*. New York: Putnam, 1987
Barthes, Roland. 'The Death of the Author,' *Image-Music-Text*. Translated by Stephen Heath. London: Fontana, 1977
Baudry, Jean-Louis. 'Ideological Effects of the Basic Cinematographic Apparatus.' In Philip Rosen, ed., *Narrative, Apparatus, Ideology*. New York: Columbia University Press, 1986 [1970]
Benjamin, Walter. 'The Work of Art in the Age of Mechanical Reproduction.' In *Illuminations*, 217–52. Translated by Harry Zohn. New York: Schoken, 1969
Bertini, Antonio. *Teoria e tecnica del film in Pasolini*. Rome: Bulzoni, 1979
Bongie, Chris. 'A Postscript to Transgression: The Exotic Legacy of Pier Paolo Pasolini.' In *Exotic Memories: Literature, Colonialism, and the Fin de Siècle*, 188–228. Stanford, CA: Stanford University Press, 1991
Brakhage, Stan. *Brakhage Scrapbook: Collected Writings 1964–1980*. Edited by Robert A. Haller. New Paltz, NY: Documentext, 1982
Brunetta, Gian Piero. *Storia del cinema*. 2 vols. Rome: Editori Riuniti, 1979
Carravetta, Peter, and Paolo Spedicato, eds., *Postmoderno e letteratura: percorsi e visioni della critica in America*. Milan: Bompiani, 1984
Comolli, Jean-Louis. 'Technique and Ideology: Camera, Perspective, Depth of Field.' In Nick Browne, ed., *Cahiers du cinéma, 1969–1972: The Politics of Representation*. Cambridge: Harvard University Press, 1990 [1971]
Corrain, Lucia. 'La grammatica della duplicazione.' *Carte semiotiche* 1 (September 1985): 97–119
Costa, Antonio. 'Pasolini's Semiological Heresy.' In Paul Willemen, ed., *Pier Paolo Pasolini*, 32–42. London: British Film Institute, 1977
Crary, Jonathan. 'Spectacle, Attention, Counter-Memory.' *October* 50 (Fall 1989): 97–106
– *Techniques of the Observer*. Boston: MIT Press, 1992
de Lauretis, Teresa. 'Re-reading Pasolini's Essays on Cinema.' *Italian Quarterly* 82–3 (Fall/Winter 1980)
– *Technologies of Gender: Essays on Theory, Film, and Fiction*. Bloomington: Indiana University Press, 1987
Faldini, F., and G. Fofi, eds. *Il cinema italiano d'oggi 1970–84 raccontato dai suoi protagonisti*. Milan: Mondadori, 1984
Fortini, Franco. 'Pasolini o il rifiuto della maturità.' *Nuovi saggi italiani*. Vol. 2. Milan: Garzanti, 1987
Goldmann, Lucien. *Per una sociologia del romanzo*. Milan: Bompiani, 1964
Greene, Naomi. *Pier Paolo Pasolini: Cinema as Heresy*. Princeton: Princeton University Press, 1990

Heath, Stephen. *Questions of Cinema*. Bloomington: Indiana University Press, 1981

Koch, Gertrud. 'The Body's Shadow Realm,' *October* 50 (Fall 1989)

Lawton, Ben. 'The Storyteller's Art: Pasolini's *Decameron*.' In A. Horton and J. Magretta, eds., *Modern European Filmmakers and the Art of Adaptation*, 203–21. New York: Frederick Ungar, 1981

Miccichè, Lino. 'Pasolini: la morte e la storia,' *Cinema sessanta* 121 (May-June 1978)

Naldini, Nico. *Pasolini. Una vita*. Turin: Einaudi, 1989

Pasolini, Pier Paolo. *Poesie in forma di rosa*. Milan: Garzanti, 1964

– 'A quattr'occhi con Pasolini.' *Lui* (1 June 1970)

– *Le poesie*. Milan: Garzanti, 1971

– *Empirismo eretico*. Milan: Garzanti, 1972

– *La divina mimesis*. Turin: Einaudi, 1975

– *Lettere luterane*. Turin: Einaudi, 1976

– *Trilogia della vita*. Milan: Mondadori, 1987

– *Il portico della morte*. Edited by Cesare Segre. Rome: Associazione 'Fondo Pier Paolo Pasolini,' 1988

Rose, Jacqueline. 'Sexuality and Vision: Some Questions.' In Hal Foster, ed., *Vision and Visuality*. Seattle: Bay Press, 1988

Vallora, Marco. 'Pier Paolo Pasolini tra manierismo e metaletteratura.' In *Per Pasolini*, 117–33. Rome: Bulzoni and Teatro Tenda Editori, 1978

Wagstaff, Christopher. 'Reality into Poetry: Pasolini's Film Theory.' *The Italianist* 5 (1985): 107–32

White, John. *The Birth and Rebirth of Pictorial Space*. Cambridge, MA: Harvard University Press, 1987 [1957]

Salò: The Refusal to Consume

NAOMI GREENE

Pasolini's violent death in 1975 deeply coloured the reception of his last film, *Salò o le 120 gionate di Sodoma*, which immediately served as a climax of the artist's often scandalous career. Many, and even some close to Pasolini, leapt to the conclusion that the film arose from the director's inner demons, that it was a confessional and regrettable work. Others, more sophisticated in their appraisal, such as Roland Barthes, saw the film as a political allegory of fascism, and attacked it as such. In this essay, Naomi Greene revisits these responses and moves beyond them, taking seriously Pasolini's pessimistic analysis of the false and finally repressive tolerance of sex in 'neocapitalist' consumer society, a frequent object of his polemics. Reading *Salò* closely as Pasolini thought it out as a filmic text, Greene argues it is a work of 'ferocious meta-cinema' in which viewers become 'perfect spectators' and yet it is a film that systematically sets out to make its spectacles unwatchable, to make its 'consumption' impossible.

Now, when Pasolini's last film, *Salò*, is included in every Pasolini retrospective, analysed by scholars and critics, available on video, it is easy to forget how shocking the film seemed when it appeared in 1975. Banned, like so many of Pasolini's films, when first released, its subsequent appearance provoked strong reactions in friends and enemies alike. Significantly, too, by that time Pasolini had been murdered and the violence of his death – apparently at the hands of a young male prostitute he had just met – cast its long shadow over the filmed atrocities. Behind *Salò* lay grisly and unforgettable newspaper photographs of Pasolini's bloody corpse; the film's sado-masochistic universe seemed to mirror the darkest impulses in the life of its director. Cries of outrage against the film were shrill, often verging on hysteria. Ugo Finetti recounts that, upon leaving the projection room, one critic – referring to Pasolini's recent death – declared: 'Luckily, they killed him.' Still another wrote: 'Rest assured that whoever is courageous enough not to see *Salò-Sade* will not miss anything' (Finetti 1976, 431).

As these remarks suggest, Pasolini's death – shrouded in an atmosphere of homosexual violence and mystery – clearly sharpened the homophobic edge that infused many, if not most, reactions to the film. For example, in a passage laced with the moralism that Pasolini had fought throughout his life, the Brazilian film director, Glauber Rocha (1981), declared that *Salò* was his favourite film by Pasolini because, said Rocha, there the director tells the truth. 'There you are,' says Rocha impersonating Pasolini,

'I am perverted, perversion is fascism, I love fascist rituals, I am making *Salò* because it is the theatre of this perversion and my character, my hero, loves torturers as I love my assassin.'

And [Rocha continues] after the film he died in an incident involving the exploitation of proletarian sex. Pasolini, a communist intellectual, a revolutionary, a moralist, abetted prostitution, that is, he paid poor boys, the '*ragazzi di vita*,' for sex. He sought the poor, the ignorant, the illiterate and he tried to seduce them as if perversion were a virtue ... In *Salò*, Pasolini accepts his true personality. (80–1)

Even those who would have disagreed with Rocha in certain vital respects, who knew that Pasolini did not see perversion as a virtue, that he scarcely painted himself among the victims, could hardly have denied that the film had a pronounced autobiographical cast. Indeed, it was for this very reason that one of Pasolini's oldest and closest friends, the novelist Alberto Moravia, expressed the wish that the director's career had ended not with *Salò*, but with the film that had preceded it, *Il fiore delle mille e una notte* (*Arabian Nights* [1974]). Unlike *Salò*, Moravia (1976) remarked, in *Il fiore delle mille e una notte*,

homosexuality is viewed ... with happiness, sympathy, with ingenuity and serenity ... In *Il fiore*, for the last time, Pasolini liked himself, that is, his own life, his own destiny, his own way of being in the world. In *Salò*, on the other hand, he hated himself in the most radical way, to the point of self-calumny. I don't know why he did it. Probably from a sense of guilt. (93–4)

There is no doubt that the scandal surrounding *Salò* was heightened by the violence of Pasolini's death. But it is also true that the double axis of the film – centred on sexuality and politics – embodied the two areas that Pasolini had embraced so controversially throughout his life.

Indeed, in his last film, he deliberately brought these two domains together by setting *120 Days in Sodom*, the novel by the Marquis de Sade that forms the basis for the film, at the time of nazism-fascism. In the film, the sado-masochistic excesses imagined by the French author are rendered, perhaps, even more unbearable than they are in Sade's prose by a clinical camera that lingers on every horrible detail. While the reader of the book might have been able to elide, to gloss over, particularly repellent scenes, no similar strategy is allowed the film viewer. Spectators are forced to witness every agony of the adolescent victims who, imprisoned in a villa by wealthy and powerful libertines, descend from one Dantesque 'circle' or *girone* to the next. From the circle of perversions (or 'mania') they go to that of shit (or coprophagia) and, finally, to that of 'blood' (torture and death). Viewers are not spared the blood that oozes from the victims' mouths when they swallow food laced with nails; or the excrement that smears their lips during a coprophagic banquet; or the final scenes of sadism and torture in which skulls are cut open, eyes slashed, and dead bodies sodomized.

It has often been debated whether or not Sade is an erotic author. No similar debate seems possible in the case of *Salò*. Indeed, the film mirrors the despair that Pasolini felt about sexuality at this time, his conviction that contemporary consumer society had turned everything, including the human body, into pure merchandise. 'Private sexual lives,' he wrote shortly before making *Salò*, 'have been subjected to the trauma of false tolerance and/or corporeal degradation: what constituted joy and sorrow in sexual fantasies has become suicidal disillusion, shapeless ennui' (Pasolini, *Trilogia della vita*, 11). Profoundly infused with this 'corporeal degradation,' this 'suicidal disillusion,' *Salò* does not resemble other films of the 1970s, which seem to find an erotic current in nazism/sadism – films such as Bertolucci's *1900* (1976) or Liliana Cavani's *Night Porter* (1974). Instead, resolutely banning any hint of sexual titillation, in *Salò* Pasolini tried to remove every cloak, every veil, conferred upon sado-masochism by a tradition of romance and/or pornography. For example, his cold and precise portrayal of sexual combinations and perversions – a portrayal that a viewer, unlike a reader, cannot soften by his own desires and imaginings – lacks the cinematic foreplay, the elements of a 'strip-tease,' that Roland Barthes, for one, considers fundamental to the representation of Western desire.[1] In *Salò*, sexual acts are totally brutal and without preamble; its victims do not undress but appear nude, lined up as if awaiting the gas chambers. In this sexual lager, no real *jouissance* is possible. Its tortured victims bear no resemblance to the heroines of a certain pornographic tradition who achieve pleasure through pain. And even their executioners, that is, the libertines, do not attain the pleasure they so endlessly seek. Meticulous bureaucrats, banal torturers, Pasolini's libertines are driven not by energy or the pulsing of desire but by impotence and frustration. Indeed, those critics who perceived the essentially anti-sexual nature of *Salò* were not wrong: one deemed it a film about 'the death of sex'; for another it was the 'funeral dirge' of eroticism (Musatti 1982, 131; Chapier 1975–6, 116). Playing on the title of *Teorema*, an earlier film by Pasolini, French philosopher Gilles Deleuze (1985) called *Salò* nothing other than a 'pure dead theorem, a theorem of death' (228).

A 'theorem of death,' the world of *Salò*, as suggested earlier, is set in the deadliest of eras. References to the period of nazism/fascism are both explicit and implicit. The title itself refers to *Salò*, the northern Italian town where Mussolini set up a short-lived republic after his flight from Rome in 1943. The first scenes of the film, which depict the victims being rounded up by armed soldiers, contain an ominous road sign pointing to Marzabotto – a town where acts of the Resistance triggered a terrible fascist massacre. As for the villa where the victims are imprisoned, it was meant, said Pasolini, to suggest a home that might have been confiscated from some 'rich deported Jew.' And the frontal, symmetrical arrangement of people on the set was to evoke what he called the solemn efficacy of nazi 'choreography.' In their combination of 'decadence and military simplicity,' the libertines of *Salò* were, he felt,

cultured in the same pseudo-way as the German and Italian party hierarchy were, with pseudo-scientific ideas and pseudo-racist rationalizations. It was what Hitler and Mussolini called a 'decadent' world, it was to be destroyed but exerted its fascination upon these louts. (cited in Bachman 1975–6a, 52)

If Pasolini's repellent portrayal of sexuality disconcerted the mass public (who had expected, perhaps, still another erotic film from the director of the 'trilogy of life'), it was the film's political allusions that seemed to enrage intellectuals. Above all, they were dismayed by the film's implicit analogy between sadism and fascism – an analogy that stemmed, of course, from the fact that Sade's novel was set in the Republic of Salò. The respected novelist, Italo Calvino, spoke for many when he declared:

The idea of situating Sade's novel in the times and places of the Nazi-fascistic republic seems the worst possible one from all points of view. The horror of that past which is in the memory of so many who lived it cannot serve as background to the symbolic and imaginary horror constantly outside the probable such as is present in Sade's word (and justly represented in a fantastic vein by Pasolini) ... The evocation of the Nazi occupation can only reawaken a depth of emotions that is the complete opposite of the paradoxical ruthlessness that Sade poses as the first rule of the game not only to his characters but to his readers as well. (Calvino 1982, 109)

Outside Italy, this view was echoed by the eminent French critic, Roland Barthes, who spoke in somewhat more theoretical terms. Drawing a distinction between 'fascism-system' (an historical phenomenon) and fascism-substance (which can circulate any time), Barthes argued that the danger and complexity of fascism-system demanded more than the 'simple analogy' offered by Salò. Conversely, he felt that one could not anchor the protean (and imaginary) phenomenon of fascism-substance in any single particular historical event since 'it is only one of the modes in which political "reason" happens to colour the death drive which, in Freud's words, can only be seen if treated with some kind of phantasmagoria' (Barthes 1981, 89).

There is no doubt that Pasolini, the most lucid and self-aware of men, knew full well that this aspect of the film was bound to anger his countrymen. According to his cousin Nico Naldini, before his death Pasolini was looking forward with 'excitement' to the release of Salò, as if to a coming 'battle.'[2] Indeed, even before completing the film, he had begun to put forth arguments justifying his choice of the fascist era. For example, he declared at one point that the fascism of Salò had to be seen as 'symbolic' or allegorical rather than real. He chose, he said, to set his film at the time of fascism/nazism simply because it was the 'last time that the human power drive expressed itself in such direct, linear, and almost symbolic terms' (in Bachman 1975–6a, 52). Still, even as he argued that the fascism of Salò was emblematic of all power, he also maintained that it represented a precise historical phenomenon. Moreover – and here he added a new twist to his argument – he insisted that, *despite the setting of the film*, this precise phenomenon was not to be equated with nazism-fascism but with what he called the 'new' fascism of neocapitalism. Defiantly calling Salò his first film about the modern world, he deemed his film the oneiric 'representation of what Marx called the commodification of man, the reduction of the body (through exploitation) to a thing. Therefore sex is ... called upon in my film to play a horrible metaphorical role' (Pasolini, 'Il sesso come metafora del potere').

Comments such as these point, certainly, to some of the personal and philosophical impulses behind the film – impulses that Pasolini was discussing at length in his controversial journalistic writings of this period. But these remarks do not tell the full story. In fact, their obvious contradictions and ambivalences suggest that *Salò* sprang from motives deeper still. It is not merely that Pasolini appears to swing from the particular (the forms taken by modern-day power) to the universal (the notion of power in general). One also wonders why, if he wanted to represent power in a general, essentially allegorical, fashion, did he pick an historical moment so deeply charged for his countrymen? Why set the film in that dangerous and controversial no-man's land between metaphor and reality, a zone of shifting contours where, as Barthes indicated, fascism-system flows insidiously, scandalously, into fascism-substance? Further, why equate the abuses of power to sexual horrors that affect viewers too viscerally to be taken in purely symbolic terms?

The answer to all these questions, I think, is that Pasolini was impelled – over and above all other considerations – by a desire to be scandalous. Indeed, in April 1975 he himself remarked to his friend Gideon Bachman that *Salò* 'goes so far beyond the limits that those who habitually speak badly of me will have to find new terms' (Bachman 1975–6b). It was precisely this desire to 'go beyond the limits' that propelled him to choose what is perhaps the most notorious text by one of history's most notorious authors. (Sade was found so intolerable that he was imprisoned by three totally different political regimes: the Monarchy, the Republic, and the Empire.) Using this revolutionary text as a point of departure, Pasolini raised scandal one notch higher by setting Sade's novel in the Republic of Salò. The film thus became the last, deliberate act of transgression in a life punctuated by scandal and controversy: its slippery political analogies outraged intellectuals, while its horrific depiction of sex repelled the mass audience.

In some sense, moreover, the scandal of *Salò* goes beyond its graphic horror, its disturbing analogies. Still other, less immediately visible factors heighten the film's power to disturb, and these factors few critics have noticed and even Pasolini barely acknowledged. Indeed, I would argue that if audiences experience a sense of numb and leaden helplessness as they watch this film, it is not only because of what they see but because of how they are positioned by *Salò*. For the very construction of film gives rise to a terrifying web of complicity with the libertines, web that forces us to see ourselves – and Pasolini – as among their number.

It has been mentioned earlier that critics were not slow to grasp at least one obvious parallel between Pasolini and the libertines: that is, the libertines' ferocious and desperate sexuality seemed to reflect an aspect of their creator. Even a friend such as Gideon Bachman, who interviewed Pasolini while he was making *Salò*, was distressed by the fact that the director seemed to echo the libertines whenever he spoke of sexuality: 'Hearing [Pasolini] discuss Klossowski's ideas of the eternal repetitiousness of the act of love, I realise the man is talking about himself, about his eternal reaching out, and his eternal disappointment' (in Bachman 1975–6a, 52). But if Pasolini, always given to self-irony, parodied his own drive in his compulsive libertines, the resemblance between him and his fascist bureaucrats did not end there. For, no less than the director of a film, the libertines incessantly turn everything into theatre, performance, spectacle. Making great use of props and costumes, they constantly stage performances that grossly parody traditions drawn from stage, vaudeville, and cinema. They themselves declaim as if they were has-been actors in a mediocre melodrama; the four female narrators they employ to excite them perform like aging night-club chanteuses. The world of the villa is, in fact, one of endless rites or performances designed by the libertines in their frenzied efforts to recreate life, to turn everything into theatre. And, as in a play by Jean Genet where opposites melt into each other and nothing is what it appears, the performances of *Salò* suggest that everything is equally unreal, equally illusory. In a mock marriage scene, for example, two of the victims are dressed as if for a 'real' wedding; but when they begin to make love in earnest after the 'ceremony,' each is seized by an aroused libertine and a new performance, a new ritual, begins. Or, the winner of a contest to determine who has the most beautiful ass is about to be 'rewarded' with a bullet in the head: but when the trigger is drawn, the bullet proves a blank and he receives only a 'false' death.

In a larger sense, the theatrical 'numbers' staged by the libertines are, of course, moments in the drama embodied in the film itself – a film that thus becomes a kind of diabolical meta-theatre. Its three 'circles,' for example, clearly correspond to the acts of a play. And, as if to emphasize the division into acts, each 'circle' is preceded by shots that depict one of the female narrators applying makeup before a mirror as if in a dressing room. The act itself begins with a theatrical 'entrance' as she descends the stairway that takes her from the second floor of the villa to 'centre stage' – that is, to the front of the room where she will perform for the libertines and their victims. Meanwhile, the camera, seemingly part of an unseen audience watching from the back, repeatedly pans along both sides of the room where, as if at the edges of the proscenium, the inhabitants of the villa have lined up to await her performance.

In this satanic world, all is theatre and, in this sense, the film becomes, as critic Franco Cordelli (1976) observes,

above all the description of its own language ... and therefore a critique of language, and auto-critique, a masterly metafilm: Isn't the recruitment of the 16 youths Pasolini's delirious desire for power – and isn't this what Pasolini is denouncing? Aren't the violence and sex above all indifference, distance, a pure spectacle, that is, the epiphany of capital ... and therefore [pure] merchandise? (91)

In this ferocious meta-cinema, Pasolini indicts himself on several counts: as a user of adolescent bodies in both life and film, he, like the libertines, manipulates bodies, tells stories, arranges numbers. He too is a master of spectacle, an organizer of rites, an expert, as *Salò* demonstrates, at turning violence into theatre. But no one is innocent in the ninth circle and, to varying degrees, we are made to share his guilt, to become – willingly or unwillingly, consciously or unconsciously – accomplices of the theatre-obsessed libertines. By the very way that he depicts the victims, Pasolini ensures that we, like the libertines, will regard these adolescents as little more than beautiful bodies or interchangeable objects. Not only are the youths easily led to denounce and betray one another but they are kept naked and mute so that they seldom emerge as individuals.

For our part, unable to feel for the victims as fellow beings, we become uneasy, unsure about the extent of our own humaneness. And this unease fuels (and is fuelled by) a still greater malaise: as the machinery of torture takes its course, we slowly become aware that the very act of watching *Salò* turns us – like the libertines – into spectators of sadistic rites, rites distanced by theatre, by style, by the formal perfection of this crystalline film. As Leo Bersani and Ulysse Dutoit (1980) remark in a very interesting article on *Salò*:

Pasolini makes us into more willing, less purposeful spectators than his sado-fascistic protagonists. In a sense, this means that we never tire of being spectators; but it is the very limitlessness of our aestheticism which constitutes the moral perspective on sadism in *Salò* (31).

If the victims become 'perfect executioners,' then we are turned into 'perfect spectators' – viewers repelled yet fascinated by the spectacle of aestheticized violence. One libertine even reminds us that our role – that of spectatorship – is a vital one: the intellectual 'joy of contemplation,' he observes, is as important to the theatre of sadistic games as the 'sublime joy of action and the abject joy of complicity.' Mesmerized by the beautiful and polished images of *Salò* – which Pasolini wanted to make the most 'jewel-like' of all his films – we cannot deny the visual pleasure offered by a theatre, a cinema, of violence.

What the libertine calls the intellectual 'joy of contemplation,' the joy that inevitably falls to us as viewers of the film, becomes totally explicit in *Salò*'s dreadful climax. Here, the hints of voyeurism that run throughout Pasolini's cinema are turned, sadistically, against the viewer. For, as the scenes of bloodshed and torture reach a frenzied apogee, we are forced to merge our gaze with that of the libertines. One after another, each libertine stands by a window and uses binoculars – which become a stand-in for the camera – to view the scenes of carnage that are taking place below in an inner courtyard. The binoculars are reversed so that each shot witnessed is, quite literally, distanced, but also framed and miniaturized like the iris shots of early films. Reinforcing this visual echo of early cinema, the sequence is silent except for light piano music in the room: the sight (but not the sound) of the victims' cries and screams heightens both the vividness and the unreality of the slaughter, a vividness and unreality that characterizes not only *Salò* but, also, the very institution of cinema.

This last scene makes it absolutely clear that *Salò* is not only, or not even primarily, a denunciation of Power in general, or of contemporary power, or of fascism/sadism. It is also, and perhaps above all, a ferocious attack on both the director and the viewer. More than its disturbing analogy between fascism/sadism, or its horrific portrayal of sexuality, it is, I think, this denunciation which is truly unbearable. For this reason, I believe that the few critics who have argued that *Salò*'s 'real' message lies precisely in its desire to be unbearable have been very close to the truth. Discussing *Salò*'s scenes of coprophagia – scenes that particularly repelled many viewers – Pasolini deemed them a metaphor for the fact that 'the producers, the manufacturers, force the consumer to eat excrement. All these industrial foods are worthless refuse' (in Bachman 1975–6b, 43). Denouncing a bourgeois public that consumes everything, every piece of 'worthless refuse,' *Salò* deliberately makes itself indigestible. In this sense, it becomes the perfect example of the totally 'extremist' art that Pasolini espoused toward the end of his life. It was his contention that such art – by unmasking both the false nature of contemporary 'tolerance' (true tolerance, he argued, had no limits) and the 'purely economic reasons governing the liberalisation of sex' – would reveal the repressive and dehumanizing nature of what he saw as the modern hedonistic, consumeristic state. Now as never before, Pasolini declared in 1974, 'artists must create, critics defend, and democratic people support ... works so extreme that they become unacceptable even to the broadest minds of the new State' (Pasolini, 'Contro la permissività di Stato,' 19). Few could deny that *Salò* was precisely such a work.

Notes

1 It was for this very reason that Barthes believed that Sade himself was not 'erotic.' See Barthes, *Sade-Fourier-Loyola* 31–32.
2 Naldini's remarks are cited in *Pier Paolo Pasolini: Une vie future* 306.

References

Bachman, Gideon. 'Pasolini and the Marquis de Sade.' *Sight and Sound* 45, no. 1 (Winter 1975–6)
– 'Pasolini on de Sade.' Interview with Pasolini. *Film Quarterly* 29, no. 2 (Winter 1975–6)
Barthes, Roland. *Sade, Fourier, Loyola*. Paris: Seuil, 1971
– 'Sade-Pasolini.' In *Pasolini cinéaste* (special unnumbered issue of *Les cahiers du cinéma*). Paris: Éditions de l'étoile, 1981. Originally in *Le monde* (16 June 1976)
Bersani, Leo, and Ulysse Dutoit. 'Merde Alors.' *October* 13 (1980)
Calvino, Italo. 'Sade Is within Us.' In Beverly Allen, ed., *The Poetics of Heresy*. Saratoga, CA: Anma Libri, 1982. Originally in *Corriere della sera* (30 November 1975)
Chapier, Henry. 'L'érotisme selon Pasolini.' *Cinéma d'aujourd'hui* 4 (Winter 1975–6)

Tetis

PIER PAOLO PASOLINI

Pasolini wrote the following essay in December 1973, during the editing of *The Arabian Nights*, the third film of the *Trilogy of Life*. It should thus be considered, along with his 'Abjuration of the *Trilogy of Life*' (see Pasolini, 'Abiura') written in 1975, one of the places in which he expressed himself most clearly regarding the *Trilogy* and the concerns raised during its production. In it Pasolini focuses on the topics of the representation of sexuality ('tetis') in cinema, sexual permissiveness in general, and he responds to those critics who held him responsible for the explosion of low-budget, pornographic versions of *The Decameron*, *Canterbury Tales*, and *The Arabian Nights*. The paper was presented by Pasolini at the 'Erotismo Eversione Merce' conference held in Bologna in mid-December 1973, and forms part of the published proceedings of that conference (see Boarini 1974).

The forms of a literary narration are not only technical-linguistic: the written page also contains certain forms that are non-verbal and thus invisible. Take for example the trajectory of the development of a character, or the evolving traits of his psychology. By way of tables and charts, structuralist criticism is capable of revealing even these internal data, though only as an abstract visibility or statistic.

The same holds for cinematic narration, because the author of a film chooses and represents certain moments from the life of a character, and the rest he leaves inside the film, within the splices or cuts of the film.

Between a character that appears laughing in the first sequence of the film, and then disappears only to reappear, crying, in the third sequence, there is a psychological passage that is not an audio-visual *form*, while it is nevertheless a *form* of the film.

However, the spectator does not apprehend this passage from laughter to tears as a *form*: he relates to it exactly as if it were a phenomenon of life. That is, he carries out a psychological interpretation, similar to the one he would carry out if, in any given moment of his life, he found himself with a laughing person and then, after awhile, with the same person crying. In real life he has at his disposal certain 'existential' elements that permit him to interpret the reality of that laughter and those tears. But certainly the author of a film will not fail to furnish him with analogous existential elements.

We thus arrive at the conclusion that the spectator, faced with the film's 'inclusions' (that is, its *audio-visual forms*), acts as an 'addressee' in reality, yet he knows that it is an illusion. However, faced with the 'exclusions' (that is, the film's *non-audio-visual forms*), the spectator acts, all the same, as an 'addressee' in reality: the scheme he adopts in order to formulate his interpretation of, or arrive at his deductions and conclusions regarding, the comportment of a character *in the film* is the same scheme he uses to interpret the comportment of a person *in reality*.

If a greater vivacity characterizes the identification of the cinematic code with the code of reality as far as the *audio-visual forms* are concerned (that is, as far as are concerned the 'included' parts of reality: shot and edited), then the identification of the cinematic code with the code of reality as far as the *non-audio-visual forms* are concerned (that is, the moments of the narration that are 'excluded' from the shots and montage) is an absolute identification.

Just as in that infinite sequence shot which is reality, in cinema the narration consists of a succession of 'inclusions' and 'exclusions.' Now, since in a film the choice is an aesthetic one, we must deduce that the first aesthetic choice for a director is what to include in a film and what to exclude.

An aesthetic choice is always a social choice. It is determined by the person to whom the representation is addressed and also by the context in which the representation unfolds. This does not at all mean that the aesthetic choice is impure or interested. Even the choices of a saint are socially determined.

Let us examine an erotic scene. A room, a man, a woman. The director is faced with the usual choice: what to include and what to exclude? Twenty years ago the director would have 'included' a brief series of passionate and nobly sensual acts, leading to a long kiss. Ten years ago the director would have 'included' much more: after the first kiss, he would have arrived at the moment in which the woman's legs and breasts were exposed, almost completely, adding a second kiss at this point clearly preceding coitus. Today, the director can 'include' much more: he can include the coitus itself (even if feigned by the actors) and even full nudity.

Not one of these three hypothetical directors can be accused of not having made some *aesthetic* choices, and of not having taken his expressive premise to its logical conclusion. He cannot be accused of not having enlarged, through an expenditure of personal effort, the space which – proportionately – the social context conceded to him.

Now it appears to me that I have been brought into this matter directly, and that I must testify, or rather illustrate or justify, an experience that is at once personal and public. Indeed, as the author of films, in these past few years, I have doubtless carried out one of those individual expenditures of effort of which I was speaking, in order to enlarge the expressive space that society has conceded to me in order to represent the erotic relationship. I have even arrived, for example – something that has never occurred before that moment – at a representation of sex in detail. First of all I must say that I myself, in previous years – both in my work and in explicitly political interventions (and, moreover, with my own being and comportment) – had given my own contribution in order that Italian society might concede to me that space within which I could exercise the effort necessary to augment even further the possibilities of the representable. It took the long struggles – by now archaic if not mythical – of the fifties and those, even more tumultuous ones, of the early sixties, to prepare the terrain for this inclination toward reform and tolerance on the part of bourgeois Italian society. The censorship that once censored an uncovered breast has now come to let pass, precisely, the detail of a sexual organ in close-up; and the magistracy which once passed sentence for a simple allusion is today forced to make the sacred 'common sense' notion of 'modesty' ever more flexible. It is true, in these months, that there is the threat of a return to order (I will not cite examples). But I think that that which has been established is established and that which has passed has passed. If this is not the case, well, whoever fought will fight again: but in order to defend the positions last reached. It is only reasonable to assume that one need not begin to struggle all over again to defend outdated or previously held positions. The threat no longer comes from the Vatican or from the fascists who, in the public opinion, have already been defeated and liquidated, although still in an irresponsible manner. Public opinion has by now been completely determined – in its reality – by a new hedonistic and completely (if stupidly) secular ideology. Permissive power (at least in certain fields) will protect this new public opinion. Eros is in the area of such permissiveness. It is both source and object of consumption. Society no longer has any need for strong and obedient sons and soldiers. It needs sons with the knowledge necessary for the new demands being placed upon them, and aware, therefore, of the new rights that they have been granted. But I will return to this later.

Why have I arrived at the exasperated liberty of the representation of sexual gestures and acts, even, precisely as I was saying, including the representation of the sexual organ in detail and in close-up? I have an explanation, which is convenient and seems right to me, and it is this: In a moment of profound cultural crisis (the last years of the sixties), which caused (and causes) us, indeed, to ponder the end of culture (and which in fact has reduced itself, objectively, to the conflict, grandiose in its own way, of two subcultures: that of the bourgeois and that of the contestation of the bourgeois), it seemed to me that the only preserved reality was that of the body. That is, in practice, culture seemed to be reduced to a culture of the popular and humanistic past – in which, indeed, the protagonist was physical reality, insofar as it still belonged to man. It was in such a physical reality – his own body – that man lived his own culture.

Now, the bourgeoisie, creators of a new type of civilization, could not help but arrive at the de-realization of the body. They have been successful, indeed, and they have made of it a mask. Today, the youth are nothing but monstrous and 'primitive' masks of a new sort of initiation (negative in pretence only) into the consumerist ritual.

The people [*il popolo*] has arrived, with slight delay, at the loss of its own body. Up until a few years ago (when I was thinking of the *Decameron* and the subsequent *Trilogy of Life*) the people was still almost completely in control of its own physical reality and of the cultural model that it emulated. For a director such as myself, who had intuited the fact that the culture (in which he was formed) had ended, that it no longer gave reality to anything, if not precisely (perhaps) to physical reality, it was a natural consequence that such a physical reality be identified with the physical reality of the popular world.

To summarize, therefore: toward the end of the sixties, Italy passed over into the epoch of Consumerism and Subculture, losing in the process every reality, which has itself survived almost entirely in bodies and more precisely in the bodies of the impoverished classes.

Thus, popular corporality has been the protagonist of my films. I could not arrive at (and this, indeed, for stylistic reasons) the extreme consequences of this premise. The symbol of corporal reality is in fact the nude body; and, in an even more synthetic way, sex. I would not have fully arrived at a representation of corporal reality had I not represented the corporeal moment by definition. The people can even be chaste, and conduct the life of a monk. But, at least up until a few years ago, the people was not divided from its own sex. The code of honour, in the south of Italy, did not mortify or repress sex: on the contrary, it exalted it. And for that matter the same held for the repression exercised by the classes in power. Chastity and sexual violence were seen with naturalness. Taboos created obstacles, not disassociations.

Naturally certain other reasons (beyond the more general and profound one I have already mentioned) contibuted to my choice of the physical reality of the people as the protagonist of my latest films. For example, one reason is that, for me, sexual relations are sources of inspiration in their own right, because I see in them an incomparable fascination, and they seem to me to be of such high, absolute importance, to warrant the dedication of far more than one film to them. Let it be said clearly: all things considered, my latest films represent a confession of this as well.[1] And since every confession is a challenge, my latest films also contain a provocation. A provocation on several fronts. A provocation of the petit-bourgeois and conformist public (which, however, did not allow itself to be provoked in the least, and simply, and finally, recognized something of its own reality – a natural reality for the popular public, a liberating one for the bourgeois public). A provocation of the critics who, by repressing the sex in my films, have repressed their content, and thus they found them to be empty, without understanding that they contained ideology (and how!), and it was right there, in the enormous cock on the screen, above their misunderstanding heads. A provocation of the moralist Left whose vestal virgins became indignant and screamed about the scandal exactly as did the vestal virgins of tradition (the journal *Potere operaio* used the same language, indeed, the same words, as the state ministries in this regard). Yes, I did not want to make so-called politically engaged cinema; nor did I want to produce a cinema of romanticized politics. Indeed, before long, many filmmakers will become embarrassed by their own films of the sixties (an embarrassment shared by their spectators). Not me. I will not be embarrassed. Already the responsibility, which was so shamelessly attributed to me, for having created a vulgar and commercial cinematic genre,[2] has faded away, and this responsibility attributed to me has been revealed as the passing and derisory moment that it was. However, I can boast, perhaps, of having established the necessary precedent for the films of Bernardo Bertolucci and Marco Ferreri. And furthermore, I *could* also boast of having had an impact upon Italian customs, and their evolution, with my films: an impact upon the liberalization of public opinion and upon the decongestion of the 'common sense of modesty.' *However, I will not boast of this.* Even though, in *The Arabian Nights*, and also in the next film [*Salò*] which will have 'ideology' as its explicit theme, I will continue to represent *even* physical reality and its blazon, Tetis, *I regret* the liberalizing influence that my films may eventually have upon the sexual customs of Italian society. In fact, my films have contributed, in practice, to a *false* liberalization, actually desired by the new reformist and permissive power, which is also the most fascist power in history. In fact, no other power has had the possibility and capability of creating models of humanity and of imposing them the way that this faceless and nameless one has. In the area of sex, for example, the model that such a power creates and imposes consists of a moderated sexual liberty that includes the consumption of what is actually superfluous yet considered essential for a modern couple. Having achieved sexual freedom (a freedom conceded to them, not earned), young people – bourgeois, and mainly proletarians or subproletarians (if such distinctions are still possible) – have quickly and fatally transformed it into an obligation. The obligation to adopt the freedom granted them; better, the obligation to take complete advantage of the freedom granted them, so as not to give the appearance of being 'incapable' or 'different': the most dreadful of obligations. The conformist anxiety of being sexually liberated transforms the youth into miserable and neurotic erotomaniacs, eternally unsatisfied (precisely because their sexual freedom is received, not struggled for and gained) and therefore unhappy. In this way even the last place in which reality resided, that is, the body, or better in the popular body, has disappeared. The youth of the people experience, in their bodies, the same mortifying disassociation, full of false dignity and stupidly wounded pride, as the youth of the bourgeoisie. Even if I wanted to continue with films such as *The Decameron*, I could not, because I would not find anymore in Italy – especially in the youth – that physical reality (whose banner is sex and its joy) which is the content of those films.

Bologna, December 1973.

Translated by Patrick Rumble

Notes

1 Pasolini is referring to the films of the *Trilogy of Life*. Shooting for *The Arabian Nights* concluded in May 1973, six months before Pasolini wrote this essay. The film was officially released soon thereafter, on 9 February 1974.
2 Several pornographic versions of *The Decameron*, *Canterbury Tales*, and *The Arabian Nights* were produced by various directors in the mid-seventies.

References

Boarini, Vittorio, ed. *Erotismo, eversion, merce*. Bologna: Cappelli, 1974
Pasolini, Pier Paolo. 'Abiura dalla *Trilogia della vita*,' *Lettere luterane*, 71–6. Turin: Einaudi, 1976

Bibliography

Poetry

Poesie a Casarsa. Bologna: Libreria Antiquaria, 1942
Poesie. Primon: San Vito al Tagliamento, 1945
Diarii. Casarsa: Academiuta de Lenga Furlana, 1945
I pianti. Casarsa: Academiuta de Lenga Furlana, 1946
Dov'è la mia patria. Casarsa: Academiuta de Lenga Furlana, 1949
Tal còur di un frut. Tricesimo-Udine: Edizione di Lingua Friulana, 1953
La meglio gioventù. Florence: Sansoni, 1954
Dal diario. Caltanissetta: Sciascia, 1954
Le ceneri di Gramsci. Milan: Garzanti, 1957
L'usignolo della Chiesa cattolica. Milan: Longanesi, 1958
Roma 1950. Diario. Milan: Scheiwiller, 1960
Sonetto primaverile. Milan: Scheiwiller, 1960
La religione del mio tempo. Milan: Garzanti, 1961
Poesia in forma di rosa. Milan: Garzanti, 1964
Poesie dimenticate. Udine: Società Filologica Friulana, 1965
Trasumanar e organizzar. Milan: Garzanti, 1971
La nuova gioventù. Turin: Einaudi, 1975
Poesie. Milan: Garzanti, 1970
Le poesie. Milan: Garzanti, 1975

Novels, Short Stories, and Correspondence

Ragazzi di vita. Milan: Garzanti, 1955
Una vita violenta. Milan: Garzanti, 1959

Donna di Roma. Sette storie. Milan: Il Saggiatore, 1960
Il sogno di una cosa. Milan: Garzanti, 1962
L'odore dell'India. Milan: Longanesi, 1962
Il vantone. Milan: Garzanti, 1963
Alì dagli occhi azzurri. Milan: Garzanti, 1965. (This volume also contains the
    screenplays *La notte brava, Accattone, La ricotta,* and *Mamma Roma.*)
Teorema. Milan: Garzanti, 1968
La Divina Mimesis. Turin: Einaudi, 1975
Lettere agli amici (1941–1945). Parma: Guanda, 1975
Amado mio-Atti impuri. Milan: Garzanti, 1982 [1943–1948]
Lettere 1940–1954. Ed. Nico Naldini. Turin: Einaudi, 1986
Lettere 1955–1975. Ed. Nico Naldini. Turin: Einaudi, 1988
Petrolio. Turin: Einaudi, 1992
Un paese di temporali e di primule. Ed. Nico Naldini. Parma: Guanda, 1993

Theatre

Calderón. Milan: Garzanti, 1973
I Turcs tal Friúl. Udine: Rivista Forum Julii, 1976
Affabulazione, Pilade. Milan: Garzanti, 1977
Porcile, Orgia, Bestia da stile. Milan: Garzanti, 1979
Teatro. Milan: Garzanti, 1988

Essays

Poesia dialettale del Novecento (co-edited with Mario Dell'Arco). Parma:
    Guanda, 1952
Il canto popolare. Milan: Meridiana, 1954
Canzoniere italiano. Antologia della poesia popolare. Parma: Guanda, 1955
Passione e ideologia. Milan: Garzanti, 1960
La poesia popolare italiana. Milan: Garzanti, 1960
Scrittori della realtà dall'VIII al XIX secolo. Milan: Garzanti, 1961
Empirismo eretico. Milan: Garzanti, 1972
Scritti corsari. Milan: Garzanti, 1975
Lettere luterane. Turin: Einaudi, 1976
Le belle bandiere. Rome: Editori Riuniti, 1977
Il portico della morte. Ed. Cesare Segre. Rome: Associazione 'Fondo Pier Paolo
    Pasolini,' 1988

Screenplays

La notte brava. Filmcritica 10, nos. 91–92 (November-December 1959)

Accattone. Rome: FM, 1961

Mamma Roma. Milan: Rizzoli, 1962

La commare secca. Milan: Zibetti, 1962; reprinted in *Filmcritica* 16, no. 161 (October 1965)

La ricotta. In *Alì dagli occhi azzurri.* Milan: Garzanti, 1965. Also found in this volume are *La notte brava, Accattone,* and *Mamma Roma.*

Il vangelo secondo Matteo. Milan: Garzanti, 1965

Uccellacci e uccellini. Milan: Garzanti, 1966

Edipo re. Milan: Garzanti, 1967

Che cosa sono le nuvole? Cinema e cinema 3, nos. 7–8 (Winter/Spring 1969)

Medea. Milan: Garzanti, 1970

Ostia (written with Sergio Citti). Milan: Garzanti, 1970

Trilogia della vita. Bologna: Cappelli, 1975; reprinted by Mondadori, 1987

Il padre selvaggio. Turin: Einaudi, 1975

Appunti per un'Orestiade africana. Turin: Einaudi, 1975

San Paolo. Turin: Einaudi, 1977

Sant'Infame (written with Sergio Citti). *Cinecritica* 13 (April-June 1989)

Porno-Teo-Kolossal. Cinecritica 13 (April-June 1989)

Filmography

Screenplays

1954   *La donna del fiume* (dir. Mario Soldati). Co-scriptwriter.

1955   *Il prigioniero della montagna* (dir. Luis Trenker). Co-sciptwriter.

1956   *Le notti di Cabiria* (dir. Federico Fellini). Co-scriptwriter.

1957   *Marisa la civetta* (dir. Mauro Bolognini). Co-scriptwriter.

1958   *Giovani mariti* (dir. Mauro Bolognini). Scriptwriter.

1959   *La notte brava* (dir. Mauro Bolognini). Scriptwriter.

1960   *Il bell'Antonio* (dir. Mauro Bolognini). Co-scriptwriter.

La giornata balorda (dir. Mauro Bolognini). Co-scriptwriter.

La lunga notte del '43 (dir. Florestano Vancini). Co-scriptwriter.

Il carro armato dell'8 settembre (dir. Gianni Puccini).
   Co-scriptwriter.

La dolce vita (dir. Federico Fellini). Co-scriptwriter.

Morte di un amico (dir. Franco Rossi). Co-scriptwriter.

La canta delle marane (dir. Cecilia Mangini). Adapted from
   a chapter of *Ragazzi di vita*.

1961   *La ragazza in vetrina* (dir. Luciano Emmer). Co-scriptwriter.

1962   *La commare secca* (dir. Bernardo Bertolucci). Co-scriptwriter.

Una vita violenta (dirs. Paolo Heusch, Brunello Rondi).
   Adapted from Pasolini's novel, *Una vita violenta*.

1970   *Ostia* (dir. Sergio Citti). Co-scriptwriter.

1973   *Storie scellerate* (dir. Sergio Citti). Co-scriptwriter.

Written and Directed

1961	*Accattone*
1962	*Mamma Roma*
1963	*La ricotta*
	La rabbia
1964	*Comizi d'amore*
	Sopralluoghi in Palestina
	Il Vangelo secondo Matteo
1966	*Uccellacci e uccellini*
	La terra vista dalla luna
1967	*Che cosa sono le nuvole?*
	Edipo re
1968	*Teorema*
	La sequenza del fiore di carta
	Appunti per un film sull'India
1969	*Porcile*
	Medea
1970	*Appunti per un'Orestiade africana*
	Le mura di San'A
1971	*Decameron*
1972	*I racconti di Canterbury*
1974	*Il fiore delle mille e una notte*
1975	*Salò o le 120 giornate di Sodoma*

Contributors

GIULIANA BRUNO is Associate Professor of Visual and Environmental Studies at Harvard University. She is the author of *Streetwalking on a Ruined Map: Cultural Theory and the City Films of Elvira Notari* (Princeton, 1993), co-editor of *Off-Screen: Women and Film in Italy* (Rosenberg & Sellier, 1991) and *Immagini allo schermo* (Rosenberg & Sellier, 1991). Her many essays have appeared in journals such as *October, Camera Obscura, Assemblage* and *Cinema Journal* as well as in catalogues for the Museum of Modern Art and the Guggenheim Museum.

PAOLO FABBRI is Professor of Philosophy of Language at the University of Bologna and Director of the Italian Cultural Institute in Paris. He is author of many essays, including 'Modelli e parabole: ragionare per figure,' in *Nuova Civiltà delle Macchine*, 2 (1987); 'Nous sommes tous des agents doubles,' in *Le Genre Humain* (Paris: Seuil, 1988); 'L'idiome esthétique,' *Le Magazine littéraire* (1989).

JOSEPH FRANCESE is Assistant Professor of Italian at Michigan State University. He is the author of *Il realismo impopolare di Pier Paolo Pasolini* (Bastogi, 1991) and of several essays on Pasolini. He has also written on Antonio Tabucchi for the *Stanford Italian Review*, *Annali d'italianistica*, and *Spunti e ricerche* and on sixteenth-century and twentieth-century Italian literary topics for *Italica, Quarderni d'italianistica, Gràdiva*, and *The Italianist*.

NAOMI GREENE is Professor of French and Film Studies at the University of California, Santa Barbara. She is the author of books on Antonin Artaud, René Clair and, recently, *Pier Paolo Pasolini: A Cinema of Heresy*

(Princeton, 1990). She has also translated Marc Ferro's *Cinéma et histoire* into English and is currently at work on a study of French cinema since 1968.

SILVESTRA MARINIELLO is Assistant Professor in the Comparative Literature Department of the University of Montreal. She is the author of *Kuleshov* (La Nuova Italia, 1990) and *El cine y el fin del arte* (Catedra, 1992).

NICO NALDINI was born in the Friulian town of Casarsa in 1929. He is Pier Paolo Pasolini's first cousin. He has published two volumes of poetry, *Seris par un frut* (Academiuta di lenga furlana, 1948) and *Un vento smarrito e gentile* (Scheiwiller, 1958). He has written or edited *Giacomo Leopardi: La vita e le lettere* (Garzanti, 1983), *Vita di Giovanni Comisso* (Einaudi, 1985), and with Andrea Zanzotto, *Pasolini: Poesie e pagine ritrovate* (Lato Side, 1980). His biography of Pasolini's early life, *Nei campi del Friuli* (Scheiwiller, 1984), was recently followed by a full biography, *Pasolini: Una vita*, which has been translated into various languages.

PATRICK RUMBLE is Assistant Professor in the Department of French and Italian at the University of Wisconsin–Madison. He is the author of a number of essays, and his study of Pasolini's *Trilogy of Life* is forthcoming from University of Toronto Press.

WALTER SITI is Professor of Modern Italian Literature at the University of Aquila. Among his books are *Il realismo dell'avanquardia* (Einaudi, 1973) and *Il neorealismo nella Poesia italiana* (Einaudi, 1980). He has published many essays on Pasolini in such journals as *Paragone* and has edited Pasolini's *Le ceneri di Gramsci* and *La divina mimesis* (both Einaudi). He is now editing the new edition of Pasolini's complete poetry for publication by Garzanti.

P. ADAMS SITNEY is Professor of Visual Arts at Princeton University. He is the author of *Visionary Film: The American Avant-Garde 1943–1978* (Oxford, 1974), *Modernist Montage: The Obscurity of Vision in Cinema and Literature* (Columbia University Press, 1990) and editor of *The Film Culture Reader* (Praeger, 1970), *The Avant-Garde Film: A Reader in Theory and Criticism* (Film Anthology/New York University Press, 1978), and *The Gaze of Orpheus and Other Literary Essays by Maurice Blanchot* (Station

Hill, 1981). His *Vital Crises in Italian Cinema (1945–1950, 1958–1963)* will be published by the University of Texas Press in 1994.

JENNIFER STONE is Associate Professor in the Department of French and Italian at the University of Massachusetts at Amherst. She is the author of *Pirandello's Naked Prompt: The Structure of Repetition in Modernism* (Ravenna: Longo Editore, 1989) and she has published numerous articles on modern Italian culture, and on literary and psychoanalytic theory.

BART TESTA teaches cinema studies and semiotics at the University of Toronto. He is the author of *Spirit in the Landscape* (The Art Gallery of Ontario, 1989) and *Back and Forth: Early Cinema and the Avant-Garde* (The Art Gallery of Ontario, 1992) as well as a number of essays in journals and anthologies.

DAVID WARD is Assistant Professor in the Italian Department at Wellesley College. In addition to his work on Pasolini, he has published articles on Giovanni Raboni, Florestano Vancini, and Stefano Benni. He is currently working on a study of Italian anti-fascism.